THE
BATTLE OF
KÖNIGGRÄTZ

THE
BATTLE OF
KÖNIGGRÄTZ

PRUSSIA'S VICTORY OVER AUSTRIA, 1866

GORDON A. CRAIG

UNIVERSITY OF PENNSYLVANIA PRESS

Philadelphia

Originally published 1964 by J.B. Lippincott Company
Published by arrangement with HarperCollins Publishers, Inc.
Copyright © 1964 Gordon A. Craig

Printed in the United States of America on acid-free paper

10 9 8 7 6 5 4 3 2 1

Published 2003 by
University of Pennsylvania Press
Philadelphia, Pennsylvania 19104-4011

Library of Congress Cataloging-in-Publication Data

Craig, Gordon Alexander, 1913–
    The battle of Königgrätz : Prussia's victory over Austria, 1866 / Gordon A.
Craig.
        p.   cm.
    Originally published: Philadelphia : J.B. Lippincott Co., 1964.
    Includes bibliographical references and index.
    ISBN 0-8122-1844-2 (pbk. : alk. paper)
        1. Kèniggrètz, Battle of, 1866. 2. Austro-Prussian War, 1866—
Campaigns—Czech Republic—Hradec Krâlovâ. I. Title.
DD439.K7 C7   2003
943'.076—dc21   2002072880

Maps drawn by John Carnes

To Phyllis

CONTENTS

MAPS

INTRODUCTION

<table>
<tr><td>

Die Schlacht bei Königgrätz,
Die haben wir mitgemacht,
Da donnerten die Kanonen,
Das hat nur so gekracht.

Mein Kam'rad ist geblieben
Und jener auch blessiert,
Doch hat uns unser Kommandeur
Auch immer gut geführt.[1] *

</td><td>

(The battle of Königgrätz—
We were there all right.
The cannons were thundering
And what a racket they made!

My comrade died there,
And someone else was wounded.
But our commander
Always led us well.)

</td></tr>
</table>

        —ANON.

ON THE EVE of the battle of Leipzig, Napoleon Bonaparte is reported to have said: *"Entre une bataille gagnée et une bataille perdue, la distance est immense: il y a des empires."* Perhaps the emperor was fey, as the Scots say, and speaking with a presentiment of his own doom, but the general truth of his remark has been borne out by many battles in history.

One such battle was Königgrätz. On the morning of 3 July 1866, as Prussian uhlans cantered forward to the Bistritz River and were challenged by Austrian batteries on the heights of Lipa, Austria was still regarded as the strongest power in Central Europe and was generally accorded the right to speak in international affairs for the German states as a whole. By nightfall, as the broken Austrian columns struggled back across the River Elbe, that proud position was irrevocably destroyed, to the general stupefaction of observers who had taken it for granted. "Events

* Superior figures refer to Notes at end of text.

ix

of so startling a character have taken place in the theater of war," wrote the *Illustrated London News*, "and present such an aspect of importance toward the future that the mind is dizzied by its attempt to estimate their real importance."[2] "Thirty dynasties have been swept away," the London *Spectator* said ominously, "the fate of twenty millions of civilized men has been affected for ever, the political face of the world has changed as it used to change after a generation of war. . . . Prussia has leaped in a moment into the position of the first Power of Europe."[3] In Paris, the chronicler of the *Revue des deux mondes* was not quite ready to accept this last conclusion, but he recognized that the world had changed. With an unconscious echo of Napoleon's words, he wrote: "One of those formidable battles which declare the irrevocable verdict of force upon the destiny of nations has been fought in Bohemia. The battle of Sadowa[4] has revealed the armed might of Prussia and has struck a perhaps irreparable blow at the political power of Austria."[5]

The political consequences of the battle of Königgrätz were so profound and so far-reaching that it is not difficult to understand why it has generally been considered one of the "decisive battles" of the modern era.[6] But this does not in itself explain why so many historians have been fascinated by Königgrätz, and one must look to other than its political aspects to explain this.

For one thing, the battle of Königgrätz was the biggest encounter of its kind in the modern era. In terms of men engaged, it dwarfed the battles of ancient times, as it did those of the ages of Gustavus Adolphus and Frederick the Great. Even at Leipzig in 1813, in the so-called "Battle of the Peoples" which saw the forces of all the great powers of Europe engaged, as well as those of some of the lesser ones, only 430,000 men stood on the field. At Königgrätz 440,000 to 460,000 contested the decision.[7] The magnitude of individual details of the battle startled contemporaries and impressed historians of a later age. European warfare had rarely witnessed anything like the massive artillery fire which the Austrians maintained throughout this long day of battle, and nothing was ever to be seen again to compare with the great cavalry fight at Stresetitz and Langenhof, in which 5,000 riders were engaged on each side. The grandiose has its own peculiar charm, and Königgrätz derived significance from its very dimensions, which were not, indeed, to be exceeded until the bloodier encounters of the First World War.

This was, moreover, the first battle in which the advanced technology of the industrial age played a significant part in the result. The transportation of so great a number of men to the battlefield and their effective control while on it were made possible only by the great strides that had been made in the field of communications in the previous two decades. Without the railway and the telegraph, the campaign would have taken a different form, and its decisive battle would probably have been fought in quite different circumstances. It was on the field of Königgrätz also that the new weapons of the future—the cast steel rifled cannon and the breech-loading infantry rifle—received their first real tests and, in the latter case at least, passed them triumphantly. At the same time, however, the experience of Königgrätz stood, and still stands, as a warning against the danger of overvaluing technical superiority, and it is particularly instructive for our own age, in which so much has been made of technological breakthroughs and "gaps" in weapons production. The superiority of its infantry weapon was of undeniable importance in the victory of the Prussian Army at Königgrätz, explaining among other things the rapid deterioration of morale in some Austrian units. But this advantage was not decisive in itself, and it is important to note that such cool observers as the French military attaché Stoffel and the future German Chief of General Staff Alfred von Schlieffen insisted that the *Zündnadelgewehr* (needle gun) had less effect upon the issue of the battle than Austrian persistence in faulty tactics and failures of command.[8]

For the student of strategy, Königgrätz is interesting because it afforded the first glimpse of a new style that was to have immense influence upon European strategical thought in the period that followed. To the dismay of most of his subordinates, the Prussian Chief of General Staff Helmuth von Moltke flouted traditional theories about the advantages of operations on interior lines and the necessity of concentrating forces before attempting significant action and demonstrated the manner in which space and movement could be used in the industrial age to encircle and destroy an army guided by conventional operational views. Daring in conception, Moltke's strategy was brilliantly successful in execution, falling short of perfection only because its executors were less willing to accept risks than its author. In our nuclear age we are understandably reluctant to speak about the beauty of military operations; in the nineteenth century, which was less inhibited in this respect, theorists of the aesthetics of war included Königgrätz in the long list of "beautiful battles," along with Arbela, Zama, Marathon, Lützen, Leuthen, Austerlitz and Waterloo. There is something to be said for this. Certainly, if one considers the economy with which Moltke employed material forces in order to achieve results according to a preconceived plan, then the victory of Königgrätz deserves to be regarded as a work of art.[9]

Finally, Königgrätz demonstrates the role which such intangible elements as heroism and will and accident play in human affairs. One of the King of Prussia's adjutants said to Bismarck after the battle was won: "Your Excellency, you are now a great man. But if the Crown Prince had arrived too late, you would be the greatest scoundrel in the world!"[10] No one who follows the wavering fortunes of the two forces on the day of Königgrätz can help wondering what might have happened if, indeed, the Prussian Second Army had been an hour later in joining the attack and the incipient panic in the Prussian center had been allowed to spread further; or, alternatively, what might have happened if Benedek's willful subordinates had not exposed the Austrian right flank to attack and he had had more freedom to develop his original battle plan.

It may be true that the historian's proper task is to explain what actually happened rather than to speculate about what might have been. But surely it does no harm to remind ourselves that great causes often depend upon the resources of courage and discipline expended upon them, that one generally has to pay a price for faltering determination or infidelity to commitments, and that in war, as in all of man's activities, will power can be as important as weaponry. There are few better illustrations of these homely truths than the battle of Königgrätz.

1

THE OPPOSING
FORCES

Wer will unter die Soldaten,
Der muß haben ein Gewehr,
Das muß er mit Pulver laden
Und mit einer Kugel schwer.[1]
—F. W. GÜLL

(If you want to be a soldier,
You've got to have a gun
And load it with powder
And with a heavy bullet.)

Der Saus und Braus,
Macht denn der den Soldaten aus?
Das Tempo macht ihn, der Sinn
und Schick,
Der Begriff, die Bedeutung, der
feine Blick.[2]
—*Wallensteins Lager*

("Must a soldier then be made
By driving this riotous, roaring
trade!
'Tis drilling that makes him, skill
and sense,
Perception—thought—intelligence.")
—S. T. COLERIDGE

IN AN ESSAY written late in his life, General Helmuth Karl Bernhard von Moltke, Chief of the Prussian General Staff, explained the origins of the war between Austria and Prussia with that lapidary conciseness which characterized his tactical and strategical writings. "The war of 1866 was entered on," he wrote, "not because the existence of Prussia was threatened, nor was it caused by public opinion and the voice of the people; it was a struggle long foreseen and calmly prepared for, recognized as a necessity by the cabinet, not for territorial aggrandizement, but for an ideal end—the establishment of power. Not a foot of land was exacted from conquered Austria, but she had to renounce all part in the hegemony of Germany."[3]

This is both frank and accurate. The war of 1866 was the culminating event in a rivalry that began with the rise of the house of Brandenburg-Prussia and found its first clear expression in Frederick the Great's unprovoked assault upon the Habsburg province of Silesia in 1740. From that time on, Austria and Prussia were involved in a struggle for supremacy in Germany. To be sure, the conflict was not continuous. In the days when Napoleon's shadow hung over Europe, the fear of French domination turned the rivals into allies; and after their co-operation had helped defeat Bonaparte they found it expedient to continue their association as a safeguard against new threats to their European position. During the thirty years that followed Waterloo, the partnership between Austria and Prussia was a constant element in the international balance of power, and their joint control of the Diet of the German Confederation at Frankfurt assured order throughout Central Europe. But even in these quiet years their collaboration was always tinged with distrust, and it was strained periodically by disputes about procedural matters in the Diet, or questions affecting the command of the contingents of the Federal Army, or conflicts of interest at the courts of the lesser German states; and, after the revolutions of 1848 swept over Germany, relations between the two powers deteriorated steadily.

In the first instance, this was Prussia's fault. The agitations of 1848 affected all the German governments, but none so seriously as the Austrian. Months after the Prussian crown had succeeded in reasserting its authority over its domestic foes, the Vienna government continued to be distracted by the disaffection of its subject nationalities, and particularly by a formidable revolution in Hungary. To King Frederick William IV of Prussia, this paralysis of Austria's energies seemed an opportunity that must not be let slip, and he sought to take advantage of it in order to extend Prussia's sphere of influence in middle Germany. Unfortunately for him, his plans—which involved the creation of a new union of states from which Austria would be excluded— took longer to achieve than he had imagined, and the Austrians had time to make an end of the war in Hungary. Once that was done, the Habsburg government reacted to the Prussian challenge with a promptness and energy that caused consternation in Berlin. Frederick William discovered that if he persisted in his plans he would have to be prepared to fight, so he reluctantly yielded to the panicky urgings of his military advisers and abandoned his projected reorganization of Germany.

At Olmütz, in November 1850, the Austrian and Prussian governments signed a convention which re-established the old German Confederation. But the harm had been done, and collaboration between the two powers inside this organization was never again as effective as it had been before 1848. The Prussians now complained that the behavior of the Austrian representatives at the Federal Diet in Frankfurt was arrogant and insulting and evinced a plain intention of asserting a new kind of primacy in federal affairs. The Austrians retorted that the Prussians were hypersensitive and more interested in balking Austrian proposals than in promoting the common interests of the German states. The Diet became an arena in which the two powers maneuvered for position and vied for allies; and their clashes were so frequent and so sharp that influential people in Berlin and Vienna began to feel that this competition could have only the most violent of ends. Minister President Otto von Bismarck-Schönhausen, who began his diplomatic career in 1850 as the Prussian representative at the Federal Diet and who served in Frankfurt for almost a decade, always maintained that he had gone there as a firm believer in alliance with Austria but had been disillusioned by Austrian tactics and convinced that a breach was unavoidable. "I realized," he wrote, "that the Gordian knot of German relations could not be untied by a friendly dualism; it had to be cut by war."[4] There were doubtless Austrian statesmen who suffered a similar change of heart.

In the unsettled period that was ushered in by the onset of the Crimean War in 1854, the opportunities for friction between the two great German powers were numerous. During that conflict, Austria's attempts to win the support of the lesser German states for a policy of intervention against Russia were fought tooth and nail by Prussian diplomats, and by 1856 exchanges between Berlin and Vienna were marked by bitterness and mutual recrimination. Three years later, when the Habsburg monarchy became involved in war with France and Piedmont, the Prussian government remained neutral, demonstrating that even hostility to France had ceased to be a tie between the German rivals and that the ideological solidarity of the first part of the century was a thing of the past. Indeed, there were probably many Prussians in 1859 who agreed with Bismarck's view that Prussia should take advantage of Austria's predicament in Italy "to break out toward the south with our whole army, carrying boundary stakes in our knapsacks and placing them either at the Bodensee or at that point where Protestantism ceases to be predominant."[5]

Three years after he had formulated this uncompromising policy prescription, Bismarck was called to Berlin, appointed as Minister President of Prussia, and charged with the direction of its foreign policy. He did not immediately attempt anything as radical as his proposal of 1859, but from the beginning the anti-Austrian note was palpable. In 1863 he disrupted an Austrian campaign for the reformation of the German Confederation because it would have blocked the realization of his private goal—the extension of Prussian hegemony over at least that part of Germany that lay to the north of the River Main. In 1864, after the Austrian and Prussian armies had intervened jointly in the confused affairs of Schleswig and Holstein and had compelled the King of Denmark to cede those duchies to them, Bismarck's behavior toward the Vienna government became more provocative. He demanded a share of the spoils so excessive that it amounted to Prussian annexation of the conquered provinces, and this made clear to the Austrians that they were really confronted with a demand for Prussian supremacy in northern Germany. With some justification, they rejected the Prussian claims, but the atmosphere was now so charged with emotion that even those people at the Prussian court who resisted the idea of a definitive breach with Austria regarded the refusal as a slight to Prussian honor and a potential threat to the national interest.

As early as May 1865 a Prussian crown council solemnly debated the advisability of forcing war upon Austria if its government did not yield on the question of the Prussian claims; and, although it was decided that such action would be impolitic in the prevailing state of national opinion, the discussion revealed a significant widening of Prussian ambitions and a patent unwillingness to suffer restraints imposed by the Germanic Confederation or the Austrians. Later in the year the disposal of the duchies of Schleswig and Holstein was settled by a provisional partition between the two powers, but this was recognized as a mere truce and soon gave rise to new disputes. On the Prussian side, indeed, Bismarck was now seizing every opportunity to provoke incidents that would further inflame the Austrians, while in Vienna the government was becoming increasingly fatalistic. "How can one avoid war," Emperor Francis Joseph was reported to have asked, "when the other side wants it?" By the spring of 1866 the Vienna government seemed to have accepted the inevitability of war and began the call-up of its army reserves. When the first mobilization orders were issued in Vienna on April 21, they had an electrifying effect in Prussia. Despite all of the alarums and excursions of the next eight weeks—the last-minute attempts to find a compromise, the halfhearted talk about an international conference, and the elaborate diplomatic maneuvering that went on between the Prussians and the Italians, between the Austrians and the lesser German courts, between both Austrians and Prussians and the enigmatic Emperor of the French—the soldiers had no doubt that the clash of arms was at hand and hastened to make their last-minute preparations.

Of the two armies that were soon to meet in Bohemia, the Austrian possessed the finer reputation, and most Europeans—even many, like Friedrich Engels, with some claim to military judgment—would not have hesitated before the war of 1866 to declare it superior to the Prussian Army.[6] The steadiness of the "white-coats," the self-reliance of the Styrian Jaeger, the dash of the Magyar cavalry were proverbial, and the memory of Radetzky's exploits in Italy in 1849 was still bright enough to cast a romantic glow upon the force that he had led. Austria's defeat at the hands of the French and the Italians in 1859 had not dispelled this, for her troops had fought stubbornly and well, and her officers had distinguished themselves by their gallantry and initiative at Solferino and Magenta. French soldiers were particularly emphatic in praising their recent antagonist, and although there were obvious reasons for the generosity of their opinion, it helped enhance the respect with which the Austrian military establishment was generally regarded.[7] Its performance in the Danish campaign of 1864 confirmed its reputation as an effective combat force. Indeed, the victories of Austrian infantry over the hard-fighting Danes had obscured parallel Prussian operations so completely that it became embarrassing, and this had led Archduke Albert to suggest in a letter to General (later Lt. Field Marshal) Ludwig von Gablenz that, for the sake of harmony between allies, some kind of a victory should be arranged for the Prussians.[8]

These external appearances of strength and efficiency were nevertheless misleading. They hid deficiencies in the organization, the weaponry, the tactical doctrine, and the command and staff system of the Austrian Army that were to impair its performance in the campaign of 1866.

The Austrian Army was a conscript force which was theoretically composed of ten classes of 83,000 men each, called up at the age of twenty and obliged to serve for eight years, with an additional two years in the reserve. When certain special troop units were added in, this gave an imperial army in excess of 850,000 men—a figure which Austrian diplomats were fond of brandishing in their negotiations with other powers. This force, unfortunately, existed only on paper. The financial difficulties that had dogged the Empire since the Crimean War made impossible the maintenance of anything so large, and the Austrian forces were always 20 to 25 per cent smaller than was generally admitted. In practice the annual contingents varied in size, and service in the different arms varied in length. Infantrymen rarely served more than three years, or artillerists and cavalrymen more than six; and it was customary to grant a furlough for the unexpired term with the understanding that the conscripts could be called back for thirty days of training a year. For financial reasons also, the reserve organization was exiguous, and there was no militia system, like the Prussian *Landwehr*, to provide a second line of reserves or to perform fortress duty and functions relating to public security in time of war.[9]

Equally important was the fact that military service was not truly universal. Graduates of universities and *Gymnasien* and members of certain professions were completely exempt, and anyone could hire a substitute for 1,000 gulden, the equivalent in the

1860's of about 250 U. S. dollars, a not inconsiderable sum that was quite beyond the grasp of the poor but could be easily raised by the propertied classes. These opportunities for exemption had the effect of depressing the educational level of the rank and file below that of the Prussian Army. The inevitable disadvantages of this were heightened by difficulties of communication in an army whose fighting men were drawn from all the provinces of the multinational Empire and, in many cases, spoke and understood German imperfectly, if at all. Nor was this the only way that the nationalities question affected the efficiency of the army. The memory of how some of the Hungarian units had joined the rebels of 1848–49 and the knowledge that there were other potential Hungarys in the Empire had led to the practice of garrisoning many of the non-German regiments (Hungarians, Italians from Venetia, and the like) in areas in which they would be unlikely to be affected by local grievances or sympathies. The net result of this was to place a good many formations far from the districts from which they were expected to draw their reserves when war came. Because of this and the general inefficiency of call-up procedures, it took the Austrian Army seven weeks to mobilize its forces in 1866,[10] and, in the end, it was able to raise only 528,000 men. When service troops, clerks, laborers, fortress garrisons, cadre troops, public security forces, and sick were deducted from this figure, the Empire had an effective fighting force of only 320,000, hardly excessive for a two-front war, and certainly a far cry from the boasts of its diplomats.[11]

This total force was divided into ten army corps, three of which were assigned to Italy. Unlike the Prussians, the Austrian Army did not recognize the divisional structure except in the cavalry arm, so there was a direct relationship between corps and brigade headquarters. A corps normally had four brigades, each comprising two infantry regiments of 2,500 men each, a Jaeger battalion, and one battery of eight 4-pound guns. In addition to these forces, each corps had at its disposal a regiment of hussars or uhlans and an artillery reserve of six batteries (48 guns), plus staff and auxiliary troops. The Italian corps were smaller than the others, and no two corps had exactly the same components or total strength; but in general the battle strength of the individual corps was in excess of 24,000 men.

Of the three principal branches of the service, the cavalry

was the most impressive. Superbly mounted on heavy chargers from the horse farms of Hungary, the three cuirassier divisions and the three light cavalry divisions (hussars, dragoons, and uhlans) had proven themselves in Italy, where the hussar regiment of Baron Edelsheim outclassed everything the French were able to put in the field against it. The onset of the war of 1866 found the light cavalry regiments in the midst of a change in side weapons, from the outmoded pistol to the short infantry rifle, and only half of the divisions had made the conversion when hostilities began. No great disadvantage resulted from this condition, however, and it was in any case matched by the incomplete conversion of the Prussian cavalry from pistol to carbine.[12] In equipment, training and confidence, the Austrian cavalry left nothing to be desired. Watching it advance toward the front on the morning of Königgrätz, the veteran British war correspondent W. H. Russell was to write: "The horse . . . seemed to me the finest cavalry by many degrees I ever saw, as it certainly was in point of numbers the largest displayed on one battlefield in recent days."[13]

The Austrian artillery had acquitted itself well in recent campaigns and, in addition, had kept abreast of new developments in ordnance more effectively than some of its neighbors. Its conversion from smoothbore cannon to rifled forward-loading 4- and 8-pounders was completed shortly after the end of the Danish war; and in 1866 the Austrian Army had 736 rifled cannon and 58 smoothbores (24 of these were rocket guns) to the Prussian Army's 492 rifled cannon and 306 smoothbores. Depending upon the type of ammunition used, their 4-pounders were effective up to 4,000 paces and their 8-pounders up to 5,000. In this respect, they were no better than the newly introduced Prussian rifled cannon and in the matter of accuracy perhaps not as good. On the other hand, the Austrians enjoyed three important advantages over their rivals: they had a significant superiority in numbers of rifled guns; their cannoneeers had had longer to accustom themselves to these weapons; and many of their batteries had trained in the area in which the battles of 1866 were to be fought and had studied the terrain and, in some places, fired measured ranges.[14]

The infantry was not so well off. Indeed, it embarked on the campaign of 1866 with an inferior weapon and outmoded tactical doctrine. The line regiments were armed with the so-called Lorenz gun, a rifled muzzle-loader firing a bullet designed by the Austrian artillery lieutenant Lorenz in 1852. This weapon was very accurate up to 400 paces and was effective against formations at twice that distance; its performance in 1859 had been superior to that of the French infantry rifle. But it could not compare with the Prussian breechloader in rapidity of fire, and in a conflict with the Prussians its relative disadvantage in this respect could be counted on to diminish its effectiveness. In 1865 a few Austrian officers urged conversion to breechloaders, but without success. The Ordance Department had not been convinced of the merits of the Prussian weapon by their observations in Denmark, and they were influenced by the fact that none of the other major powers had adopted breechloaders. They remained true, therefore, to the weapon that they had used in 1859, a decision that proved to be a costly mistake.[15]

It was perhaps less so, however, than prevailing Austrian views with respect to infantry tactics. In the Italian war the Austrians had seen the advantage which they derived from the possession of superior infantry weapons vitiated by the tactics employed by their opponent. The French relied upon offensive speed to overcome the range of the Lorenz gun, using very open skirmish lines to bring the fight close to the Austrian lines, and then, after a volley of aimed fire, launching massed bayonet charges, usually with a battalion front of 100 men, six men deep. The success of these tactics was due in part to factors which the Austrians did not properly assess: the fact, for instance, that the projectile from the Lorenz rifle followed a curved trajectory and did not properly sweep a field across which troops were advancing rapidly, thus allowing the French to come to grips without prohibitive losses; and the additional fact that the tighter Austrian battalion formations, and their reluctance to maneuver, made them particularly vulnerable to the bayonet charge. Failing to appreciate these things, they made the mistake of overvaluing shock tactics and, in the new drill regulations of 1862, prescribing them. Little emphasis was placed henceforth on the fire fight or on skirmishing; and battalions were kept closed up until the time came for their charge, which was usually delivered on a front less than half as wide as that employed by the French in 1859.[16] Against well-dispersed troops using a rifle that fired four times as rapidly as the Lorenz, this was to invite disaster, but few suspected this before 1866—or, if they did, had the temerity to say so, particularly in view of the Emperor's strong views on the subject. Especially after the victories in Jutland in 1864, Francis Joseph was ungracious to the point of brusqueness with critics of the bayonet and was the most zealous upholder of the tactical doctrine which was to prove the gravest handicap to Austrian operations in 1866.[17]

The imperial army was led by an officer corps whose devotion and courage was beyond question, but whose discipline and appreciation of the intellectual aspects of modern warfare were more dubious. Neither religion, nor social origin, nor nationality was an insuperable barrier to advancement—*Feldzeugmeister* Ludwig August von Benedek, for example, the commander-in-chief of the Northern Army in 1866, was a Hungarian Protestant from the lesser nobility—and, if the highest places were reserved for members of the six hundred ruling families, the bulk of the officer corps came from old soldier stock and from the middle class, with a not inconsiderable number coming from the lower nobility of the states of central and southern Germany.[18] At all levels war was perhaps regarded, as Benedek was to admit ruefully after the Austrian defeat,[19] with less seriousness than in the Prussian officer corps. Among the highest ranks were many great noblemen who looked on their occupation as a kind of sport, while among those from the German states were adventurers and soldiers of fortune whose views were no less frivolous. In general, in an army that revered the name Radetzky, gallantry and dash were more widely respected than the methodical but inconspicuous work that turns an armed force into a well-functioning machine. Because of this, obedience to the directives of higher commanders tended to be imperfect in time of war; to win the Maria Theresa Order, which was awarded for conspicuous bravery, was every officer's highest ambition and had a corrosive effect upon discipline. On the morning of Königgrätz the commander-in-chief publicly warned Major General Leopold Freiherr von Edelsheim-Gyulai, commander of the First Light Cavalry Division, that he would tolerate no individual strokes on his part and would court-martial him in the event of any deviation from his orders.[20] The fact that Benedek felt it necessary to take this extraordinary step is revealing in itself; and it is interesting in addition to note that if his warning seems to have hobbled the brilliant but impulsive Edelsheim in the day's operations, it had, unfortunately, no similar effect on other unit commanders who were as self-willed as he.

In view of all this, it is not surprising that staff work was not highly regarded in the Austrian Army, and that the staff system was ineffective. In 1854, the Prussian military attaché in Vienna had found it impossible to interest his Austrian colleagues in the *Kriegsspiel* used to train Prussian staff officers once he admitted that it was not a game at which one could win money[21]; and Lieutenant Colonel (later *Feldzeugmeister*) Friedrich Freiherr von Beck, who was serving on the staff of the Vienna Army Command at about the same time, admitted that among his fellows there were only one or two officers with even a rudimentary understanding of their jobs.[22] Ten years later, when Beck was a member of the Geographical Bureau of the General Staff, he was charged with the job of making a military-geographical study of central Germany. He was supposed to base his report on surveys and maps sent to him by one of his superiors, who had gone to Germany to prepare them. This officer, however, preferred to spend his time in the casinos at Bad Ems and answered Beck's pleas for material by writing that he could find everything that he needed in Baedeker![23]

In Radetzky's time, the army had had a brilliant chief of staff, in the person of Heinrich Freiherr von Hess; but his influence was resented and resisted by court generals like the Emperor's Adjutant General, Karl Ludwig Count Grünne von Pinchard, and Hess was not combative enough to fight for the things he believed in. As a consequence, the "pedants" and "scribblers," as Grünne was wont to call them, were bypassed or ignored throughout the 1850's[24]; and, thanks to this, Austria went to war in 1859 under an incompetent commander-in-chief whose *chef* was a cypher and whose staff were so unversed in their profession that they had not even provided the army commands with detailed maps of the theater of war.[25] Defeat led to some measure of reform: steps were taken to reduce the influence of the *Adjutantur*, previously the chief obstacle to the influence of the General Staff, and the War Ministry was completely reorganized.

But the position of the General Staff remained ambiguous; the relationship between its Chief and the head of the Operations Section of the War Ministry was never made clear; and the General Staff was permitted to have no effective influence over the selection of *chefs* for the different army corps. When Lt. Field Marshal Alfred Freiherr von Henikstein was appointed Chief of the General Staff in 1864, he resisted the preferment precisely because the authority of the position was still obscure; and he was told by his predecessor, in language that hardly comforted him, that he needn't worry about that, since, if anything exciting like a war came along, he could always hand the job over to an interim appointee and take command of a corps.[26] This persistent refusal to take the staff problem seriously was unfortunate even in peacetime. As war approached, it menaced the very security of the state.

This was particularly true because of decisions taken with respect to the command of the army. When mobilization began for what it was now realized would be a war fought against both Prussia and Italy, the Emperor appointed supreme commanders for the two theaters of war. His choice was limited, for only two names came seriously into question, those of the Archduke Albert of Austria and *Feldzeugmeister* Ludwig August von Benedek. Among the best judges, it was generally held that the former, the son of Austria's most famous soldier of the Napoleonic era and a lifelong student of every aspect of the military art, probably possessed more of the qualities necessary for supreme command and that he should, for this reason, be sent to the crucial Bohemian front. But it was also recognized that this would be an unpopular, and from the dynastic point of view possibly dangerous, choice. Archduke Albert was remembered chiefly as the commander of the royal troops in Vienna during the insurrection of March 1848 and as governor of Hungary in 1860; in neither position had he endeared himself to the masses. His great military talents and his services to the state in 1859 and 1864 were neither understood nor appreciated by most people, and his appointment to the northern command in 1866 would have appeared to them as the rankest kind of favoritism. As such there was a danger that it would recoil upon its authors in the event of a major Austrian defeat. This would almost certainly be attributed to royal interference in the military sphere and would weaken, and possibly topple, the dynasty.

Benedek, on the other hand, was the most popular Austrian soldier since Field Marshal Josef von Radetzky. The son of a Protestant doctor in Ödenburg, Hungary, he had entered the Wiener-Neustadt Military Academy at the age of fourteen and begun his active service in the Twenty-seventh Regiment in Capua four years later. He distinguished himself in the suppression of disorders in Galicia in 1846 and drew so much attention to himself by his exploits during the Italian campaigns of 1848 and 1849 that his name began to appear regularly in the columns of Vienna newspapers, usually with flattering descriptions—"the restless and indefatigable Benedek," "the idolized hero of the army," "the army's Bayard," and (in a poem that appeared in 1849) "Radetzky Number Two." This kind of praise turned to downright adulation in 1859. If the battle of Solferino was an Austrian defeat, it was, nevertheless, a personal triumph for Benedek and represents the peak of his military career. Under his command, the right wing of the embattled Austrian force not only held but broke the enemy attack and might have swept the field, if it had not been for the crumbling of the center and the incompetence of *Feldzeugmeister* Count Wimpffen, who commanded the Austrian left.[27]

Benedek was not, therefore, a man who could be lightly passed over in 1866. In addition to the support he had in the press and in the country as a whole, he was universally adored by his troops for his personal bravery and for more homely qualities— his ability to speak language that the common soldier understood, his rough and ready humor, which heartened them in moments of danger, and his unfailing generosity to old soldiers down on their luck, which often left him in straitened financial circumstances. Some of his fellow officers felt that he had a tendency to curry favor with the ranks, but even these critics admired his valor in the field, as well as his loyalty to his subordinates, his forthrightness in denouncing abuses regardless of their origin, and his steadfast opposition to incompetence and injustice. They would no more have understood his being passed over for the northern command than would the common soldiers or the newspaper readers.

There were other factors that made Benedek's appointment seem advisable. He was a Hungarian, and his preferment might, for that very reason, help confirm the loyalty of his homeland. Moreover, it was hoped that the luster of his reputation might encourage the lesser German states to be somewhat more enthusiastic about military collaboration with Austria than some of them appeared to be. The Bavarian minister von der Pfordten had told an Austrian diplomat that assurance that Benedek would be the commander in Bohemia would be worth 40,000 troops.[28] It would be folly to fly in the face of this kind of opinion.

The only one who seemed openly to object to Benedek's appointment as commander of the Northern Army was the general himself. Benedek was a friend and admirer of Archduke Albert and did not wish to appear to be taking precedence over him. Moreover, although only sixty-two years old, he had for some time been suffering from periods of bad health and was honest enough to doubt the advisability of the Emperor's choosing a weapon that might break in his hand. Most of all, he felt uncomfortable at the prospect of having to fight outside Italy, where he had soldiered all his life. When he first heard what was in store for him, he grumbled, "So now I am supposed to study the geography of Prussia! What do I know about a Schwarzer Elster and a Spree? How can I take in things like that at my age?"[29] He tried to decline the post when it was first offered to him and yielded only when the Emperor appealed to his sense of duty and his devotion to the Habsburg house. After that, he packed his kit and bade a gloomy farewell to Archduke Albert, who took over command of the southern theater.

It was at this point that the question of staff became vitally important, for, with all his good qualities, Benedek was not competent on his own to fulfill the demands of his mission. It was not only that he was called upon to fight in terrain unfamiliar to him; more important was the fact that, although he was a very good corps commander, he had no idea of how to maneuver an army of 230,000 men. In 1849, he had said in a moment of self-revelation: "I am too little the scientifically arrogant strategist; I conduct the business of war according to quite simple rules and am no friend of complicated combinations."[30] In the direction of armies, unfortunately, some complexity is unavoidable.

Benedek's fault was that, unlike Archduke Albert, he had not kept up his studies. Even during the years which he had been forced to spend as Chief of General Staff, from 1860 to 1864, he had shied away from operational and strategical studies and taken refuge in administrative tasks and troop inspections. What he needed now was someone to supplement his own talents, someone who could be what Gneisenau had been to Blücher and Hess to Radetzky.

Such persons are rare, and one cannot blame Benedek for having failed to discover one. He might, nevertheless, have exercised better judgment than he did in dealing with the important staff problem. In choosing a *chef*, he took the advice of Archduke Albert and appointed Major General Gideon Ritter von Krismanic, a former chief of the Topographical Bureau, apparently because he had some knowledge of the geography of Bohemia and southern Germany. This was hardly enough to qualify a man for the direction of an army's operations, and it was unfortunate that more attention was not paid to Krismanic's strategical views, which were rigidly conservative and, in application, cautious to the point of timidity.[31] Having made this appointment, Benedek added a needless element of confusion to conditions at headquarters when he acceded to a request from the current Chief of General Staff in Vienna, Lieutenant Field Marshal von Henikstein, and permitted him to join his staff too. Despite Henikstein's agreement to refrain from interfering in operational matters, the presence of two chiefs of staff at army headquarters (with none in Vienna to co-ordinate the movements of the Northern and Southern Armies)[32] was bound to cause confusion, not least of all in the transmission of instructions to corps staffs. Aside from this, Henikstein, who combined a cynical view of life with a sarcastic and wounding wit and was given to the kind of destructive criticism that always sees flaws in other men's plans,[33] was privately convinced that Austria could not win the war. Thus, Benedek, who was ordinarily a daring and optimistic commander, went to the front accompanied by one adviser who was excessively cautious and another who had accepted defeat in advance. This was a combination that was hardly designed to hearten him when difficulties appeared.

Like the weaknesses in organization and weaponry, these deficiencies in the headquarters staff were not apparent before the war began. Nor were there many officers and men who felt as Henikstein did. As the conflict neared, the prevailing mood was one of confidence. After all, what victories had the Prussians won in the last half century?

At the end of the Prussian Army's autumn maneuvers in 1861, a French visitor was heard to mutter: "They are compromising the whole profession."[34] This was not a unique view. In the early 1860's, the impression that the army of Frederick the Great and Blücher had fallen on evil days was widespread, despite the reforms pushed so energetically by King William I and his War Minister, General Albrecht von Roon. These, it was assumed, were vitiated by the constitutional difficulties attendant on them[35]; and, in any case, the effectiveness of military weapons could be maintained only by use. "Prussia has had no great war for fifty years," wrote Friedrich Engels in the *Manchester Guardian* of 20 June 1866. "Her army is, on the whole, a peace army, with the pedantry and martinetism inherent to all peace armies. No doubt a great deal has been done latterly, especially since 1859, to get rid of this; but the habits of forty years are not so easily eradicated."[36]

The army's lack of experience when compared with the Austrian Army worried some Prussian officers, too. In the days before mobilization began, the artillery commander Colonel Prince Kraft zu Hohenlohe-Ingelfingen was having lunch with his cousin, the Duke of Ujest, at Hiller's on Unter den Linden, and they were joined by Major General Karl Leonhard Count von Blumenthal, who was slated to be the Crown Prince's chief of staff. The talk turned on the likelihood of war, and Ujest expressed some concern over the superiority of the Austrian infantry, particularly the Jaeger battalions, in wooded terrain. "In wooded terrain," said Blumenthal comfortably, "we'll be better than they are because our officers are better trained than the Austrian ones." "All right," said Ujest, "but what about on the plains?" "Then I'm just sorry for them," Blumenthal answered as he sipped a glass of red wine, "because there we will shoot the poor fellows dead!"[37]

General Blumenthal's confidence was more realistic than the

judgments of foreign military publicists. The reformed army of King William I was better than its lackluster performance in Denmark had made it appear, and its strength lay in those very aspects of military organization and practice in which the Austrians were weakest.

Despite the budgetary difficulties caused by the parliament, the Prussian government had since 1860 carried through a series of reforms designed to eliminate the kind of furloughs that interrupted the active training of Austrian recruits, to improve reserve training and facilitate the call-up of reserves in time of war, to define the wartime functions of the older classes of the militia, and to create a coherent over-all command system.[38] Partly as a result of these reforms and partly in accordance with long practice, the peacetime army was already organized in the corps, divisions and regiments in which it would take the field; and, with the exception of the Guard Corps, which drew its members from the country as a whole, each army corps was stationed in the district from which it would draw its reserves. This facilitated fast and effective mobilization; and in 1866 it took the Prussian Army less than half the time required by the Austrians to mobilize, most corps bringing up their reserves in fourteen days. Moreover, although the population of the Kingdom of Prussia was only 18 million to the Habsburg Empire's 35 million, the fighting force raised in that time was roughly equal to the Austrian (a total of 355,000 men, of whom 254,000 could be employed against Benedek in Bohemia); and Prussia, unlike her adversary, still had reserves who could be called if needed.[39]

On the eve of war, the Prussian Army, like the Austrian, was organized on a corps basis. There were eight of these corps, each comprising two infantry divisions, an artillery reserve, and auxiliary forces (engineers, sanitary corps, baggage trains, field police, and the like). In battle conditions, great autonomy was given to the individual divisions, and in the war of 1866 the corps structure was to be superseded entirely in a large part of the army. At war strength, the Prussian infantry division included four infantry regiments, four squadrons of horse, four batteries of six guns each, and one or two companies of engineers. The normal division totaled about 15,000 men, 700 horse, and 24 guns.

Of the three principal branches of the army, the cavalry and the artillery were at less than peak efficiency in 1866, and neither was to distinguish itself particularly in the campaign in Bohemia. The art of cavalry employment had been neglected in recent years by Prussian theorists. Clausewitz had placed little emphasis upon it, despite the uses to which his model Napoleon had put his horse; and cavalry training did not bulk large in the military schools. Of the modern commanders, Prince Frederick Charles of Prussia was the one most interested in the role of cavalry in war, but he seems to have thought primarily in terms of a *Schlachten-kavallerie*, which would be held in reserve until the turning point of the battle and then used to break and pursue the enemy, and he was constantly urging the creation of a concentrated cavalry corps to serve these ends. His advice was not followed, and the Prussian horse was parceled out among the infantry divisions where it could not be used for the purposes envisaged by Frederick Charles and where it was not employed effectively for the other important duties of cavalry—intelligence and maintaining contact with the enemy.[40]

The deficiencies of the artillery stemmed largely from administrative conservatism and penny-pinching, although current doctrine also contributed to them. During the term of General von Hahn as Inspector General of Artillery from 1854 to 1864, every innovation was regarded with suspicion and accepted, if at all, only after long delays. Hahn's prejudice against rifled cannon was the main reason for the retention of the short smoothbore 12-pounder long after it should have been realized that, with a maximum range of 1500 meters (less than half of that of some of the Austrian and Prussian rifled guns), it was virtually unusable in war. Hahn's resistance to change and his caution in expenditure were responsible also for the fact that, while Prussian guns were capable of firing grapeshot and canister, as well as projectiles that exploded on contact, they had—unlike the Austrians—no shrapnel that detonated in mid-air by fuse.[41] Finally, the possibility that the Prussian Army might have converted from bronze guns to the more durable cast steel guns at an early date was lost as a result of the laborious and protracted testing procedures used by the Ordnance Department.

As early as 1843, Alfred Krupp was trying to interest the army in cast steel gun barrels forged at Essen; but, although tests demonstrated their superior qualities, he had no success and was, indeed, selling his products to the governments of Egypt and Russia long before he could overcome the Ordnance Department's indifference. Thanks to the intervention of Prince (later King) William, Krupp got his first order from the Prussian Army in 1859, for 300 cast steel rifled barrels; but in the subsequent period he made no progress whatsoever in his attempt to convince the ordnance experts that his tubes would work most effectively when combined with breech mechanisms of his own design. Hahn's successor, Lieutenant General Gustav Eduard von Hindersin, brought a more liberal approach and a greater urgency to the job of rearming the Prussian artillery, but the harm had been done, and the army entered the war of 1866 with a third of its batteries still armed with smoothbore 12-pounders. The rest had rifled, breech-loading 4- and 6-pounders, and these included about 160 cast steel guns. These last, however, had imperfect breech mechanisms, and five of them were to explode during the campaign, with deleterious effects upon battery morale out of all proportion to the number of incidents of this kind.[42]

In its operations, the artillery was handicapped by a doctrine of extreme caution. The loss of a gun to the enemy was regarded as a cardinal crime and, in order to prevent this during the advance of the army, it was held that the artillery should be carried in the rear. Prince Hohenlohe's fear that artillery was beginning to be regarded as a kind of ballast was not exaggerated,[43] and the performance of the Prussian guns in the 1866 campaign suffered as a result.

No similar flaws affected the most important branch of the service, the infantry, which in human matériel, equipment and doctrine was probably the best in Europe. Its merits derived in part from the fact that in Prussia the principle of a universal military obligation was rigorously applied,[44] which made the army a genuine cross section of the national population, and partly from the excellence of the state system of education. It is perhaps an exaggeration to say that the Prussian schoolmaster won the battle of Königgrätz, but there was doubtless a direct connection between the relatively high educational level of the rank and file and their discipline, adaptability, fortitude under fire, and patriotism. With respect to the last of these qualities, the homogeneity

of the national population was also a contributory factor, for the
Poles were the only subject nationality in the Kingdom of Prussia; and, while there were temperamental and other differences
between Rhinelanders, Berliners and Pomeranians, these did not
represent the kind of problem that the Austrian high command
had to cope with.

The whole of the Prussian infantry was armed with the
breech-loading rifle. This was not, as has often been supposed, a
new weapon. Guns with a movable breech, into which projectiles
could be placed without passing through the muzzle, had been
experimented with for at least 200 years; sportsmen had long used
them when going after pheasant and partridge[45]; and the breech-
loading principle was currently employed in both the Colt re-
volver and the infantry weapon used in Sweden and Norway.[46]
As Engels explained in an article written five years before the
Austro-Prussian war, the obstacle that had stood in the way of
widespread adoption of breechloaders had been the difficulty of
constructing a gun in which a movable breech was fastened to a
barrel in such a way as to be strong enough to withstand the ex-
plosion of the charge. Once this problem was solved, the breechloader had obvious military advantages. It could be loaded from
any position, unlike the muzzle-loader which exposed its user to
counter-fire; it could be reloaded and re-fired more quickly than
the muzzle-loader; it was capable of greater range, since it could
take a projectile larger in diameter than the bore, which when
propelled by the charge would "fill the grooves with its excess
of lead, take the rifling," and, after leaving the muzzle, travel with
a lower trajectory and with less possibility of windage than other
rifles; and it could be cleaned easily. Moreover, since the weight
of the breech brought the weapon's center of gravity closer to
the shoulder, it could be aimed more accurately.[47]

All of these advantages were enjoyed by the needle gun
(*Zündnadelgewehr*) invented by Nikolaus von Dreyse of Som-
merdä as early as 1835. This weapon took its name from the fact
that, unlike the Swedish breechloader, it was fired by means
of a striker with a long, sharp, needlelike point, which was released by a spring activated by the trigger and then penetrated the
explosive material fixed in the cartridge. The gun was simple of
construction and strong enough to withstand the requisite charges

of explosive; and its only weaknesses were the fragility of the needle (which necessitated each soldier's carrying a spare) and the great effort required to close the breech, which tempted infantrymen with tender hands to employ stones for this purpose, with resultant damage to the weapon.[48] To offset these minor flaws, it was capable of firing five aimed rounds a minute, with 65 per cent accuracy against man-sized targets at 300 paces and with 43 per cent accuracy against formations at 700 paces. The rapid rate of fire was enough in itself to interest the Prussian Army. Its first orders went to Dreyse in 1841, and eight years later the needle gun was used by fusilier detachments in the suppression of revolutionary disorders in Dresden and Baden. Satisfaction with its qualities was almost general, and it was issued to the army as a whole as fast as the military budget allowed. By 1866 all of the line infantry regiments were armed with new models of the Dreyse rifle, needle guns were beginning to be given to *Landwehr* units scheduled for front-line service, and a start had been made in arming the light cavalry with Dreyse carbines.

After some initial uncertainty, tactical doctrine was based firmly on this infantry weapon. The success of French tactics in the Italian war had caused some wavering; and Prince Frederick Charles had warned his brother officers against too great dependence on firepower, and particularly against the notion that wars could be won by defensive tactics alone. But the experience of Denmark, where Prussian losses were always a mere fourth to a tenth of Danish casualties, considerably lower than Austrian losses against the same adversary,[49] was enough to prevent the rise of a school in Prussia favoring shock tactics. Approved tactical doctrine emphasized the offensive, as Prussian tactics had always done since the days of Scharnhorst and Gneisenau, but called for advance by open order and aimed fire. In this connection, the Infantry Regulations of 1847, which were theoretically still in force, and which emphasized movement and deployment in closed battalions, were generally ignored. The basic unit in the new tactics was the company, and battalions on the offensive advanced in parallel company columns, with the forward companies fanning out by platoons and feeding the skirmishing line in the van.[50] Against massed units this flexible open order was equally effective in offense and defense, provided a decent amount of fire discipline was maintained. There was always the possibility that the ease with which they could reload would make troops "fire-happy" and lead to rapid exhaustion of ammunition. It is a tribute to the Prussian system of command that this was not permitted to happen very often.

The infantry and, for that matter, the other branches of the service as well were led by competent noncommissioned officers[51] and an officer corps which, since the time of King Frederick William I, had formed a brotherhood of arms with its sovereign and had been characterized by the equality of its members, in status if not in rank, and their devotion to the state interest. The feudal aspects of the officer corps had been amended but not destroyed by the work of the reformers of the Napoleonic period, who had sought to break the aristocracy's monopoly of commissions and to raise the intellectual standards of the corps as a whole. With the departure of the last of the reformers from office in 1819, the privileges of the nobility were largely restored, especially in the line regiments, and there was considerable evasion of the educational innovations introduced by Scharnhorst, Boyen, Grolman and their colleagues. But the memory of the defeat at Jena was enough to prevent any complete return to the caste prejudice and intellectual slackness that had caused it. Gifted soldiers of middle-class background might find it difficult to gain a commission and to make their way to posts of authority, but they could do so, as former Chief of General Staff von Reyher and other officers proved.[52] And if regimental officers were sometimes allowed to side-step the legal educational requirements, the general level of education remained higher than it had been in the old regime. This was particularly true of the curricula of the schools preparing officers for work in the technical services and of the *Allgemeine Kriegsschule,* which supplied the General Staff with its officer candidates.[53]

No part of the work of the reformers of 1807 had been more permanent than the General Staff system. The principles laid down by Scharnhorst and Grolman continued to guide their successors Müffling, Krauseneck, and Reyher, who carried further the systematization of the duties of the staff corps, established topographical and historical sections, and made annual reconnais-

sance tours (*Generalstabsreisen*) a regular feature of staff training. They also improved the critiques of annual maneuvers,
prompted the accumulation of intelligence about foreign armies,
and as early as the 1830's established a commission to study the
military significance of railroads. Most important of all, by ac-
customing the whole army to the regular alternation of officers
between the General Staff in Berlin and the corps and divisional
staffs, they diminished the once strong distrust of the intellectuals
with the red stripes down their trousers.[54]

Until the Danish war the position of the Chief of the General
Staff in the command structure of the army had been as ambiguous as it was in Austria. The General Staff was merely a subordinate department of the War Ministry, and its chief had no access
to the King except through the Minister and no contact whatsoever with the commanding generals in peacetime or in war. It was
the chaos that existed in Field Marshal Friedrich von Wrangel's
headquarters during the Danish campaign that changed this situation, for it led the King, in the hope of relieving it, to replace
Wrangel's chief of staff, General Vogel von Falckenstein, with
Helmuth von Moltke, who had succeeded Reyher as Chief of the
General Staff in 1857.

The King's decision marked the beginning of the real career
of one of the best strategical minds of the modern period and,
among German chiefs of staff, certainly the most successful. Born
in Mecklenburg, Helmuth von Moltke had begun his military
career, like his father before him, as a lieutenant in the Danish
Army, but he had transferred to the Prussian service in 1822, had
been sent to the war academy a year later, and had been a member of the General Staff since 1833. In the years 1835–39 he had
served as special military adviser to the Sultan of Turkey and had
seen the army that he had tried to reform routed by the forces
of Mehemet Ali of Egypt. Aside from this frustrating tour of
duty, he had had no direct experience with troop leadership or
the actual business of war, devoting himself to staff functions and
theoretical studies, with particular attention to problems that were
assuming growing importance: the effect of changes in weaponry
on infantry tactics, the role of railroads in modern war, and the
varied problems of mobilization in the industrial age.

Moltke's intellectual gifts were generally acknowledged by

those who read his essays, and they doubtless played a part in his appointment as Chief of the General Staff in 1857. But what was not suspected, at least before he went to Jutland in 1864 in response to the King's call, was that those talents were accompanied by others, and that Moltke indeed possessed the peculiar genius that had characterized great captains of the past like Gustavus and Frederick and Napoleon. The Danish war gave the first intimation that he had the kind of imagination which, amid the fog of war, immediately grasps all the possibilities in a given situation, that he possessed the additional ability to decide without hesitation what the best course of action should be in these circumstances, and that he was strong-willed enough to insist that his decisions be carried out. Bismarck once said that Moltke was "unconditionally reliable and, at the same time, cold to the very heart," and he meant this as a tribute to the Chief of Staff's sureness of judgment and his immunity to doubt and hesitation once he had determined his course and issued his operational commands.[55]

It was this side of Moltke that impressed those with whom he worked during the last stages of the Danish campaign. Once he had arrived in Jutland, the muddle that had characterized the work of his predecessor disappeared, and a new energy and confidence was discernible in every aspect of Prussian operations. Moltke's sure touch was apparent particularly in his direction of the successful attack upon Alsen which brought the war to a close, and his performance here seems to have won the admiration and the permanent confidence of his sovereign. In the tense years that followed the war, King William always included Moltke in the group that attended the crown councils which discussed relations with Austria, and this was both a mark of respect and an indication of the growing authority of the Chief of Staff. More tangible evidence of this followed, after it became apparent that war was inevitable. On 2 June 1866 a royal memorandum stated that henceforth the orders of the General Staff would be communicated directly to the operational commands, without the mediation of the War Minister or anyone else.[56]

This order gave Moltke a degree of authority that the Austrian Chief of the General Staff did not possess. It made him, for the time being, the King's principal military adviser. Under royal authority he would direct the army's movements during the period of mobilization and deployment, and at the start of the critical phase of hostilities he would accompany the King to the front and, standing at his elbow, use his paramount influence to make sure that the great objectives were not lost sight of in the turmoil of battle. This corresponded to the view of command relations which Moltke had expounded in his essay on the Italian war of 1859. In this monograph, which was published in 1862, he had criticized the confused state of the Austrian headquarters during the war and had argued that a commander-in-chief should not have to rely upon a committee for advice, but should have a single adviser in whom he had trust and confidence, and from whom he could expect unequivocal opinions when he needed counsel.[57] When Moltke was given that kind of authority himself in 1866, he brought to Prussian command relationships the kind of order and co-ordination that were to be missing from the Austrian staff system as conspicuously in 1866 as they had been in 1859.

This command structure did not fill all Prussian hearts with confidence. In March 1866, the King's Adjutant General, Lieutenant General Leopold Hermann von Boyen, said to a friend: "The King in command, at the age of seventy, with the decrepit Moltke at his side! What will come of it all?"[58] The question was an appropriate one to be posed by the son of one of Scharnhorst's collaborators, and it was doubtless inspired by the memory of the way in which superannuated commanders had contributed to the Prussian defeat at Napoleon's hands in 1806. But Boyen's gloom was unnecessary. Moltke was 66 years old, but he was in full command of his powers, as his direction of the deployment of the Prussian Army was now to demonstrate.

2

THE
PRELIMINARIES

Wohlan, die Zeit ist kommen,
Mein Pferd, das muß gesattelt sein;
Ich hab' mir's vorgenommen,
Geritten muß es sein.[1]
— Nassau Folk Song

(Now then, the time has come!
My horse must be saddled,
For I have decided
That I must ride.)

Wir ziehn! Die Trommel schlägt!
Die Fahne weht!
Nicht weiß ich, welchen Weg die
Heerfahrt geht.
Genug, dass ihn der Herr des
Krieges weiß—
Sein Plan und Losung! Unser
Kampf und Schweiß![2]
— C. F. Meyer,
"Huttens letzte Tage"

(We're off! The drum sounds and
the flag is flying!
Which way our expedition goes I
do not know.
But if the war lord knows, that is
enough—
His plan and command! Our
struggle and sweat!)

I n a collaboration that extended over thirty years, Bismarck and Moltke had many differences, but they had no difficulty in agreeing with the proposition that strategy, whether employed in diplomacy or military operations, was not an exact science. The sciences dealt with calculable factors; strategy had to cope with the fortuitous and the accidental. It is true, of course, that Bismarck planned his diplomatic campaigns, but he did so knowing full well that the intrusion of imponderables would probably make strict adherence to his designs impracticable. For him diplomacy was an art of the possible, and the successful statesman was one who could adjust his dispositions to meet changed circumstances and to counter sudden turns of the wheel of fortune.

Moltke looked on military strategy in much the same way, having none of that reverence for "the Plan" which, later in the century, was to inspire the disciples of Alfred Count von Schlieffen. Strategy, he once said, was no more than the expedients which a *Feldherr* used to advance his objectives amid the confusion of war. To regard it as more would be dangerous, particularly after the beginning of hostilities. "It is only the layman who thinks that he sees in the course of a campaign the previously determined execution of a minutely detailed and scrupulously observed plan. To be sure, the *Feldherr* will keep his great objectives always in view, undistracted by the varying course of events, but the roads on which he hopes to reach them can never be delineated long in advance."[3] To attempt to chart the course of a campaign and to hold field commanders to rigid prescriptions would be to destroy the kind of initiative and opportunism that wins battles.

The proper sphere of planning was before the fighting began. Here the strategist should provide his supreme commander with a plan that would give his army maximum protection during the period of deployment and would, in addition, direct the combat forces to that part of the theater of war where they would have the greatest possible advantage in the subsequent fighting. But even this operational plan had to be flexible and capable of being adapted to meet difficulties created by enemy movements or other factors.

It is just as well that Moltke felt this way, for the spring of 1866 was filled with problems for Prussian planners which might have exasperated another Chief of Staff and goaded him into dangerous decisions.

In the event of an Austro-Prussian war, an offensive-minded Habsburg army had two options: it could drive into Silesia, the rich province that Frederick the Great had wrested from Austria in the war of 1740–45, or it could advance through the mountains of Bohemia and strike directly at Berlin. To counter this double danger by effective deployment was the task of Prussian planners, and Moltke had been pondering it ever since he became Chief of the General Staff.

In his first memorandum on the subject, which was written in 1860, Moltke assumed that the Austrians would fight not a limited war but one intended to destroy the Kingdom of Prussia, and that their main drive would be directed against Berlin, the capture of which would disrupt Prussian communications and fatally injure morale. For Prussia, this would necessitate the retention of relatively light forces—"hardly more than an army corps"—in Silesia, and the deployment of the greater part of the army farther west. The Austrian advance on Berlin should not, however, be met frontally, but from the flank by forces which operated from the Elbe bridgeheads of Torgau and Wittenberg, threatened the enemy's lines of communication, and, if fortune smiled on them, forced him off his northward line of march and pressed him back toward Silesia. If the flanking attacks could start even farther upstream, greater success might be expected. Thus, a strong Prussian force established at the outset of the war at Dresden could probably deny an enemy the use of the Elbe gap in the Erzgebirge and inflict grave losses on his columns if they tried to pass through the Lusatian passes.[4]

This memorandum of 1860 is interesting on a number of counts. It assumed that the Austrian option made some division of Prussian forces necessary, although it showed a preference for deploying the bulk of the army so as to counter a thrust from northern Bohemia. It revealed a disinclination to fight a war from fixed defensive positions and a preference for one in which the enemy would be checked by the skillful use of space and movement. It breathed an offensive spirit that was remarkable when one considers that Moltke, throughout the memorandum, assumed that the Austrian Army would be the stronger of the two antagonists. Finally, it indicated that Moltke took it for granted that Prussia would not hesitate to improve its offensive capability by overrunning Saxony at the beginning of a war. "If we could occupy Dresden before the Austrians," Moltke wrote, "and establish ourselves there, we could compel the Saxons to go with us. If that didn't work, then the Saxon army would have either to withdraw to Bohemia or to barricade itself in a secure position at Pirna. In either case, we would make ourselves masters of the rich resources of the country."[5]

The salient features of this paper were repeated in later writings, and the offensive note became stronger. In a memorandum of 1862, in which he considered the problems of a war against Austria and the states of southern Germany, Moltke wrote: "Prussia's advantage lies in the initiative. We can mobilize our forces more swiftly than any of our German opponents. Success depends entirely upon their immediate and unconditional employment." Once more he talked of a swift assault on Dresden, adding that it should be followed by an offensive with 160,000 men against the Austrian center of Prague.[6] The same ideas appeared in a longer memorandum of the winter of 1865–66 which proposed dividing the Prussian forces between Lusatia and Silesia in the ratio of 3½ to 1, and which laid down the principle that "the first day of mobilization should also be that of the declaration of war . . . and, as soon as one of our neighbors begins to arm, we should declare war and announce mobilization simultaneously, for in no case should we permit ourselves to lose the initiative."[7]

The emphasis upon the offensive that emerges from these early strategical writings seemed all the more justifiable in the spring of 1866. It was abundantly clear that the sympathies of most of the larger German states—and particularly Saxony, Electoral Hesse, Hannover, Bavaria, Württemberg, and Baden— were on Austria's side and that, if they were willing to give her military support, they might add as many as 150,000 troops to an army that was already larger than Prussia's. Despite their alliance with Piedmont, which was signed on April 8 and which promised to force the Austrians to deploy for a two-front war, the Prussians were in a potentially awkward position, so far as numbers were concerned; and a strong Austrian offensive that effected a juncture with the forces of the South German states might lead, if not to an immediate defeat, to a war so protracted that it would exhaust Prussian resources. Offensive action by the Prussian Army might, on the other hand, remove this potential danger before it became actual.

Once Moltke became convinced that war was inevitable—and

he seems to have done so as early as February 1866—he wanted to bring it on before Austrian preparations were complete and while the lesser German states were still debating their best course of action.[8] But here he had his master to contend with, and, despite his frequent irritation with the policies of the Vienna government, King William was reluctant to become involved in a conflict which he regarded as being akin to a war between brothers and which he feared would always be remembered to his discredit. Throughout the spring of 1866, he became increasingly restive. He viewed Bismarck's negotiations with Napoleon III, and subsequently with the Italians, with distaste and approved the Piedmontese alliance only because he was assured that it was a necessary defensive measure. To persuade him to take the offensive—to launch what would have been a preventive war—would have been impossible; it was difficult enough to get him to approve even partial measures of mobilization.

Although the Austrian call-up had begun on April 21 and had been accelerated on April 27, it was not until May 3 that the first Prussian countermoves were made, and not until May 12 that a reluctant authorization was given for something resembling complete mobilization. The various army corps were ordered to call up their reserves, to purchase horses, to organize their baggage and ammunition trains, and to make other necessary preparations. At the same time, the pattern of command was completed by the formation of two principal army headquarters. First Army, based in Lusatia, was tentatively to comprise III and IV Army Corps and the Cavalry Corps of Prince Albert. As its commander, the King appointed his nephew, Prince Frederick Charles, who, like William himself, had devoted himself since his youth to the study of the art of war and had written extensively on problems of command, cavalry organization, and other questions. He was a careful and methodical commander of troops, whose attention to detail often irritated more dashing subordinates; and during the Danish war, in which he had commanded the Prussian Combined Corps, his laborious preparations before launching the assault on Düppel had led the Chief of Military Cabinet, Edwin von Manteuffel, to warn him that his behavior was beginning to make people think he lacked determination.[9] This suspicion was ungrounded. Once his preparations were complete, Frederick

Charles demonstrated, at Düppel and during the war of 1866, that he was a commander of energy and will, steady of nerve, and undaunted by misfortune.[10] His chief of staff was Lieutenant General Konstantin Bernhard von Voigts-Rhetz, an opinionated soldier who was almost jealously critical of Moltke, but possessed undoubted intelligence and grasp and great personal courage,[11] and his Quartermaster General was Major General Wolf von Stülpnagel, who had been his *chef* in Denmark and who, unlike Voigts-Rhetz, was on the warmest possible terms with Moltke. Stülpnagel did the housekeeping for a large staff that included the future Field Marshal Haeseler and the future head of Admiralty and Imperial Chancellor Caprivi.

The Second Army, with its headquarters in Silesia, was initially to comprise V and VI Army Corps. Its commander was the Crown Prince Frederick William (later Emperor Frederick III), a vigorous, handsome, bearded man of 35 years who had served on Wrangel's staff in Denmark and had gradually absorbed many of the functions of that aged incompetent. Assigned to him as chief of staff was General von Blumenthal, who had been Prince Frederick Charles's *Chef* in Denmark, an arrogant and hotheaded man with a contempt for desk generals and the kind of *Schlachtenbummler* (battle tourists) who attach themselves to headquarters staffs, but a soldier whose talents were universally admitted and admired.[12] Blumenthal was delighted with his assignment, writing in his diary: "The job is just what I wanted. The youthful freshness and happy temperament of the Crown Prince suit me better than Prince Frederick Charles' earnestness. Warm blood is suited to war."[13] The Quartermaster General was Major General Albrecht von Stosch, short of speech and gruff in manner, but with intellectual capacities that belied his appearance (he was an anonymous contributor to Gustav Freytag's journal, *Die Grenzboten*) and of pronounced liberal views in politics. A manysided figure who was to have two careers, as soldier and later as chief of the Admiralty, Stosch endeared himself to the Crown Prince, who shared his political views and relied on him with complete confidence in 1866 and, indeed, for the rest of his life.[14] The Second Army headquarters staff was as well endowed with brains and energy as that of First Army and included, among others, the future War Minister, Major Julius von Verdy du

Vernois, whose memoirs supply us with one of the most detailed accounts of Second Army operations in the war of 1866.

With this command and staff structure Moltke was well content. He was less pleased by the inactivity to which all this talent was condemned by the hesitations of his sovereign, which also had a disruptive effect upon all his previous planning. The Chief of the General Staff was forced, indeed, to go over to a highly tentative policy, which to many observers seemed formless in conception and potentially dangerous in result. Aware that the Austrians had a long lead in mobilization, Moltke sought to recover some of the lost ground and to give his country reasonable protection by dispatching all available troops as quickly as possible to what promised to be the main theater of war. Making skillful use of Prussia's highly developed railway system, he pushed his army corps forward until they stood on an arc 275 miles long, stretching along the borders of Saxony and Bohemia and extending into Silesia.[15] III and IV Corps, assigned to First Army, were already gathering in Lusatia between Torgau and Cottbus, in accordance with earlier orders. On May 16 they received the promise of additional support when Moltke instructed II Corps to move by rail from Pomerania over Berlin to Herzberg. On the same day, the command of I Corps in East Prussia received orders to move its units toward the Königsberg–Kreuz rail line for transportation to Goerlitz, near the Saxon border. Here it was to serve as the link between First Army and the Crown Prince's Second Army, which was now assembling in Silesia, with V Corps at Schweidnitz and VI Corps at Neisse-Frankenstein. Finally, the Chief of Staff directed the Guard Corps to march from Berlin to Cottbus, and—at the risk of denuding western Germany of Prussian troops[16]—ordered VIII Corps and the 14th Division of VII Corps to advance toward Halle, where they would be poised for a blow against the Saxon capital of Dresden or, if need be, against an advancing Bavarian army. The rest of VII Corps was left at Minden where it could join with Manteuffel's division from Altona for action against the Kingdom of Hannover, if that should prove to be necessary.

The dispersal of the army along so wide a front aroused criticism on the part of traditionalists who believed that armies should be concentrated before they went into action. Many of these saw in Moltke's initial dispositions a return to a cordon system of deployment that was an open invitation to disaster since it could not withstand strong pressure at any point; and more than a few felt that Moltke was proving that he was not up to his job.

This kind of criticism was based on a misunderstanding of the Chief of Staff's intentions and of the limitations under which he had to operate. It was idle in May 1866 to talk of concentration. Where was it to take place? To have concentrated the bulk of Prussian forces in Silesia, as some critics desired, would have taken up to six weeks after the completion of mobilization and given the Austrians a chance to move into northern Bohemia without serious opposition. Alternatively, to have tried to concentrate the whole army in Lusatia would have placed too great demands on the resources of that district, and abandoned Silesia to the enemy, and the King had told Moltke explicitly that this could not be tolerated.[17] Some division of the army was therefore necessary and had, in any case, always been taken for granted by Moltke. If it now appeared to go further than anything he had planned in the past, this was because there seemed no better way of mobilizing the army so that it could give at least some resistance to any possible enemy thrust. Moltke's critics overlooked this, as they did the speed and efficiency with which the movement was executed.

They also failed to appreciate that, in Moltke's view, the dispositions made by rail were not the end of the army's deployment, but the beginning, for, as he wrote to General von Steinmetz, the desired concentration of forces would come in due course, when the King authorized an advance, and would take place "forward," by means of concentric movement towards the enemy.[18] Moltke hoped, indeed, that the King might be persuaded to declare war on Austria as soon as the rail movement was complete, on or about June 5. When War Minister von Roon, at a crown council of May 25, urged William to start hostilities on that date, it was obviously with Moltke's foreknowledge and approval. But the King not only refused to accept this suggestion but also turned down Bismarck's proposal that an ultimatum be sent to Dresden, offering the Saxon government the choice between neutrality and invasion.[19]

The King's refusal to authorize a general advance that would

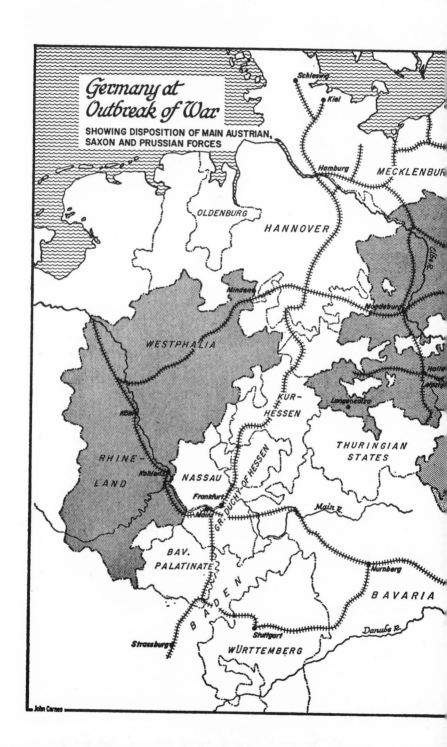

Germany at
Outbreak of War

SHOWING DISPOSITION OF MAIN AUSTRIAN,
SAXON AND PRUSSIAN FORCES

Schleswig
Kiel

Hamburg
MECKLENBURG

OLDENBURG
HANNOVER

Minden
Magdeburg

WESTPHALIA
Halle

Köln
Leipzig

KUR-
HESSEN
THURINGIAN
STATES

RHINE-
LAND

Koblenz
NASSAU

Frankfurt
Mainz
GR. DUCHY OF HESSEN
Main R.

BAV.
PALATINATE
Nürnberg

B A D E N
BAVARIA

Danube R.

Strassburg
Stuttgart

WÜRTTEMBERG

John Carnes

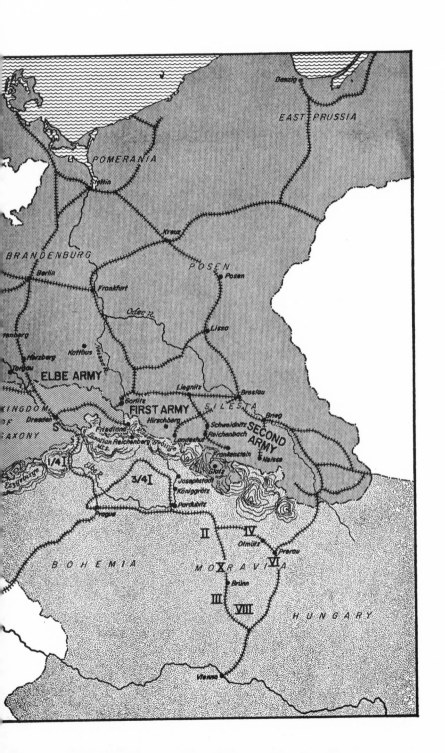

have relieved the present fragmentation of the army compelled Moltke to indulge reluctantly in a very risky maneuver—a shortening of the army's lines in the interest of increased strength by means of what was essentially a flank march along the border. Although an Austrian attack while this was going on might have been fatal, he ordered a leftward movement of the total force and the shift of I Corps from Goerlitz to Hirschberg in Silesia. As this elaborate movement neared completion on June 10, he received a message from the chief of staff of Second Army, advising him that the enemy, instead of planning a drive into Bohemia, was massing its forces at Olmütz in Moravia for what promised to be a blow against the Silesian capital of Breslau. In response to Blumenthal's urgent plea, Moltke authorized the Second Army command to move its forces farther east to the Neisse River and ordered the Guard Corps to entrain for Brieg, to the east of Breslau, to serve as Second Army reserve.[20] Simultaneously, he ordered the components of First Army to continue their eastward movement toward Goerlitz.[21]

These movements involved a marked departure from the kind of disposition outlined in Moltke's early writings about an Austrian war, and they were awkward in their results. The shift of I Corps and the Guard Corps to Silesia made the Second Army just as big as the First,[22] whereas Moltke's memoranda of 1860, 1862 and 1865–66 had all favored an unequal division with the stronger force behind the Lusatian Mountains. In addition, the leftward movement had not appreciably tightened the Prussian line; the separate corps were still strung out; the gap between First and Second Armies was still wide enough to seem dangerous; and the distance between First Army and the so-called Elbe Army, composed of the 14th, 15th and 16th Divisions and brought from the Rhineland and Westphalia to the borders of Saxony during the past week, was even greater. This disturbed many Prussian officers, including some on Moltke's own staff;[23] but it was the inevitable result of two things: Moltke's lively respect for Benedek's combative nature, which had led him to expect an Austrian advance into Bohemia and, when this did not materialize, seemed to lend plausibility to Blumenthal's fears; and the limitations placed on him, as long as he was forbidden to enter enemy territory, by geography.

In point of fact, he need not have been so concerned over the imminence of an Austrian thrust. The advantages that the Austrians had gained by starting their mobilization early were offset by the inefficiency with which they carried it out and by the inadequacy of their railway net. Whereas Moltke had five railroad lines at his disposal, the Austrian advance into Moravia had to be accomplished by means of a single line. The delays caused by this were compounded by the caution of Benedek's staff and his willingness to tolerate it. His operations chief, Krismanic, was a man who seemed to believe that armies should move *en masse*, and he countered all pleas for forward movement by saying that nothing could be done until the reserves had joined the main body. Thus, although Benedek joined the headquarters of the Northern Army at Olmütz as early as May 26, he and his forces were still sitting there two weeks later with no apparent intention of moving north.

On June 6 Lieutenant Colonel von Beck of the Emperor's staff of adjutants arrived at Benedek's headquarters. A forceful and intelligent officer with a grasp of strategy which was to bring him in time to the highest post in the army, Beck had been thinking about a German war almost as long as Moltke had, and he had concluded that Austria's best strategy would be to join her south German allies in northern Bohemia just as quickly as possible and then make a joint advance upon Berlin. To lay the foundations for this, he had been advocating the conclusion of military conventions with the German governments and, when he received no encouragement from the Austrian Foreign Office, had tried a little personal diplomacy in the hope of persuading the Bavarians to join the Austrians in Bohemia at the outset of a war. He had been unsuccessful,[24] but he had not given up hope. An energetic drive northward might, he felt, change the view of the south German governments; and, when he reached Olmütz, he urged this on Benedek. The *Feldzeugmeister* told him that he was satisfied with his staff's plans and that, in any case, his army wasn't ready to move. Both he and Krismanic proved unresponsive to the argument that delay might mean that Prussia would separate Austria from her allies in Germany, Krismanic saying coldly that, if that happened, it could be remedied in due course, and that, for the meantime, the concentration in Moravia had to be completed.

In a subsequent talk, Krismanic countered Beck's arguments by accusing him of being an agent of the retired Field Marshal Hess, and demanded that Benedek protect him from backstairs influence. Beck decided that no useful purpose would be served by further discussion and returned to Vienna to report to the Emperor.[25]

In contrast to his behavior during the Italian war, Francis Joseph had resolved to refrain, as much as possible, from interference in the direction of the pending war. Even so, he seems to have been puzzled and disturbed by the inactivity of Northern Army headquarters, and he may have instructed Beck to intimate as much to Benedek. In any event, Beck stopped off at Olmütz a few days later on his way to Dresden and had another talk with the *Feldzeugmeister*, who this time agreed to instruct I Army Corps at Prague, which was commanded by General Eduard Count von Clam-Gallas, to advance with the First Light Cavalry Division of General Baron von Edelsheim to the Iser River in northern Bohemia. Benedek also authorized Beck to talk with Clam-Gallas about arrangements for a fusion of his forces with the Saxon Army, if he was able to get any assurance in Dresden that the Saxons were going to come into the war.

Somewhat heartened by this, Beck went on to Dresden, where he discovered to his dismay that the Saxons were as divided in their councils as the Bavarians had been earlier. Crown Prince Albert of Saxony, a very competent soldier who was a personal friend and hunting companion of the Emperor Francis Joseph, was in general agreement with Beck's view that the Saxon Army should move to the Iser River as quickly as possible, and was grateful for the invitation to assume command over the joint force; but the Saxon chief of staff, Major General von Fabrice, wanted to retain the army's freedom of action, and the ministerial council could reach no clear decision with respect to Saxony's position in a war. The net result of the talks was a tacit agreement to await Prussian action and let that shape the course of events.[26]

Benedek's reluctance to move from Olmütz and the indecision of Austria's friends in Germany represented the first in a series of lost opportunities. While the Prussian Army was confined to its own territory and Moltke was shifting forces to guard against an invasion of Silesia that was never contemplated by his enemy, the beginnings of an Austro-German concentration might have been made in Bohemia, and the shape of the war to come might have been different. But ironically the very circumstances that provided the Austrians with this opportunity helped to prevent them from exploiting it. Using techniques first employed during the American Civil War, Austrian agents in Silesia had managed to tap the telegraph wire connecting the headquarters of the Prussian Second Army with Berlin; and the intercepted messages were interpreted by Colonel von Tegetthoff's intelligence staff and passed on to Krismanic. In this way Benedek's operations officer learned of Moltke's decision to send the Guard Corps to Second Army, and this persuaded him that the Prussians were massing for an attack from Silesia and that, in consequence, the Austrian Army must remain based on Olmütz.[27] Thus, the Austrian chance was let slip.

This was unfortunate, for now, after the period of waiting on Moltke's part and delay on Benedek's, events began to move with frightening speed. In the Elbe duchies the squabbling of the two great powers over their relative rights and privileges had never stopped. Now, wearied beyond endurance by a long series of provocations on the borders of Holstein, the Austrian government repudiated the provisional partition that had been made in 1865 and referred the Schleswig-Holstein question to the Germanic Confederation. The Prussians responded on June 12 by occupying Holstein with troops, the Austrians retiring without resistance. The Vienna government then appealed to the Federal Diet and asked for the mobilization of all federal troops, exclusive of the Prussian contingent; and on June 14 the majority of the Diet voted approval. Bismarck immediately announced that this represented a dissolution of the federal bond, and on June 15 the Prussian government—taking a leaf out of Moltke's memorandum of 1865-66—declared war on the Kingdoms of Hannover and Saxony and the Electorate of Hesse. Prussian troops began to move into those territories without delay.

The occupation of Saxony and Kurhesse presented no great difficulties. At three o'clock on the afternoon of June 16, the Elbe Army—comprising three divisions of infantry, 26 squadrons of horse, and 144 guns and commanded by General Herwarth von

Bittenfeld—crossed the border of Saxony and headed for Dresden.[28] Now that the decision had been made, the Saxon Army did what Beck had urged it to do earlier. Thirty-two thousand strong and under the leadership of the King and the army's effective commander, Crown Prince Albert, it fell back toward the Bohemian frontier, which it reached early on the morning of June 18. The King watched his troops cross the border, their rifles garlanded with oak leaves from their country's forests, and with the words, "Now then, in God's name!" followed them. The march to the Iser began.[29]

The elector of Hesse had no time to mobilize his forces, and a single Prussian division, based on Wetzlar and led by Major General Friedrich Gustav von Beyer, overran the country and ended resistance within three days. The case of the Kingdom of Hannover proved to be somewhat more difficult, although there is good reason to believe that this was largely due to the incompetence of Prussia's commanding general in western Germany, Vogel von Falckenstein, the same general whom Moltke had replaced in Denmark two years earlier. Falckenstein had Manteuffel's division from Altona and Goeben's from Minden at his disposal, enough to deal with the Hannoverians if he acted with speed and determination. His failure to do so or to appreciate the necessity of preventing the Hannoverian Army from establishing contact with the Bavarians to the south led Moltke, most reluctantly, to intervene in the actual direction of operations. This violated his firm belief in the advisability of leaving the initiative in the hands of local commanders, but it had the happy result of blocking the escape route southward and forcing the King of Hannover, after his honor had been saved by a hard-won fight at Langensalza, to lay down his arms on June 29.[30]

These events were a mere prelude to the greater clash of arms that was now to come in the east, but they represented a major strategical victory for Prussia. With the employment of very small forces and with little spilling of blood, the Prussians had cleared all of north Germany, linked up the scattered territories of their own kingdom, and detached states with rich resources and a population of six millions from the Habsburg alliance. The occupation of Saxony had placed the passes of the Erzgebirge in their hands, a weapon of inestimable value in the offense and the defense.[31] Moltke now had no reason to fear complications in the west while he was dealing with the Austrians, for, once the Hannoverians had surrendered, the federal forces that were left in the west (the VIII Bundeskorps and the Bavarians) lost any martial enthusiasm that they might have had earlier and were isolated and defeated with relative ease by Falckenstein's forces, now renamed the Army of the Main.

These events broke the deadlock farther east, where the two armies had been waiting uneasily in expectation of action in Silesia. On the same day that Prussian troops entered Saxony, Emperor Francis Joseph telegraphed to Benedek: "The events in Germany make the beginning of operations imperative. Nevertheless, since military considerations are paramount, I leave it to you to determine the time for the beginning of the advance and await telegraphic information concerning your decision."[32] It was clear from this and from a spirited manifesto to the people issued on June 17 that the Emperor had no intention of leaving Austria's allies in the lurch and that, when he spoke of an advance, he was thinking of an offensive in the direction of the Iser River and beyond.

Benedek was thinking of the same thing, although for somewhat different reasons. He had been making some rough calculations on the basis of intelligence reports and had concluded that, as things stood, he was in danger of being outnumbered. Unless he broke out of Olmütz and managed to link up with the Saxon and, hopefully, the Bavarian armies, he could not hope to meet the enemy on equal terms.[33] With an urgency that had been lacking in his past behavior, he pushed on his preparations and, on June 18, a hot summer day, the Northern Army, 180,000 strong plus trains and administrative staffs, started its march in three parallel columns toward the fortress of Josephstadt on the upper Elbe. The same day came news from Munich that Benedek need not expect to find the Bavarian Army at the trysting place; the Bavarian government had decided that its mission was to defend the Main River line and nothing more. This was a blow, but it did not dampen the army's spirits, which were heightened by the liberation from long inactivity and the knowledge that they were moving against the enemy at last.

The Austrian advance had two effects in Prussia. It helped

persuade the still hesitant King that he was justified in removing the restrictions that had till now hampered his soldiers' freedom of action, at least with respect to Austria. And it clarified Moltke's mind with regard to Austrian intentions. As late as June 18, he was writing to General von Stülpnagel at First Army headquarters, expressing his gratification about the course of events in Saxony but saying that this in itself proved nothing, since the decision would come in the east. The problem was to find the place where this was going to happen. "It is difficult at the moment," he wrote, "to decide whether the First Army should support the Second Army directly, or the Second the First. That depends on whether the Austrians turn their main force toward Silesia or Lusatia. . . . It is very easy to give orders for something that doesn't turn out right later on, and consequently we must wait for more light. . . . Day and night my thoughts turn to the question of how we can make both armies as strong as possible, no matter which of them the main Austrian army attacks. Happily each of them is 130,000 to 150,000 men strong, and an army like that doesn't let itself be overrun. As soon as General Herwarth is available, I think we will, in God's name, march into Bohemia."[34]

The next day intelligence reports indicated that Benedek was moving toward northern Bohemia, and Moltke's doubts began to lift. There was always a chance, of course, that the reports were mistaken or that the Austrian movement was a feint, and Moltke's first orders to the separate armies, while ordering a general advance toward Bohemia, were cautious and placed restrictions on Second Army.[35] By June 22, however, the direction of the enemy march was confirmed beyond reasonable doubt, and at noon on that day the Chief of General Staff sent a laconic wire to the Crown Prince and Prince Frederick Charles. "His Majesty commands," it read, "that both armies march into Bohemia and seek a juncture in the direction of Gitschin. VI Corps will remain at disposal on the Neisse."[36]

The drama to which the campaign in the west had been the curtain raiser was now about to begin.

3

THE CAMPAIGN IN BOHEMIA:

The First Encounters

Nun adjö, Lowise, wisch ab das
Gesicht,
Eine jede Kugel, die trifft ja nicht,
Denn träf jede Kugel apart ihren
Mann,
Wo kriegten die Könige ihre
Soldaten dann!

Die Musketenkugel macht ein
kleines Loch,
Die Kanonenkugel ein weit
größeres noch;
Die Kugeln sind alle von Eisen
und Blei,
Und manche Kugel geht manchem
vorbei.[1] —WILLIBALD ALEXIS,
"Fridericus Rex"

("Well, adieu, Louise. Wipe your
face off!
Every bullet doesn't strike home.
For if every single bullet hit its
man
Where would the kings get their
soldiers then?

The musket ball makes a little hole.
The cannon ball makes a much
bigger one.
Bullets are made of iron and lead,
And lots of bullets miss lots of
people.")

BOHEMIA—an ancient battleground, whose hills once watched
Field Marshal Traun teach the great Frederick the art of maneuver and heard the Old Dessauer pray, "Lord, if you won't
help me, don't help those scoundrels on the other side!"[2]—

juts like a bastion into the southern flanks of Saxony and Silesia. Its frontiers are delineated by an irregular mountain chain that extends eastward for more than three hundred miles from the limits of northern Bavaria to the environs of Cracow in Galicia. Behind what Carlyle called "the wizard solitudes and highland wastes" of this outer range, the land falls away in great swelling hills and ridges towards the south, the steeply ascending ranges of foothills alternating with deeply cut river valleys. It is a land of water as well as of hills. Near Libau, the Elbe bursts forth from its eleven legendary springs in the Riesengebirge and flows southward to Pardubitz, fed as it goes by the streamlets from Glatz and the more considerable Aupa, Mettau and Adler rivers. At Pardubitz it turns sharply to the west and, joined by the waters of the Cidlina and the Bistritz and the Iser, which also spring from the roots of the Giant Mountains, winds its way to the vicinity of Prague, then angles northward past the confluence of the Moldau and flows through a gap in the Erzgebirge to the city of Dresden and beyond.

Along this beautiful river and its tributaries nestled the most important of the towns of northeastern Bohemia: the fortress towns of Josephstadt and Königgrätz on the upper Elbe; Miletin, Sadowa and Nechanitz on the Bistritz; Gitschin, Smidar and Chlumetz on the Cidlina; Turnau, Münchengrätz and Jung-Bunzlau on the Iser—all names that will recur in our story. In 1866, their inhabitants, like the people of the countryside, were Czechs and Germans, according to the census of 1857 in proportion of three to two, but so mixed that there was no discernible language frontier between them, as boundary commissions were to discover in 1919 and in 1938–39. Predominantly German towns like Reichenberg and Trautenau were surrounded by Czech villages, and Czech communities were to be found in the most heavily Germanic rural areas. The town inhabitants were imperial officials and civil servants, merchants, shopkeepers, handicraftsmen, and workers in small plants like brick kilns, breweries and glass manufactories. Except in Prague, there were few signs of large-scale industrialization, and the most visible sign of the new age was the railway. The main line from Vienna and Olmütz ran over Pardubitz, westward to Prague, and northwest to Dresden; and from Pardubitz another line ran north to Josephstadt and northwest to Turnau, where one could get connections for Prague to the southwest or for Zittau and Lobau in Saxony. But the smoke from the occasional locomotives did not long disfigure the blue skies or the green fields dotted with villages. The main industry was still agriculture. Bohemia had long been known for the fertility of its soil, and Bohemian fruit and hops were famous and sought after. All told, the country in which the war was to be fought was a pleasant and prosperous parkland, its fields filled with cultivated fruit trees and waving grain.

In his fascinating history of the Austro-Prussian war, the Berlin novelist Theodor Fontane pointed out that, as a theater of military operations, Bohemia fell into three parts.[3] The westernmost sector was bounded by the Elbe and Iser rivers and the mountains of Lusatia. The central section extended east of the Iser and was limited on the north by the Riesengebirge and on the south by the central Elbe. The easternmost sector lay between the upper Elbe and the Adler and was also bounded on the north by the Riesengebirge.

Moltke's plan called for the penetration of all three of these sectors by Prussian armies, and the eventual union of these separate forces at or near Gitschin on the Cidlina. Once it had finished mopping up in Saxony, the Elbe Army of General Herwarth von Bittenfeld would move through the pass at Rumburg into the western sector and head for Münchengrätz on the Iser River. The First Army would invade the central section, using the defiles through the Lusatian Mountains at Zittau and Friedland. It would move toward the Iser line at Turnau and Podol and, once that was broken, toward Gitschin. East of Friedland there was no practicable pass through the Riesengebirge for 40 miles, but at the end of this forbidding escarpment was the pass of Landeshut, famous in Frederick's wars, and east of it the passes that led from Braunau and Reinerz, in the county of Glatz, into the valleys of the Aupa and the upper Elbe.[4] Through these defiles the army of the Crown Prince was to make its way and, having done so, effect a rendezvous with the First Army.

To some military publicists this was a plan fraught with danger, and Friedrich Engels, known to his political associates as "the General," made sport of it. If anything like this, he wrote in an article that was not published until July 3, were suggested by a lieutenant in a war academy examination, it would cause his dismissal from the service. "It would be completely inexplicable how such a plan could ever be discussed, much less adopted, by a body of such unquestionably capable officers as form the Prussian staff," he added, mounting one of his favorite hobbyhorses, "if it was not for the fact of King William being in chief command. But nobody could possibly expect that the fatal consequences of kings and princes taking high command would come out so soon and so strong."[5]

If we leave aside Engels's stubborn conviction that Prussia was bound to lose the war because its ruler would not stay at home like his fellow sovereign in Vienna,[6] his basic criticism was that the Prussian plan of advance exposed the First and Second Armies to the danger that Benedek would get his forces in between them and, by taking advantage of interior lines, defeat them singly before they could combine. But the Prussian plan was not something foisted on a reluctant staff by a willful monarch. It had been devised by Moltke without royal interference, and it was based on as realistic an appreciation of the situation in Bohemia as that of his amateur critics. Given the difficulties of the terrain, it was indeed more than likely that Benedek would get his forces into a central position; but what then? Moltke was not as impressed by the hoary tradition concerning the advantages of interior lines as some of his contemporaries. An army in the middle has an advantage only when the separate detachments of the opposing force are more than a day's march apart. Its position deteriorates rapidly as the enemy's armies converge upon it, and there comes a time when it dare not move against one of them for fear of being hit in flank and rear by the other.

Moltke never had any intention of satisfying those critics who believed that the army should be concentrated for a breast-to-breast encounter with the enemy. From the beginning his advance was designed to come at Benedek, wherever he might be found, from at least two directions; and the possibility of encircling the Austrian Army was never absent from his mind, although this never became actual until the day of Königgrätz and then was narrowly missed.[7] The assignment of Gitschin as the rallying point for the Prussian armies had no absolute significance in Moltke's mind. He had merely calculated that this was about as far as Benedek could get, if he were reasonably energetic in his advance from Olmütz, before the Prussian armies caught up with him. But Moltke had advised Prince Frederick Charles that he should be prepared to follow victory in another direction, depending on how things developed.[8] The Chief of Staff did not want to prescribe an exact course for the First Army, and he had written to his friend Stülpnagel to say that opportunities for tactical victories should not be avoided when they presented themselves. "I think," he wrote, "that you will bump into the heads of columns and have a chance for some pretty fights."[9] But the important thing was a realization of the relationship between the advance of the First Army and the vulnerability of the Second in the passes east of Landeshut.

It was also imperative that the Second Army realize the risks it would have to take and not increase them by an unwise plan of march. On June 24 Moltke wrote to Blumenthal: "Just be sure of real and precise leadership!" The staff would have to take care that it used all available routes through the mountains, so that the crossing was not dangerously slow, and that it timed the advance so that no single column got too far ahead and opened itself to attack by superior forces when support was not possible. When Blumenthal received Moltke's orders, he saw the point and was in general more appreciative than Engels had been. His strategical sense leaped to the possibilities inherent in the projected concentric operations, and he confided to his diary that it was a good omen that Moltke and he seemed to be thinking the same way. "I don't deny," he added, "that our march over the mountains is a truly dangerous operation, which quite possibly can come a cropper. But it is absolutely necessary, if we don't want to lose time."[10]

Time! The whole of Moltke's plan depended upon a sense of time, upon an urgency in execution, upon an awareness of the necessity of speed in the interest of that kind of co-ordination that would secure the single armies against disaster in the first difficult days of the advance. Blumenthal, at least, seemed to appreciate this. The question was whether Prince Frederick Charles did.

The first Prussian troops crossed the Bohemian border on the Dresden-Rumburg road on June 22. These were the King's Hussars (Seventh Regiment), the Rhenish Jaeger (8th Battalion), four battalions of fusiliers, and two batteries of guns—all forming the advance guard of Herwarth's Elbe Army. The bulk of his forces, which comprised the 15th and 16th Divisions from the Rhineland and the 14th Division from Westphalia, followed without delay.[11]

The troops of Prince Frederick Charles were gathered in Lusatia—the 3rd and 4th Divisions (II Corps, Pomerania), the 5th and 6th Divisions (III Corps, Mark Brandenburg), and the 7th and 8th Divisions (IV Corps, Prussian Saxony). In every case but that of the Pomeranians, the corps structure had been set aside for the duration of the war, and the division commands were placed directly under the First Army commander. The Prince ordered the advance on the morning of June 23 and, led by the Magdeburg and Brandenburg divisions, the army began to move on the roads that led from Zittau, Seidenberg and Marklessa respectively towards the Bohemian town of Reichenberg. They crossed the border with bands playing and troops cheering. An eyewitness of the passage of the 7th and 8th Divisions described the scene later. "A toll house with a black and yellow crossing barrier," he wrote, "marked the border between Saxony and Bohemia. Here the Prince stopped. Uhlans, who formed the advance guard, crossed the border first; then came the infantry. Whenever the forward ranks of a battalion reached the barrier and saw the Austrian colors, they raised a joyful shout, which was taken up by the rear ranks and repeated over and over, until the troops reached the toll house and saw their 'soldier prince' standing by the border marker. At the sight of him the hurrahs turned to a jubilant roar, which stopped only when replaced by the sound of a war song which was taken up and repeated by every battalion as it crossed to Bohemian soil. The commander stood quietly on the highway, watching the passing regiments with silent pride. And well might he have felt this way, for never had an army crossed a foreign border that was better armed, better supplied, and inspired with a higher feeling than the one that crossed from Saxony to Bohemia."[12]

Like much of the reporting of the day, this is remarkable

more for its patriotic tone than for any critical sense, and in one respect it went far astray. The army was not as well supplied as it may have appeared when crossing the frontier, and this was one reason why the First Army, and the Elbe Army as well, was soon moving more slowly than Moltke desired.

In the period before the actual outbreak of hostilities, little had been done to think through the problems of provisioning the army during the campaign. War Ministry officials indulged in unreal assumptions about the ability of local recruiting areas to supply their troops by rail (apparently expecting bakeries in Königsberg and Cologne to send bread all the way to the Bohemian border), but did not take the time to draw up a systematic schedule of food trains or a list of denominated food stations. At the same time they seemed to believe that, once the fighting had begun, the armies would be able to live off the land, and—in the interest of economy—resisted army and corps requests for vehicles in which to transport food and fodder beyond the railheads. It was not, for example, until June 13 that the First Army was able to persuade the War Ministry that it must be permitted to purchase wagons with which to supply advancing troops, and the Elbe Army never received such an authorization. Even in the case of the First Army, the permission came too late to enable the staff to organize an effective service of supply, and the progress that was made was vitiated in large part by the decision to hire civilian drivers for the food trains rather than to rely on military personnel. The results were not gratifying, the drivers showing a marked tendency toward panic or drunkenness whenever danger threatened.

For both the Elbe Army and the First Army confusion increased once the frontier was crossed. The former, with no magazines or provision trains, tried to live off the land and found it impossible. "Despite the best intentions of the inhabitants," wrote the leader of the advance guard at the end of the second day's march, "it is simply impossible for them to supply sustenance for 6,000 men." The commander of the 16th Infantry Division prophesied a quick breakdown of morale unless food was brought from the rear and administrative officers appointed to see that it was equitably distributed. The First Army was soon in even worse condition, for its food columns were completely undisciplined and soon clogged the roads behind the army, and the inhabitants of the mountain regions did not try to co-operate, but filled up their wells and fled to the forests with their food and cattle, so that requisitioning did not work. "Nothing to live on unless we carry it ourselves," Prince Frederick Charles wired to the King on June 28, and two days later: "First Army completely exhausted. Needs several days rest."[13]

That the constant preoccupation with the problem of food supply helped slow down the progress of the Elbe and First Armies is unquestionable. But this was not the only reason for the failure of the two armies—now both under Prince Frederick Charles's over-all command—to live up to Moltke's expectations. As has already been indicated, Frederick Charles was a prudent commander, who justified his caution by appealing to Clausewitz. He once said: "The best strategy is always to be really strong, first in general, and then at the decisive point. There is no loftier or simpler law in strategy than to hold one's strength together."[14] During the advance into Bohemia, he carried this philosophy to excessive lengths, because he was convinced that the enemy would be waiting for him in strength at Reichenberg or, if not there, on the Iser River. In consequence, he kept his own forces bunched up, so that by the time they reached Reichenberg they had too narrow a front and a depth of over a day's march. This not only made for slow progress but increased the difficulty of provisioning. Apart from this, the prince was reluctant to move forward until Herwarth's forces had fallen in on his right or until he had established some contact with the I Corps of General Eduard von Bonin, which formed the right wing of the Second Army's advance. Since Herwarth was as methodical as Frederick Charles, and Bonin was on the other side of the pass of Landeshut, this promised to be a lengthy business.[15]

Frederick Charles's apprehensions concerning the enemy might have been relieved if he had employed his cavalry for purposes of reconnaissance. But his staff had decided that cavalry could not be used in the difficult mountain terrain, and in the army's order of march the horse brought up the rear. It remained there, indeed, even after the mountains had been crossed.[16] With no patrols fanning out ahead, Frederick Charles was deprived of the knowledge that there were no enemy forces at Reichenberg, and that those which were on the Iser line numbered only 50 to 60,000 instead of the 135,000 that the First Army's staff believed were massing at Jung-Bunzlau.[17] The bulk of the Austrian Army was, in fact, at the fortress town of Josephstadt, where Krismanic was once more insisting that no forward action could be taken until the rear units had come up, a process that was to take until June 28.[18] Moreover, the enemy forces on the Iser were in a state of some disorganization because of delayed and contradictory messages from Benedek's headquarters, and the commanders were uncertain about the possibility of making any real stand west of Josephstadt.[19]

An appreciation of the true situation came to Frederick Charles only slowly. First Army reached Reichenberg on June 24 and found it unoccupied, although there was a brush with a detachment of Austrian hussars, and five horses were wounded or killed.[20] Instead of pushing on, the First Army commander decided to wait until he had a clearer picture of the whereabouts of Herwarth's forces, and he gave his army a day's rest on the 25th and prolonged this, for most of them, for another day on the 26th. At the same time, he was somewhat shaken by a peremptory wire from Moltke—a message that had been written three days earlier and delayed in transmission—which pointed out that to make the movements of the First Army dependent upon Herwarth's progress might result in the Crown Prince's forces being caught in the mountain passes and which stated emphatically that "only a vigorous advance by the First Army [could] disengage the Second."[21] It was this message which, in all probability, induced Frederick Charles to take the step that led to the first significant victory of the campaign. On June 26 he ordered the 8th Division, led by Lieutenant General Heinrich Friedrich von Horn, to make an exploratory movement in the direction of Turnau on the Iser.[22]

At Sichrow, Horn's advance guard encountered the Austrian cavalry division of General Baron von Edelsheim, the hero of Solferino, and that able and energetic soldier proceeded to give the Prussians a lesson in the proper co-ordination of cavalry and artillery. He used his batteries to such effect, indeed, that Horn found it necessary to deploy his whole division against the smaller Austrian force, and even then Edelsheim gave way only after

Frederick Charles had brought up the 7th Division of Lieutenant General Eduard Friedrich Karl von Fransecky in support. The Austrians then retired towards the Iser, having suffered only trifling losses.[23]

From the Austrian point of view, this brilliant performance had one unfortunate consequence: it released Frederick Charles from his earlier inhibitions. Thoroughly aroused, he ordered his two forward divisions to pursue the retreating Austrians in the direction of the Iser bridgeheads. Horn's troops, somewhat chewed up, stopped for an evening meal before pushing on towards Podol; but Fransecky's forces pelted ahead toward Turnau, which they were surprised to find unoccupied, although the wooden bridge across the river had been destroyed. They took over the town, and the engineers began immediately to construct a pontoon crossing.[24]

This unexpected prize was due to the disarray of the Austro-Saxon forces on the Iser. Because of delays in the transmission of messages from Benedek's headquarters, the Saxon Corps had not joined the Austrian I Corps on the Iser until June 25. Command of the combined force was vested in Crown Prince Albert of Saxony, but he decided to leave responsibility for the defense of the river crossings north of Münchengrätz in the hands of the Austrian corps commander, Count Clam-Gallas, while he defended the upper river. This was not a happy division of authority. According to Benedek's last vague order, the Austro-Saxons were supposed to hold the river line unless the losses suffered in doing so promised to be prohibitive, in which case they were to retire to Miletin, west of Josephstadt. Clam-Gallas was the wrong man to whom that kind of freedom of choice should have been given, for he was neither an energetic nor a sanguine commander. When it had been suggested, on June 25, that a strong defense could be built on the western bank of the river if he would assign infantry units to Edelsheim's command at Sichrow, Clam had refused to countenance this, an indication that he had little confidence in his ability to hold the Iser by any means. On June 26 the Prussians owed their unopposed seizure of Turnau to this attitude and to his customary lassitude.[25]

However, the day was not yet over. At two in the afternoon, Prince Albert received a telegram from Benedek which made it clear that he intended to advance with his whole army against the Prussian First Army and that the Iser line must, therefore, be held at all cost. The Saxon Crown Prince went immediately to Clam-Gallas and galvanized him into unwonted activity, the two commanders deciding that the enemy must be thrown out of Turnau and that the way to effect this would be to secure Podol and then to advance on Sichrow, where Edelsheim had fought that morning. The advance on Sichrow would in itself force the Prussians to pull out of Turnau by threatening their communications, and the seizure of this high ground would secure the bridgehead. The first step was Podol, and the "Iron Brigade" of Major General Ferdinand von Poschacher von Poschach, so-called because of its exploits in Denmark, was ordered to advance on it.

Earlier in the day—although this was not to be known to either Frederick Charles or the Austro-Saxons for another twenty-four hours—a fire-fight had taken place at Hühnerwasser on the Elbe Army front between Herwarth's advance guard and an Austrian brigade led by Major General Leopold Count von Gondrecourt. The Austrians had relied on bayonet charges against infantry concealed in woods and had suffered losses of 270 to the Prussian loss of 50.[26] This was the first real demonstration of the efficiency of the needle gun, and, on a larger scale, it was repeated at Podol, a picturesque little village with a single street lined with wooden blockhouse-like dwellings, which now witnessed savage and bloody conflict.

The Austrian advance began at 8:30 in the evening. In the absence of General von Poschacher, who was at Clam-Gallas's headquarters, Colonel von Bergou took command of the brigade. He sent a column of two infantry battalions, supported by the brigade artillery, to Laukow, the crossing below Podol (where it, rather oddly, stayed during the ensuing struggle), while he himself led an advance with the rest of his force along the Podol highroad to the stone bridge over the river. An hour before his advance got under way, fighting had already started at Podol, between the advancing Magdeburg Jaeger of Horn's division and two Austrian companies which had been stationed there as a bridge guard; and by the time Bergou was ready to mount his attack the Magdeburgers had forced the defenders to retire by wading across the shallows and threatening to cut them off. Colonel Bergou's attempt to retrieve this situation lasted for almost two hours, during which time his forces, led by the 18th Jaeger Battalion, stormed the bridge and drove the Prussians out of the town, only to be subjected to murderous fire from the heights beyond. A Prussian fusilier wrote later that, in one phase of this fighting, his company fired 5,700 rounds in 33 minutes, an average of 22 per man.[27] The effect of this upon the close-packed Austrian columns was devastating; and, shortly after ten, General von Poschacher and Count Clam-Gallas called off further attacks. They hoped at least to hold the crossing, however, and Clam-Gallas ordered two brigades forward to support Poschacher in this attempt; but the first companies to approach the bridge suffered such heavy losses that, soon after eleven, Clam-Gallas ordered a general retirement. The Prussians had won the bridgehead at a cost of 12 officers and 118 men. The Austrians had employed 17½ companies in the fight and, according to their own General Staff history, had lost 33 officers and 1,015 men.[28]

This setback at Podol made it impossible for the Austro-Saxons to retake Turnau, unless reinforcements arrived speedily from the main army. But on June 27, at his headquarters in Münchengrätz, Crown Prince Albert received the dampening news that there was no hope of this, for a wire from Benedek made it clear that he was still at Josephstadt, although he expected to be in Gitschin by the 30th. In the circumstances, the Saxon commander decided to abandon the already breached Iser line and ordered his subordinate commands to make preparations for a march to Gitschin on the morning of the 28th.[29]

One might have supposed that Prince Frederick Charles would already have been on his way to that point too, not only because of Moltke's emphasis upon the necessity of closing the distance between the First and Second Armies, but also because a rapid advance might make it possible to cut off the Austro-Saxons before they could join Benedek's army. But Frederick Charles had apparently decided that the Austro-Saxons were going to stay at Münchengrätz and that, in consequence of this, any Prussian advance to the east would be exposed to a flank attack from that direction. It would be a measure of prudence to destroy Prince Albert's force where it stood, but it would be unwise to attempt even this before the First Army reserve and Herwarth's divisions, which were still a day's march to the north-west, had reached the river. That the enemy was not going to wait for him at Münchengrätz never seems to have occurred to the First Army's commander, for, as usual, he had neglected to use his horse and had no way of detecting Prince Albert's already well-advanced preparations to retreat towards Gitschin. Methodical as ever, Frederick Charles spent June 27 in planning a massive push against what was to prove to be an open door. As he did so, violence erupted in the eastern mountains.[30]

Had the command of the Second Army been as dilatory and as disposed to violate the spirit of Moltke's operational plan as First Army, Benedek might have escaped the dilemma that was, very shortly, to confront him. But Crown Prince Frederick William's staff showed both energy and the ability to overcome the kind of difficulties that plagued Frederick Charles's forces. The supply problem, for instance, was never as acute as upon the western front, largely because unit commanders refused to accept the theory that armies could both fight and forage for food and insisted that provisions and fodder be brought from the rear.[31] The awkward disposition of forces that had been caused by Blumenthal's earlier demand for reinforcements in the Neisse area was corrected swiftly and in a way that showed a willingness to take reasonable risks which was in marked contrast to Frederick Charles's caution. Moltke's order of June 22 had stipulated that VI Corps be left on the Neisse as a precaution against a change in the Austrian plan. The Crown Prince suggested that, instead, VI Corps should move westward into Glatz where it could, if need be, protect Silesia, but would also be in a position to support the operations of the rest of the Second Army in Bohemia. This change of plan, concurred in by Moltke, proved to be of significance in the subsequent development of the campaign.[32] By June 24, the Crown Prince's forces were disposed for the mountain crossing: Bonin's I Corps was standing at Landeshut; the Guard Corps was in the Eulengebirge behind Silberberg; V Corps was moving from Glatz toward the

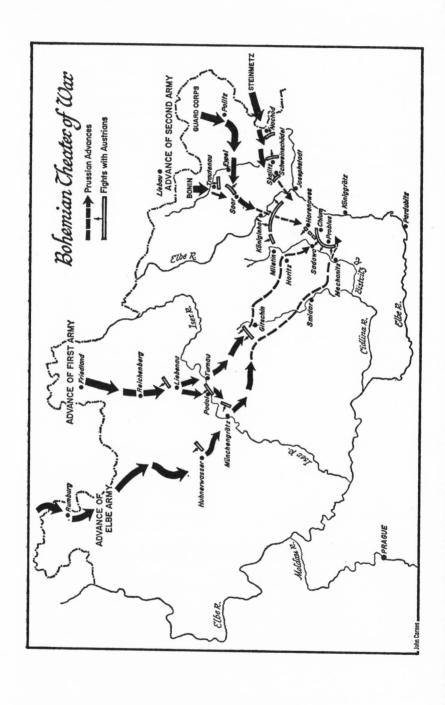

Bohemian Theater of War

Prussian Advances
Fights with Austrians

ADVANCE OF SECOND ARMY

GUARD CORPS

STEINMETZ

Liebau

ADVANCE OF FIRST ARMY

BONIN

Pölitz

Nachod

Trautenau

Eypel

Stalitz

Schweinschädel

Josephstadt

Königinhof

Königgrätz

Soor

Horenowes

Chlum

Elbe R.

Probus

Miletin

Sadowa

Hořitz

Mechanitz

Friedland

Reichenberg

Liebenau

Turnau

Isec R.

Gitschin

Podoll

Smidar

Bistritz

Elbe R.

Hühnerwasser

Münchengrätz

Iser R.

Cidlina R.

ADVANCE OF ELBE ARMY

Rumburg

PRAGUE

Moldau R.

Elbe R.

Pardubitz

John Carnes

Reinerz-Nachod road; and VI Corps was shifting westward from the Neisse. Two days later, everything was ready for the jump-off.

These preparations were not, of course, lost upon Benedek's staff at Josephstadt, for Austrian cavalry patrols were active and on June 25 had brought accurate reports of the massing of the Prussians at the northern ends of the defiles. In other circumstances, this might have been enough to persuade Benedek to direct his blows against his nearer antagonist—perhaps, as a Prussian staff study was later to suggest, by allowing the Crown Prince's forces access to the Upper Elbe and then engaging them frontally with three of his corps and hitting them in the flank with two more from the line Josephstadt–Nachod. In such event, the Prussian corps, separated during the passage of the defiles and not yet reunited, would have been in serious trouble, and Frederick Charles's fixation about Münchengrätz would probably have prevented his army from starting to the rescue of the Crown Prince until June 28 or even 29, when it might have been too late.[33]

Benedek's chief of operations, however, set his face against any such attack. The army's plan, as announced in Benedek's wire to Crown Prince Albert of Saxony on the morning of June 26, was to advance westward in force against Prince Frederick Charles and the Prussian First Army; to change this plan now would, he insisted, merely cause confusion. It would be enough to detach a corps or so to keep Crown Prince Frederick William and the Prussian Second Army under observation. As usual, thanks to his own stubbornness and Benedek's apparently unshakable confidence in his abilities, Krismanic had his way. On the evening of June 26 all corps and cavalry division commanders received detailed orders for the projected march to the west and were instructed to hasten the completion of their concentration at Josephstadt. Two corps—those of Gablenz and Lieutenant Field Marshal Wilhelm Freiherr von Ramming— were ordered to march toward the mountains and act as a screen for the Northern Army's offensive against Frederick Charles.[34] On the other hand, no exact date was set for the offensive; and on that same evening Benedek still seemed very indefinite on this point, telegraphing to the Emperor's Adjutant General, Lieutenant Field Marshal Count Franz Folliot de Crenneville, that he expected to move "within a few days."[35]

Benedek was not to be given a few days. He had already delayed too long, and the Prussian forces on his right flank were nearer and stronger than the confident Krismanic believed. Ramming was to discover this all too clearly the next day, when the Prussian V Corps cut through the mountains and struck a hammer blow at Nachod.

The commander of the Prussian V Army Corps was General Karl Friedrich von Steinmetz, who had fought as a lieutenant in the war of 1814, won a *pour le mérite* in Denmark in 1848, participated in the fighting in Baden and Hesse in 1850, and received his corps command in 1864. He had always been a man of forthright character—his divisional commander in 1848 called him "a really outstanding staff officer, who must, however, be handled firmly if he is to be kept under control"—and his behavior became increasingly violent and uncertain after 1854, when his only daughter died. For years thereafter he suffered from visions in which she came to him at his table, and this probably contributed to his moodiness, his intermittent rages, his controversies with his superiors and with civilian authority, and the willfulness that was to cost him his position in the war of 1870. Despite this, he was a competent officer, quick at assessing a situation and reaching a decision, never afraid of responsibility, and always capable of inspiring his troops. In the war against Austria, he was to be more successful than any other single commander.[36]

Verdy described Steinmetz as he appeared in 1866 as a small energetic man with a sharply chiseled soldier's face, eyes that showed intelligence and energy, and full white hair upon which he wore "a campaign cap covered with black oilcloth, just like the one he had worn as a very young lieutenant in the wars of liberation."[37] The cap was against regulations, but Steinmetz permitted himself liberties of this sort and was, indeed, given to certain tactical irregularities also, which were, however—at least in 1866—usually successful.

His relaxed and confident approach to his first encounter with the Austrians showed this tendency toward unorthodoxy; and Schlieffen was later to accuse him of having endangered his troops

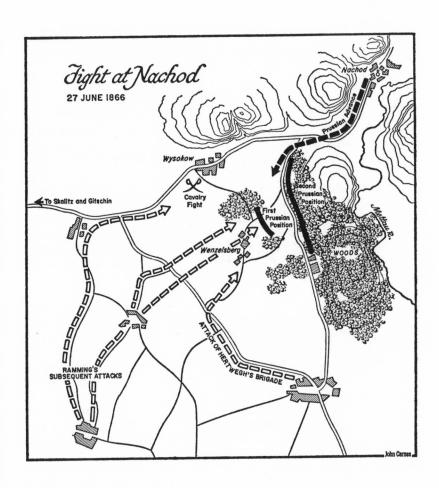

Fight at Nachod
27 JUNE 1866

Nachod

Prussian Advance

Wysokow

Cavalry Fight

To Skalitz and Gitschin

Second Prussian Position

First Prussian Position

Metteau R.

Wenzelsberg

WOODS

ATTACK OF HERTWEGH'S BRIGADE

RAMMING'S SUBSEQUENT ATTACKS

John Carnes

by starting his advance through the mountains on the morning of June 27, instead of moving during the previous night, as Napoleon would have done.[38] If this was a mistake, Steinmetz did not have to pay for it. His advance guard—battalions of the Thirty-seventh and Fifty-eighth Infantry Regiments (Westphalians and Poseners), four companies of Jaeger, four squadrons of dragoons, and two batteries of 4-pounders—started at Nachod, a little border town known for having been the birthplace of the brilliant but ill-fated Wallenstein, and moved briskly through the narrow defile to the plateau above the village of Wysokow, arriving there before the first detachments of Ramming's VI Austrian Corps reached the scene. If the Austrians were now to catch Steinmetz's main force in the defile, they would first have to clear the plateau. The commander of Ramming's first brigade, Major General von Hertwegh, sought to accomplish this with his artillery, but soon tired of this and made the same mistake that Colonel Bergou had made at Podol. He sent his infantry up the slope in battalion columns, and they were mowed down by rapid fire from the plateau.

The bravery of the Austrian troops left nothing to be desired. The 25th Jaeger Battalion in particular distinguished itself by its reckless courage and stormed forward in repeated attacks until it had reached Wenzelsberg on the Prussian flank, only to be taken under fire by the second battalion of the Prussian Thirty-seventh Regiment deployed in the orchards above the village, and thrown back down the slope. By ten o'clock in the morning, Hertwegh's brigade was broken.

Even so, the crisis of the fight had not been reached. The Austrian corps commander, Lt. Field Marshal Ramming, a soldier of deservedly high reputation in the Austrian Army—he had served with distinction under Baron Haynau in 1848 and 1849 and collaborated with Hess in 1859[39]—now appeared at Wysokow and threw two more brigades into the fight, and these almost turned the tide. By noon their repeated assaults had driven the Prussians back to the far edge of the plateau, where they were in danger of being pressed down into the hollow where the defile from Nachod debouched. If this had happened, Austrian guns could have commanded the exit from the mountains, and Steinmetz would have had to retire.

Ramming was suffering in these crucial days from severe

neuralgic facial pains, and these may have blunted his judgment. In any case, at this critical juncture he made the mistake of thinking that the fight was won, called off the infantry attack, and ordered his cavalry forward to drive the Prussians into the ravine. Steinmetz, who was now directing the fight in person, met horse with horse, and a protracted fight ensued between the Eighth Prussian Dragoons and West Prussian Uhlans on the one hand and, on the other, three-and-a-half squadrons of the Kaiser Ferdinand Cuirassiers and the second squadron of the Hessen-Kürassiere, a regiment that claimed descent from the Pappenheim cuirassiers of Wallenstein's army in the Thirty Years' War.[40] This fight was spirited and surprised onlookers by its duration, the units meeting and passing through, re-forming, and fighting hand to hand in small groups[41]; but, although it was later much celebrated in song and story, it was essentially a mere episode in what Schlieffen described as a contest between the bayonet and the bullet, the blade and the gun. It gave Steinmetz time to get more battalions on to the plateau, and as these West Prussian and Brandenburg grenadiers of the 10th Division came into the fight, Austrian fortunes sank rapidly.

As the Prussian fire increased, Ramming lost control over his subordinate commanders, some of whom led their men against the Prussian lines with a berserker fury but with little co-ordination and with a complete indifference to flanking tactics. The resultant losses were heavy. Some of the Magyar battalions broke and fled, and the whole assault line wavered. As it did so, it was hit repeatedly in the flank by the Eighth Dragoons, and when it tried to re-form to meet these blows, it was subjected to volley after volley of aimed infantry fire. The assault line began to melt away and by one o'clock the issue was settled, and the Austrians were retiring in the direction of Skalitz.[42] Their losses were significantly high—232 officers and 5,487 men (1,106 officers and men dead, 1,178 wounded, 2,344 prisoners, 1,091 missing) as opposed to Prussian casualties of 62 officers and 1,060 men, of whom 19 officers and 264 men were dead. Superior firepower had again told heavily, but so had the skill with which the Prussian junior officers had handled their units, maneuvering them against the Austrian flank or front as needed, and bringing support to the right places in the line at the right time.[43]

The news of Nachod was telegraphed to Berlin, where it was

released on June 29 and where it immediately put an end to the lack of enthusiasm for the war and the general pessimism that had impressed Blumenthal and others during the mobilization period.[44] In the outburst of patriotic rapture that followed, Bismarck discovered that he was popular and, for the first time since becoming Minister President, found cheering crowds wherever he went; while King William's stubborn fears concerning his subjects' reaction to the war were at last laid to rest as happy throngs besieged the palace and citizens' groups bombarded him with fulsome messages of support and affection.

The enthusiasm was perhaps premature. Steinmetz's victory was not a definitive one; his enemy had regrouped at Skalitz and was prepared to renew the fight; his own losses had not been inconsiderable; and he had no prospect of additional support. Prince Frederick Charles was still on the Iser, waiting for the Elbe Army to come up so that he could try a double envelopment of Münchengrätz. Moreover, on the same day as the victory at Nachod, the Prussian I Corps of Bonin had suffered a sharp defeat at Trautenau, while coming through the mountains.

Unlike Steinmetz, General Bonin was not to cover himself with glory during the Bohemian campaign, perhaps because his first encounter was so shocking to him. His opponent at Trautenau was Lt. Field Marshal Ludwig von Gablenz, commander of the Austrian X Corps, a curious mixture of military talent, political ambition, and personal vanity, who in 1874 was to end a chequered career by his own hand as a result of unwise speculation. Sometimes called "the lucky mushroom from Saxony," Gablenz had been in the Austrian Army since 1833, had won the Ritterkreuz of the Order of Maria Theresa at Kaschau in Hungary in 1849, had distinguished himself at Magenta in 1859 and Veile in Denmark in 1864, and had served most recently as the Austrian Governor of Holstein. He was cool and resourceful in battle, had great personal bravery, and understood the use of terrain and of all weapons; and he was highly regarded by such a good judge as Archduke Albert. His weakness, made manifest in Denmark, was a willingness to accept excessive losses in order to gain his objectives.[45] All in all, he was too much soldier for Bonin, a timorous and unenterprising troop leader.

Bonin's mission was to secure Trautenau and push ahead to

Pílnikau, a village only two or three days' march from Gitschin and a point at which he might hope to make contact with advance units of the First Army. He was so intent on this objective that he failed to watch his left flank or to seize the three hills—the Galgenberg, the Johannesberg and the Hopfenberg— that protected it. It was from this direction that he was hit by

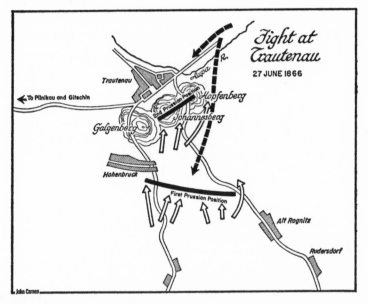

Gablenz's forward brigade as his corps was passing through Trautenau on the Pílnikau road. A stubborn seesaw fight followed in which superior numbers counted and the Austrians were pushed off the hills. Without reconnoitering to the south, Bonin ordered a resumption of the advance, and some of his troops left the positions that they had won with considerable cost. Gablenz seized this opportunity to bring up two fresh brigades, which, by a combination of frontal and flanking attacks, overran the forward Prussian line at Hohenbruck before Bonin was fully aware of what was happening and, by five in the afternoon, retook the Galgenberg and the Johannesberg and stood athwart the Prussian line of communications. Bonin's belated attempt to retrieve a situation caused in large part by imperfect reconnaissance was now ruined by muddles in communications which Gablenz exploited with great skill. Even so, the Austrian regiments, particularly the Italians and Ruthenians, took fearful punishment in the hill fighting; and it was not until Gablenz's reserve, the Brigade Knebel, had entered the fight that the Hopfenberg fell in a bloody contest between Silesian and East Prussian regiments. Then, as the Austrian Brigade Grivicic began a flanking movement around the town of Trautenau, their victorious comrades began to attack from the high ground. Faced with encirclement, Bonin started to retreat and, having done so, didn't stop until his bone-weary troops were back on the other side of the mountains, in the bivouac area which they had left the day before.[46]

Bismarck later called the fight at Trautenau a slap that rocked the whole Prussian Army, and this was no exaggeration. Although Gablenz's losses had been over three times those of Bonin—191 officers and 4,596 men against 56 Prussian officers and 1,282 men[47] —Bonin's corps was *hors de combat* for at least a day by virtue of his withdrawal, and this left Steinmetz in a dangerously exposed position. This was all the more true because Crown Prince Frederick William, who had intended to send the Guard to support the V Corps, had felt it necessary to change his mind after Trautenau. Never dreaming that Bonin had lost all contact with Gablenz, he ordered the Guard to advance through the pass at Eypel, the third doorway to Bohemia, and to move forward toward Trautenau, taking Gablenz in the flank and rear while Bonin renewed the fight frontally.[48] This decision gave Benedek a splendid opportunity to change the face of the war by overwhelming Steinmetz on June 28.

"That a *Feldherr* should not lightly abandon a plan once it has been completed is certainly understandable and commendable, but he is worthy of still higher praise if he seizes the opportunity of the moment for a decisive blow."[49] Such was the judgment passed by Moltke's greatest successor upon Benedek's conduct at this stage of the war. With fatal obstinacy, the Austrian commander-in-chief clung to his plan and remained deaf to all advice save that of Krismanic. To be sure, he was not entirely unmoved by the events in the defiles; and he formed a defensive screen of 70,000 men in front of the Prussian Second Army by ordering the IV Corps of Lieutenant Field Marshal Tassilo Count Festetics de Tolna to come up in support of Ramming's corps and that of Archduke Leopold, which were standing at Skalitz. This caused some confusion, since IV Corps had already started its march westward. But having taken these precautionary measures, Benedek went on with his preparations for the advance to the west, apparently believing that he could still bring six army corps to bear against Frederick Charles's four and a half, and thus destroy the Prussian First Army before Crown Prince Frederick William and the Prussian Second Army could take effective action. His intelligence chief, Colonel Karl von Tegetthoff, who had been at Nachod, pleaded it was too late for this and urged him to turn against the nearer and more threatening enemy; but Tegetthoff was warned sharply by Krismanic to mind his own business.[50]

On the morning of June 28, Benedek rode with his staff to Ramming's headquarters. As he passed, he was cheered by the troops, who felt that the time for decisive action had arrived and that "Father Benedek" had come to watch the discomfiture of the Prussians. Benedek inspected the VI Corps of Ramming and listened to that commander's arguments in favor of an attack upon Steinmetz; he then crossed the Aupa and rode forward to Skalitz to inspect the dispositions of Archduke Leopold's VIII Corps. He found the Archduke's brigades poised on the heights along the river, facing eastward and straining for a chance to attack Steinmetz's columns, which could be seen off to the east, an hour's march distant. Benedek's inspection, however, merely seemed to confirm opinions that he had already arrived at. The Prussians were not going to seek battle, he concluded; they were moving northward to establish contact with the Guard. This being so, it was safe to withdraw; and so he instructed Ramming and Archduke Leopold to start for the Iser, with Festetics's corps behind them as a rear guard. Having issued these orders, Benedek rode back toward Josephstadt, abandoning what was probably the best opportunity offered during the whole campaign.[51]

Had they known of his decision, the commanders and staff of the Prussian Second Army would have been perplexed. The Crown Prince's staff awoke on the morning of June 28 expecting that this would be a bloody and perhaps disastrous day for them, and as the hours passed their anxieties mounted. The Crown

Prince had spent fourteen hours in the saddle on the previous day at Nachod, often in circumstances of considerable danger; he had intended to spend this day, too, with Steinmetz; but in view of the pending operation at Trautenau, to which he had despatched the Guard, he decided to take up his position at Kosteletz, where he could be in touch with all his corps.[52] It was here that Hohenlohe found him later in the morning, sitting astride a tall chestnut mare and wearing the blue undress uniform of a general, with shoulder boards and the star of the Order of the Black Eagle, and—although he rarely smoked in peacetime—carrying a short pipe with a decorated bowl. He said to Hohenlohe, "You see, this is the decisive day for my army, the one that tells whether we're going to succeed in getting over the mountains on these divided lines of march. If one of my wings is beaten, it's all up with the other, for it will have to go back, and I shudder at the thought of a retreat through the defiles we've just come through." The hardest thing to bear, he added, was sitting here doing nothing, but since he had designated this as the command post, there was no alternative. "So," he said, puffing at his pipe, "there's nothing left for me but to smoke one nose-warmer after another."[53]

All told, it was a worrying day for the Second Army staff. To add to its preoccupations, telegrams arrived announcing what appeared to be a Prussian setback at Langensalza in western Germany and what clearly was a smashing victory for Archduke Albert of Austria over the Italians at Custozza. Of more immediate concern was the lack of news from Bonin's corps, which made it clear that he must have lost contact with the enemy and that the Guard might find itself in serious straits when it reached Trautenau. Finally, from behind the hills to the south came sounds of a cannonade so heavy that it was assumed that Steinmetz was being attacked by as many as three corps. This depressed everyone except Blumenthal and the Crown Prince. The chief of staff said: "What a shame we can't be with Steinmetz! I'd just like to watch how the old fellow finishes them off!" The Crown Prince, as usual, was quiet and unruffled. He asked if anyone could think of something that had been left undone and, receiving no suggestions, said simply, "Well then, we've done our duty and taken care of everything that good will and our limited understanding make possible. Now it's up to God!"[54]

The sound of the firing was misleading, perhaps distorted by a freak electrical storm that passed over the hills. This completely obscured the cannon's sound from Benedek, so that he rode back to Josephstadt thinking that his orders had been carried out and, having got there, wired the Emperor that he was starting his push toward the Iser. It magnified the cannonade for the benefit

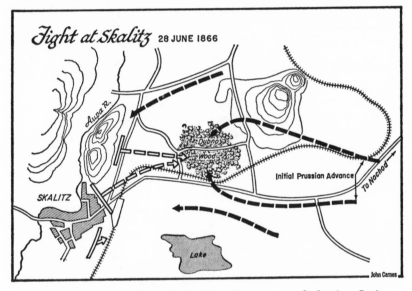

Fight at Skalitz 28 JUNE 1866

Aupa R.

Dubno Wood

Initial Prussian Advance

To Nachod

SKALITZ

Lake

John Carnes

of the Crown Prince's staff, leaving them to conclude that Steinmetz was outnumbered and later—when it brought dust clouds that looked from Kosteletz like retreating troops—leading them to suppose that he had been defeated.[55] Both Benedek and the Second Army staff were mistaken.

When Benedek had ordered the retirement of the three corps around Skalitz, two of them had obeyed. Archduke Leopold, however, could not persuade himself that this was justified and—in another demonstration of the administrative and disciplinary ills that plagued the Austrian Army—opened an attack upon Steinmetz's advancing columns, without communicating his intentions either to army headquarters or to Ramming or Festetics, who might have supported him. The Archduke's conduct of the fight that followed to the west of Skalitz was as muddleheaded as his act of insubordination. After causing heavy casualties among the King's Grenadier Regiment and Brigade Hoffman by well-aimed artillery fire from the heights east of the Aupa, he left the direction of the fight in the hands of his brigade commanders, who fed their regiments piecemeal into Dubno wood, where the Prussians had taken cover. Lack of co-ordination in the attack and the usual reliance upon bayonet charges cost Leopold over 5,500 casualties against the Prussian loss of 1,365 officers and men, and he retired from the fight with two of his brigades so badly chewed up that they could not be expected to fight again in the near future. By two o'clock in the afternoon, Steinmetz was in Skalitz and the road to Gradlitz was open.[56]

Meanwhile, the breakdown of Austrian communications had led to another blow to Benedek's hopes. Although Gablenz had won his fight with Bonin on June 27, he discovered that evening that the extraordinary losses had shaken the morale of his troops, and he felt it wise to appeal for reinforcements, particularly in view of intelligence that the Prussian Guards were advancing from Eypel toward Trautenau. This was a wise request. A strong defense at Staudenz by fresh troops would probably have prevented the Guard from coming through the Eypel pass. It was precisely this sort of thing that their commander, Prince August von Württemberg, feared, and if he had not had explicit orders from the Crown Prince to proceed, he might well have decided to stand at Eypel. But although Benedek first answered Gablenz's plea by ordering Festetics's IV Corps to send a detachment to the vicinity of Praussnitz–Kaile–Staudnitz, and although he informed Gablenz that he had done so, he later countermanded the order *without* telling him. The result was that Gablenz walked into a trap. Dividing his forces, he led three brigades to join the expected reinforcements at Praussnitz, with the intention of turning against the Prussians as they emerged from the pass, and simultaneously he sent Brigade Grivicic over Alt-Rognitz to hit the enemy in the right flank when they were engaged. But the enemy was through the pass, and the reinforcements were not there; Gablenz's forces were driven apart and defeated separately. While Lieutenant General Friedrich Wilhelm Freiherr Hiller von Gärtringen's 1st Guard Division inflicted heavy losses upon his

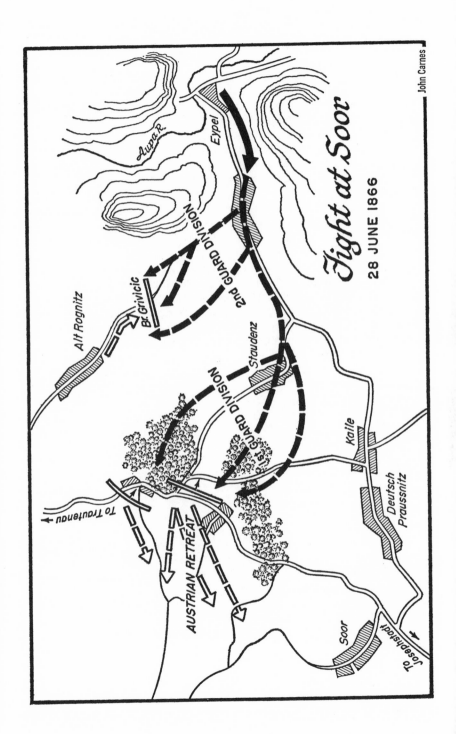

Fight at Soor

28 JUNE 1866

John Carnes

Aupa R.

Epel

2nd GUARD DIVISION

Br. Grivicic

Alt Rognitz

1st GUARD DIVISION

Staudenz

Kaile

Deutsch Praussnitz

To Trautenau

AUSTRIAN RETREAT

Soor

To Josephstadt

main force and drove them in retreat towards Soor,[57] the 2nd Guard Division (Lieutenant General von Plonski) virtually destroyed Grivicic's Brigade, which had already suffered heavily the day before, and which now lost three fifths of its effectives.[58] Despite the rigors of its two days' march through the mountains, the Guard Corps lost only 28 officers and 685 men this day, while Gablenz's corps reeled out of the fight with a loss of 123 officers and 3,696 men (207 dead, 311 wounded, 2,908 captured, 393 missing).[59]

Thus, while Benedek was drafting the telegram in which he announced to the Emperor the long-planned advance against Prince Frederick Charles and the Prussian First Army, the Crown Prince of Prussia was making good his passage into Bohemia. There was still perhaps a possibility that the Prussian Second Army could be held in check long enough to permit Benedek to strike out against the First Army—Schlieffen, at least, seems to have believed so[60]—but, if so, it was disappearing hour by hour. For, on the same day in which Steinmetz and the Prussian Guard cracked their way through the mountains, Frederick Charles at long last began to move also.

4

THE CAMPAIGN IN BOHEMIA:

The Eve of Battle

Sharp shoots the Prussian Rifle, which
Has to be loaded at the breech;
Five times for each mouth-loader's one:
What a formidable weapon is the needle-gun!
Oh, that unerring needle-gun!
That death-dispensing needle-gun!
It does knock over men like fun.
What a formidable weapon is the needle-gun![1]
(Tune: "The Dog's Meat Man")
—*Punch*, 21 July 1866

THE PLAN that Prince Frederick Charles and his chief of staff Voigts-Rhetz had worked out for their operation at Münchengrätz was well-conceived. It called for an attack by the Elbe Army, which had now arrived on the Iser, against the Austrian troops on the west side of that river, and a simultaneous advance from the north by the 6th, 7th and 8th Divisions, which would strike the enemy's flank and rear. As has often been remarked, the plan had everything but an enemy to be affected by it, for the Austro-Saxons, in accordance with Crown Prince Albert's orders, had started for Gitschin at four o'clock on the morning of the

28th, with Edelsheim's cavalry leading the way. As Fontane wrote later, the operation, in consequence, "gave the impression of a massive weapon employed for a blow against a place for which a light rapier blade would have sufficed."[2]

When the attack began at seven in the morning, most of the Austro-Saxon force had made good its withdrawal. The Brigade Leiningen, which had been ordered to protect the retreat, held off the advance guard of the Elbe Army until ten o'clock, the time that had been designated for its own retirement. At that time, new orders arrived from Prince Albert, asking its commander to hold on until noon if possible. This proved difficult, for one of the regiments, composed largely of Italians, had already begun to show signs of collapse and surrender; but the other battalions —Germans, Magyars, and Serbs—held on despite heavy losses and finally retired across the river in good order. Meanwhile, the Prussian flank attack from the north had been held off by Austrian artillery on the Musky Berg to the east of the town. The batteries were finally forced to retire by a spirited attack of the 7th Division, which took the hill; but the advance of the other divisions of the Prussian First Army was contained by a rear-guard action by Brigade Abele until Prince Albert's forces had disappeared behind the hills to the east.[3]

If this rather disappointing fight did not convince Prince Frederick Charles that there is such a thing as being too elaborate in preparing an operation, the sequel may have done so, for he discovered now that he had so many troops concentrated in so small a space—100,000 men within one square mile—that it was impossible either to move them or to feed them. On the evening that followed the fighting, there were many hungry men in Münchengrätz—even the Prince's staff, quartered in a castle that had once belonged to Wallenstein, had to make do with potatoes and a few bottles of champagne—and the next morning, as Frederick Charles prepared to start his advance toward Gitschin, he decided to leave the Elbe Army behind on the Iser until it had some room in which to move.[4]

On the morning of June 29, the First Army commander received a number of anxious wires from Moltke, urging a speedy advance westward. The first of these, dated the morning of June 28, reported the victory at Nachod and Bonin's setback at Trautenau and pointed out that a successful crossing of the mountains by the Second Army would depend on the First Army's progress. A second, of later date, said peremptorily: "His Majesty expects that the First Army will by the speediest possible advance disengage the Second Army, which despite a number of victorious fights is still momentarily in a difficult position."[5] It is unlikely, however, that Frederick Charles needed this kind of prodding now. He had been disappointed by the previous day's engagement and was hot on pursuit. He had, indeed, already anticipated Moltke's orders by despatching six cavalry squadrons and an infantry division (the 5th) toward Gitschin on the previous day. Now, at 9:30 in the morning, he started for that rendezvous with his main force, the 3rd Division of Lieutenant General August Leopold Count von Werder in the van.[6]

In 1866, Gitschin was a pleasant town of some six thousand inhabitants, most of whom were Czechs, situated in the beautiful and fertile region of the Český Raj (Bohemian Paradise). During the Thirty Years' War, it had been the residential center of the Duchy of Friedland, created by Emperor Ferdinand II for his brilliant *Feldherr* Wallenstein after the battle of the White Hill in 1620. Here, around an arcaded square, Wallenstein had built a baroque palace, a treasury building and a mint, and a richly endowed Jesuit college; and here he had rehearsed scenes of magnificence that caused the Prince of Hohenzollern, whose family had acquired in those days neither opulence nor power, to blink his eyes in astonishment.[7] In 1813 Emperor Francis I of Austria had lived for five weeks in Wallenstein's palace, and it was there that Metternich, Wilhelm von Humboldt, and Nesselrode had conducted some of the negotiations that aligned Austria, Prussia, and Russia in war against Napoleon.[8] Since that time it had not bulked large in the annals of Austrian history; and its appearance there now was less illustrious than its previous ones, associating the name "Gitschin" not only with defeat but also with ineptitude. In his authoritative analysis of the Austrian defeat in 1866, Heinrich Friedjung has speculated on the role played by national character in the debacle and has pointed out that, at every crucial point in the campaign, slackness, imprecision, procrastination, and lack of urgency caused mistakes that had fearful consequences. In the drama that was enacted now in Wallenstein's capital, these things were not absent.

Crown Prince Albert of Saxony reached Gitschin early in

the morning of June 29. His latest advices from Benedek were to the effect that the Northern Army would reach Gitschin on the following day, and he assumed from this that it was his duty to hold the town. Still, he wanted some confirmation, and at noon he telegraphed to Josephstadt, asking for further orders. This wire may have gone astray; in any event there was no answer. At two in the afternoon, however, a courier arrived from Benedek's headquarters with a comprehensive and detailed description of the projected advance on Gitschin. This was dated June 27, although this may have been a mistake, for the message appears to have been a copy of the one that Benedek had drafted the day before, while he was still unaware of what was happening at Skalitz. However that may be, it had taken at least nineteen hours to reach Gitschin, although the riding distance between that point and Josephstadt was only three and a half hours,[9] and it no longer represented Benedek's intentions. But the Saxon commander had no way of knowing that, and he took up the defense of Gitschin in the belief that support was on its way.

His direction of the fight that followed demonstrated that this thirty-eight-year-old prince, who had received his baptism of fire at Düppel in 1849, possessed military gifts of the first order, an impression that was to be confirmed at Königgrätz and again during the Franco-German war of 1870, in which he commanded the Prussian Army of the Meuse.[10] The Prussians advanced on Gitschin from two directions, the 3rd Division of General von Werder approaching the town from the west, along the road that led over Sobotka and Lochow, and the 5th Division of Lieutenant General Ludwig Karl von Tümpling using the road from the north via Kniznitz. Prince Albert made his dispositions so as to meet both threats and took advantage of every terrain feature that favored the defense. Thus, as Werder approached from Sobotka, he found his way blocked by the Austrian Brigade Ringelsheim, well positioned on a plateau overlooking the village of Unter-Lochow; and, despite repeated attempts, his battalions could shake the enemy neither by frontal nor by flanking attack. After three hours of stubborn fighting, the Austrians were still firm and apparently unwearied. At this point, however, Ringelsheim received unexpected orders to break off the fight and retire on Gitschin. The reasons for this we shall have occasion to

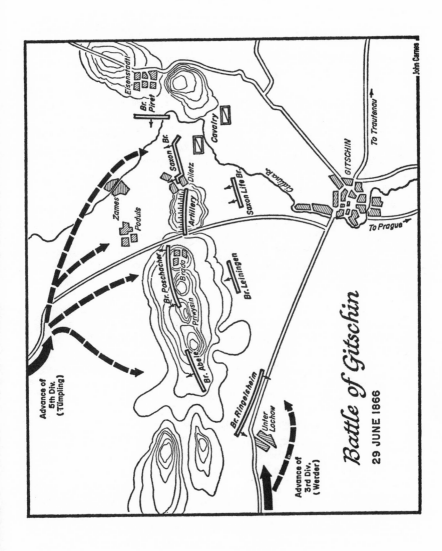

Battle of Gitschin

29 JUNE 1866

John Carnes

Eisenstädtl

Br. Piret

Cavalry

GITSCHIN

To Trautenau →

Saxon ½ Br.

Dietz

Gidlina R.

To Prague →

Zames

Poduls

Artillery

Saxon Life Br.

Br. Poschacher

Broda

Br. Leiningen

Prwysin

Br. Abele

Advance of
5th Div.
(Tümpling)

Br. Ringelsheim

Unter
Lochow

Advance of
3rd Div.
(Werder)

consider; the immediate consequences were unhappy. In order to win enough room to begin his withdrawal, Ringelsheim ordered the Württemberg Regiment to storm the lines of the Pomeranian battalions which were in the Prussian van, and in the ensuing melee the Württembergers left six hundred dead on the field. Their sacrifice did, however, permit Ringelsheim to detach his brigade and, behind strong artillery fire, to retreat toward Gitschin.[11]

While this fight was going on in the late afternoon, the Prussian 5th Division was finding it impossible to crack the line of defenses to the north of the town. The heights to the west of the road from Kniznitz were held by Brigade Abele and Poschacher's Iron Brigade, already blooded at Podol; the right flank of the Austro-Saxon position, where the Cidlina brook flowed toward the town, was commanded by Brigade Piret at Eisenstadtl and by a line of 56 guns stretching from the village of Diletz to the height of Brada and backed by the Cavalry Division Edelsheim. The center was weaker than the flanks, but Prince Albert had two Saxon brigades and one Austrian brigade in reserve. Successively, Tümpling tried a direct approach toward Poduls-Brada, a wide flanking attack around the height of Priwysin to the west, and an approach via the Cidlina over Zames to Diletz. None of these was successful, and the Prussian commander's assault on Diletz with fifteen companies at 7:30 in the evening was contained also. By that time Tümpling was beginning to worry about his position, for he had used up his reserves, while Prince Albert still had uncommitted troops to put into the fight.

At 7:30 P.M., however, a courier brought Prince Albert a message from Benedek that caused the collapse of all his hopes. Dated June 29 at Josephstadt, it read: "I find it necessary to call off my movement to the Iser today; in the course of this present day the army will take the positions spelled out in the attached annex. Your Royal Highness will direct your present movements with the objective of uniting with the main body of the army and, until this union is achieved, will avoid any major encounters."[12]

The Saxon commander consulted his Austrian colleague Clam-Gallas, and they decided they had no alternative to obedience. But they were, nonetheless, confronted with a wretched task. Nothing is harder than to detach troops from a fight in progress;

there is always the danger that a retirement will turn into a rout and, even if it does not do so, the effect on troop morale will be depressing. To pull troops out of Diletz, where new Prussian attacks were being pressed, was doubly difficult. A Saxon report said later: "Because of the nature of the fight in the village and the exhausted condition of the troops, the evacuation of Diletz by the 1st Infantry Brigade (Crown Prince) could not take place in regular order. The companies were all mixed up together, some of them deprived of leaders, and they had to retire over completely open terrain, traversed with ditches and ravines. The enemy, pressing quickly into the village, therefore inflicted great losses upon them with infantry fire."[13] Repeated diversionary assaults by Edelsheim's horse and a flank attack upon the Prussian infantry by Brigade Piret from Eisenstadtl helped the Saxons make good their withdrawal, but these attacks, like that of the Württemberg Regiment at Unter-Lochau, were costly.

Worse was to come. The orders to retire had now been transmitted to almost all units, and from north and west they fell back on Gitschin, where the roads were soon clogged with gun carriages, wagon trains, and weary troop detachments. Some order was restored by Prince Albert and Clam-Gallas, who met in front of the town and intervened personally; and the two commanders determined also to hold the town for the rest of the night in order to secure the retreat. Brigade Ringelsheim was designated as the rear guard, but it soon became clear that it was too worn out by its fight at Unter-Lochow to accomplish this task, which was consequently assigned to the relatively fresh Saxon Life Brigade.

These preparations failed to take into account the speed with which the Prussians were now moving. Scenting victory, they bore down upon the town, and before the Life Brigade had arrived there, the forward units of Werder's 3rd Division, Pomeranian fusiliers of the Regiment Frederick William IV, broke into Gitschin from the west. It was after eleven at night, and Clam-Gallas's chief of staff was dictating march instructions to the troop commanders when the sound of Prussian guns was heard. The result was confusion and near panic. Clam-Gallas was a soldier whose talents were conspicuous only when the going was good; his performance at Magenta and Solferino showed a strong tendency toward discouragement when under pressure, and he gave in to that now. Leaving his *chef* to finish reading the march orders, he left the town with the rest of his staff. Behind him his command disintegrated, rushing out of town pell-mell with little idea of where they were going, so that the next day units from his forces were to turn up in such far separated points as Miletin, Horitz, Smidar, Nobidschow and Josephstadt.[14]

At 11:30 at night, the Saxons entered Gitschin and at once attacked the Pomeranians and drove them out of the town. They then protected their comrades' retreat until nearly one o'clock, finally giving way, slowly and stubbornly, before the first units of the Prussian 5th Division, which now entered the town from the north.[15] In contrast to Clam-Gallas's forces, the Saxon corps kept its order and marched off with its spirit unbroken toward Smidar, which it reached on the afternoon of the following day. Its total losses amounted to 27 officers, 586 men and 58 horses, considerably lower than the Austrian casualties of 184 officers, 4,714 men and 222 horses. The Prussians lost 71 officers, 1,482 men and 56 horses.[16] Among their wounded was General von Tümpling, hit in the arm during the fighting around Diletz. He received a congratulatory message from Prince Frederick Charles, which read: "It is fine when a Prussian general bleeds. It brings the army luck."[17] What Tümpling thought of this sentiment is not recorded.

The Prussian forces were exhausted by this hard-won victory and made little attempt to pursue, bivouacking in and around Gitschin. Frederick Charles and his staff rode in the next morning, and the scenes they viewed on their way moved Voigts-Rhetz to write: "The battlefields were dreadful to look at, and the worst thing is that there was no means of carrying the wounded to lazarets as quickly as one would have desired. Often one finds these hapless persons days later lying half dead in the fields. The inhabitants have all fled, and there are seldom people in the villages and, when there are, they themselves have nothing to live on, so how can anything be done for the sick and the wounded?"[18]

The defeat at Gitschin awakened in the whole Austrian Army the thought that the war was lost, and no one was more profoundly affected by this feeling than the commander-in-chief himself. Skalitz had destroyed the possibility of an offensive war that would have been in keeping with his temperament. The setbacks of June 29—not only the one at Gitschin, but new Prussian blows on the upper Elbe, where the Prussian Guard battered Gablenz in an artillery duel at Königinhof, and Steinmetz inflicted 1,440 casualties on Festetics's IV Corps in an unintentional encounter at Schweinschädel[19]—made it clear that he was being caught in a remorselessly closing ring of steel; and the news from all fronts of the casualties inflicted by the *Zündnadelgewehr* had a shattering effect upon his spirit.[20] The knowledge that his own hesitations and his reliance on bad advice had contributed to his present plight must also have borne heavily upon him, although he thought less of himself than of the army he commanded. On June 30, he wrote to his wife, recalling his appointment to the command of the Northern Army. "I told the Emperor in that conference, honorably and confidentially, that, if he wished, I would sacrifice my civil and military honor for him—and that has now happened. How and why the army, whose units have been inspired by the greatest courage unto death, has come into such a desperate condition, you will read and hear about in a thousand versions, true and false; but I am not going to waste a single word on that. . . . It is possible that I'll see you again. It would really be better if a bullet got me, but I would be willing to suffer personal shame if, by doing so, I could perform a last service for the Emperor and the army."[21]

On that same day, Lieutenant Colonel Beck of the Emperor's *Adjutantur* arrived at Königgrätz, whither Benedek had decided it would be expedient to move. Beck found a staff that was thoroughly fed up with the methods employed by Krismanic and a commander-in-chief who seemed tired and dispirited and inclined to surrender. Benedek held a war council in the presence of the visitor at which he explained that all his units, with the exception of the II Corps, had now been badly mauled, and that unless peace were made quickly the army would suffer a disaster. This seems to have impressed Beck, and he told Benedek that, if things were as bad as that, the news should be passed on to the Emperor at once. Benedek therefore drafted and despatched a wire to the Emperor in which he said, "I beg Your Majesty urgently to make peace at any price. Catastrophe for the army is unavoidable. Lieutenant Colonel von Beck is returning at once."[22]

This was not the kind of advice that one could give a Habsburg ruler. Although he recognized the perils of the situation, Francis Joseph also believed that great powers do not—indeed, must not—surrender unless compelled to do so. The knowledge that Austria could be defeated only by a supreme effort, that she would fight to the end and inflict great losses on her adversary, was a prerequisite of her position in Europe. Therefore, the Emperor's answer to Benedek's request was a flat refusal. "To conclude peace is impossible," Francis Joseph wired. "I order you, if it is unavoidable, to begin a retreat. Has a battle taken place?"[23] The Emperor also, a day later, ordered Benedek to relieve Krismanic, Henikstein and Clam-Gallas of their duties and to choose a new chief of staff.

Beck discovered later that the last sentence in the Emperor's wire was an addition made by Crenneville, the Emperor's Adjutant General, who admitted this and, when Beck suggested that the words were superfluous, said: "Yes, but how can one begin a retreat without losing a battle?"[24] It has been held that Benedek regarded the words in question as an order to fight a major battle before embarking upon a retreat, and there may be some truth in this. It is equally possible that the more he thought about retreat the less he liked the prospect and that he concluded that the losses in a running fight with the Prussians would exceed those suffered in a battle on ground which he chose himself. Finally, the possibility must not be excluded that Benedek's mercurial temperament played a role in his decision. The wire to the Emperor had been sent under the influence of the news from Gitschin, when Benedek's spirits were at their lowest ebb. But he spent the next two days in the saddle, visiting troop units and inspecting the terrain around Königgrätz, and as he did so his belief in the possibility of victory revived. By July 2 the tone of his messages to Vienna had lightened, and his subordinates were noting that he was more like the old Benedek than he had been during the whole campaign.

He had, in fact, for whatever reason, decided to fight rather than retreat, and his reconnaissance rides had convinced him that the place to fight was not behind the Elbe, as many critics later believed,[25] but in front of it—on the hill chain of Lipa-Chlum eight miles northwest of Königgrätz.

On June 30 the King of Prussia issued a general order to the soldiers of his army, in which he said: "I come to you today . . . and offer you my royal greeting. . . . Your bravery and devotion have won results that are worthy of comparison with the great deeds of our fathers. I look upon the assembled units of my loyal army with pride and look to the approaching events in this war with confidence. Soldiers! Countless foes stand arrayed against us. Let us therefore trust in God the Father, the ruler of all battles, and in our just cause. Through your bravery and endurance, He will bring new victories to our triumph-accustomed Prussian banners!"[26]

After this rhetorical exercise, the King and his headquarters moved toward the front by rail. The staff was numerous enough to fill six trains, which will not surprise anyone who reads the list of those who found an opportunity to be with their sovereign on this historical occasion. Among the more legitimate members were the King's chief minister of state, Count Bismarck; Moltke, freed at last from his preoccupations with operations in western Germany; War Minister von Roon, Chief of Military Cabinet (Major General) Henning von Tresckow, the *Generalfeldzeugmeister* Prince Carl of Prussia, Quartermaster General (Major General) Theophil von Podbielski, the Inspectors General of Artillery and Engineers von Hindersin and (Lieutenant General) von Wasserschleben, the King's Adjutant General (Lieutenant General) Gustav von Alvensleben, and Moltke's Chief of Operations, Major General Hermann Wilhelm Count von Wartensleben. In addition, there were members of the Foreign Office staff, foreign diplomatic and military observers, the King's personal physician and other body servants, and any number of his friends and associates. Finally, everyone of any importance had brought his own adjutants and assistants, and this made up an imposing number, which worried those who had to provide for their sustenance and other needs.[27]

Bismarck was worried for another reason, for he was nervous about the personal safety of his sovereign. His quick eye had noticed, when headquarters had reached Reichenberg at the beginning of enemy territory, that it was protected by only three hundred *Trainsoldaten*. In view of rumors that there were Austrian and Saxon regiments at Leitmeritz, only six miles away, he asked Moltke whether this was not dangerous. "*Ja*," said Moltke coolly, "in war everything is dangerous."[28]

On the way over Reichenberg to Gitschin, which he reached on July 1, Moltke despatched an order that was intended to guide the operations of the army in the immediate future. "The Second Army," he directed, "is to maintain itself on the left bank of the upper Elbe, its right wing ready to unite with the left wing of the advancing First Army over Königinhof. The First Army will advance without pause in the direction of Königgrätz. Sizable enemy forces on the right flank of this advance shall be attacked by General Herwarth and pushed away from the enemy's main force."[29]

This instruction did not mean that Moltke had any precise information about Benedek's plans or even his location. Indeed, the exact whereabouts of the Austrian force was a matter of worrisome conjecture at Prussian headquarters, for both Prince Frederick Charles and Crown Prince Frederick William had succeeded in losing contact with their foe, the former by not pressing the pursuit after Gitschin, the latter when Gablenz and Festetics withdrew from the Elbe after the encounters of June 29. What Moltke's order *does* show is that he was still thinking in terms of encirclement. By keeping the Crown Prince on the other side of the Elbe and by keeping a wing out to the right, he was preparing to slide one force at least around Benedek's flank and rear wherever he was found and whether he retreated or stood to fight.

Schlieffen was probably correct in intimating that Moltke's army commanders never perfectly understood or agreed with this conception. They were not thinking in terms of pursuit and encirclement, because, despite their victories, they regarded everything that had happened so far as a mere testing of strength, an introduction to the real fighting that was to come, and for that they wanted the whole army to be massed. While Moltke wished to retain the flexibility that separation made possible, the army commands had an instinctive tendency to huddle together, and this was strengthened by the fear that the missing Benedek might suddenly appear while they were still divided and defeat them separately.[30] Their differences with Moltke were voiced on July 2 in a war council held in the presence of the King, in which *Generaladjutant* von Alvensleben, Voigts-Rhetz, and Blumenthal, who had made the long and hazardous ride from Königinhof by carriage, argued for a union of the armies, each propounding novel theories as to where Benedek might be.[31] Moltke, however, had his way, and it was decided to keep the First and Second Armies separated at least until the last point was clarified. Meanwhile, the next day, July 3, was to be a day of rest for most of the army, except for I Army Corps, which was supposed to move to positions which would facilitate its contact with the First Army's left wing, and Herwarth's forces, which were ordered to advance toward the bridgeheads on the Elbe below Pardubitz and to secure them.

The general feeling at the conference was that Benedek had by this time withdrawn across the Elbe. Moltke himself believed so, and, for this very reason, wished to keep the Second Army on the left bank of the river. But even while the discussions at Gitschin were going forward, this impression was being corrected, and in dramatic fashion.

Prince Frederick Charles had established his headquarters at Kamenetz and sent detachments forward toward the valley of the Bistritz River. The most advanced of these was the point of the 7th Division, commanded by Colonel Franz Friedrich von Zychlinski, which had established itself on the night of July 1 at Schloss Cerekwitz, on the river bank about five miles north of Sadowa. Zychlinski noticed numerous campfires on the heights to the east, and on the following day, after reporting his observations to headquarters, sent a cavalry patrol to investigate. His riders bumped into an Austrian infantry detachment and managed to escape with a prisoner. Under interrogation at Cerekwitz, their captive told Zychlinski that the Austrian III Army Corps was encamped on the heights of Chlum and Lipa. At about noon, the colonel sent this news off to Schloss Kamenetz.

Prince Frederick Charles had already decided that Zychlinski's earlier reports required investigation and had ordered Major von Unger of his general staff to reconnoiter the Bistritz valley and see what he could discover. With a lance corporal and sixteen uhlans, Unger started for the hill of Dub, which he imagined would give him a view of the whole valley. Before reaching this objective, he came to a little stream bed and met an Austrian cavalry patrol on the other bank. The Austrians seemed on the point of passing without recognizing them as Prussians, but one of Unger's troopers fired at them and they fled—two of them, however, falling from the saddle. Unger's men seized them and, as they rode on, forced out of them the intelligence that not one but at least four enemy corps were in the area between the Bistritz and Königgrätz. This was corroborated by villagers whom they met on their way.

Unger's patrol rode on to the village of Dub, passing more Austrian cavalry who waved in a friendly fashion, obviously mistaking them, as their comrades had done earlier, for Saxons. Thanks to this, the little troop was actually able to reach the top of Dub hill and to see, stretched out before them, evidence that a considerable part of the Austrian Army was bivouacked in the river valley and on the neighboring hills. They had no time to estimate numbers, however, for now at last they were recognized as Prussians, and a squadron of Galician uhlans started from Sadowa in pursuit. There followed a pell-mell chase over hedge and ditch and stream bed. Unger himself was almost killed by a Polish lance, but he got away without casualties to his patrol, and between six and seven in the evening was back in Kamenetz with the news that the whole army had been waiting for.[32]

If Frederick Charles had erred on the side of caution on earlier occasions during this campaign, he showed no similar hesitation now. Unger's information inspired him to what his biographer has called the greatest and most consequential decision in his military career:[33] the decision to attack the enemy with all of his forces at dawn. Working swiftly, he and Voigts-Rhetz had the plan of attack worked out by nine in the evening. It called for an advance by the First Army along the Horitz–Sadowa–Königgrätz road, led by II and IV Corps, which would jump off at 2 A.M., and followed an hour later by III Corps (Divisions Tümpling and Manstein). The cavalry corps, characteristically, was to remain in its bivouac area until called on. Simultaneously, Herwarth's Elbe Army was to move in the direction of Nechanitz. The orders to the divisional commanders were despatched immediately, and at 9:30 P.M. Frederick Charles also sent a message to the Crown Prince, telling of his projected attack and asking him to detach the Guard Corps, or other units if he could spare them, for the support of his operation.

It was only after these things were done that the prince sent Voigts-Rhetz to royal headquarters in Gitschin, where he arrived some time after ten o'clock and found that the King had retired. At his insistence, an aide-de-camp awakened the sovereign, who recognized the importance of the news and sent him to Moltke. The Chief of Staff rose from bed with the words "*Gott sei dank!*" He may have been somewhat less thankful after he had learned of the steps taken at First Army headquarters. Prince Frederick Charles seemed to be assuming that only part of the Austrian Army was in front of him; Moltke sensed intuitively that it was all there and that the decisive battle was at hand. If that were so, it was idle to think—as the First Army commander seemed to be thinking—that the enemy could be defeated by a frontal attack by the First Army alone, plus whatever units the Crown Prince might see fit to send to his aid. Since orders had already gone out to the divisions, however, a radical change of plan would probably produce nothing but confusion. The best that could be done was to order the Crown Prince to commit not part but all of his forces and to bring the Second Army, with all speed, against the enemy's right flank. Since time was of the essence, this meant that no troops could be kept on the left side of the Elbe, and this would inevitably squeeze the Second Army's four corps between the Elbe and the Bistritz rivers and reduce the possibility of an attack against the enemy's rear. This was unfortunate, but in the circumstances unavoidable.[34]

With these thoughts, or thoughts like them, in his head, Moltke confirmed the instructions issued by Frederick Charles to his divisional commanders, but in his own battle order asked the Crown Prince to make immediate preparations to come to the assistance of the First Army "by moving with all forces against the right flank of the presumed enemy order of battle, attacking him as soon as possible."[35] A copy of this was given to the King's aide-de-camp Lieutenant Colonel Count Finck von Finckenstein, who rode off through the night by way of Miletin to the Crown Prince's headquarters at Königinhof. Because of the importance of the message, Voigts-Rhetz took another copy back to Schloss Kamenetz in order to send it to the Crown Prince by a different route.

The precaution was commendable but unnecessary. Although he had to make many detours to avoid enemy patrols, Finckenstein rode into Königinhof at four o'clock in the morning, and the Crown Prince's staff began to draft the orders for the battle that was now at hand.

5

THE BATTLE:
The Fight Along the Bistritz

Erhebt euch von der Erde, *Ihr Schläfer aus der Ruh!* *Schon wiehern uns die Pferde* *Den guten Morgen zu.* *Die lieben Waffen glänzen* *So hell im Morgenrot,* *Man träumt von Siegeskränzen,* *Man denkt auch an den Tod.*[1]	(Rise from the ground And from your rest, ye sleepers! Our horses are already whinnying A good morning to us. The weapons we love are gleaming So brightly in the red of the dawn, And we dream of victory wreaths, And we also think of death.)

—MAX VON SCHENKENDORF,
"Soldaten-Morgenlied"

T HE BISTRITZ RIVER is a small stream that rises to the north of Miletin and then flows in a southerly and westerly direction, parallel to the course of the upper Elbe. Along its eastern bank the land rises in undulating slopes to a chain of hills of no very majestic stature but of sufficient height to dominate the western approaches. Of these heights the most considerable are Lipa and Chlum, which lie about eight miles northwest of Königgrätz, on the northern side of the road that runs from that town to Gitschin; and these are flanked on the right by the hills of Maslowed and Horenowes, and on the left by those of Tresowitz, Popowitz, Problus and Prim. At the foot of the hills, along the

87

river, are a series of villages—Sadowa, where the Königgrätz-Gitschin road crosses the Bistritz; Benatek, three miles to the northeast; Dohalitz, Mokrowous, and Nechanitz to the south—and these are separated by thick woods, the largest of which are the *Holawald* and the *Swiepwald*, behind Dohalitz and Benatek respectively, and those around the village of Prim to the south.

In making his battle plan, Benedek took full advantage of these features of the terrain, and, whenever possible, used artifice to improve upon nature. For the past two days, his General Inspector of Artillery, Archduke William of Austria, had been painstakingly reconnoitering the area, making note of all positions with a clear field of fire and measuring and marking ranges; and on the heights of Lipa and Chlum he had positioned batteries in tiers so that they commanded the bridge at Sadowa and the rim of the Dub valley beyond.[2] During the same period the Chief of Engineers, Colonel Franz Karl Freiherr von Pidoll zu Quintenbach, had laid out an elaborate system of trenches and field works and had ordered the trees on the wood above Sadowa to be cut down and their tops and branches set toward the direction from which the enemy would come, so as to form an abattis. As a writer for the London *Spectator* correctly noted, Benedek had learned from the severe conflicts on open ground at Skalitz and Soor and "had determined to find some compensation for an inferior armament by using the spade" and the axe.[3]

The Austrian commander placed the center of his order of battle on the Chlum bastion, where he concentrated 44,000 men and 134 guns. The III Corps of Archduke Ernest of Austria stood on the heights to the north of the highway with a brigade pushed forward towards Sadowa village. To its left was the X Corps of Gablenz, its forward units extended forward to Dohalitz and Mokrowous. The left wing of the battle array extended southward to block the approaches from Nechanitz, seven miles south of Sadowa. Here the Saxons were to stand, on the heights of Tresowitz and Popowitz, supported by the Austrian VIII Corps, the vanquished of Skalitz, now commanded by Major General von Weber in place of the hapless Archduke Leopold. Together the Saxons and VIII Corps comprised 40,000 men and 140 guns. Weaker than either of these positions was that of the right wing, whose mission was to guard against a flank attack by the Prussian

Second Army. Gun emplacements and entrenchments had been constructed along the ridge that ran from Chlum eastward to the village of Nedelist, but these were dominated by the heights of Maslowed and Horenowes further north which also obscured the view in the direction from which the Prussian Crown Prince would presumably come. Despite this disadvantage, which was to have a sorry sequel, Benedek ordered IV Corps (Festetics) and II Corps (Lieutenant Field Marshal Karl Count von Thun-Hohenstadt)—55,000 men and 176 guns all told—to take the positions delineated by Pidoll's earthworks.[4]

The flanks were secured by cavalry—the 1st Light Cavalry Division of Edelsheim at Ober Prim with the Saxons, the 2nd Light Cavalry Division of Major General Emerich Prince von Thurn und Taxis on the extreme right at Nedelist. Behind these forward positions, Benedek concentrated the rest of his army—the I Corps of Clam-Gallas, now commanded by General Gondre-court, Ramming's VI Corps, three divisions of heavy cavalry, and the reserve artillery—a very considerable reserve of 47,313 infantry, 11,435 cavalry and 320 guns.

Since battle positions in front of rivers have obvious disadvantages, the commander-in-chief had considered it necessary to increase the number of Elbe crossings by building pontoon bridges at Lochenitz and Placka and at points below Königgrätz.[5] This was a measure of prudence rather than a gesture of resignation, for as the battle approached, Benedek's spirits rose to meet it. He wrote to his wife early on the morning of the 3rd: "Now comes . . . a great decisive battle. If my old luck does not desert me, I can bring it to a successful issue; if things turn out differently, then I'll say humbly 'as God wills.' I am rested and ready, and, once the cannon begin to thunder near me, I shall be fine."[6] Nor did he have any intention of fighting a purely defensive battle. The very size of his reserve shows that he was hoping to do what Archduke Albert had done so successfully eight days before at Custozza—to wear down the enemy by a defensive battle from a favorable position, meanwhile keeping the reserves intact, and then, at the crucial moment, to break his center.[7] The enemy in this case would be Frederick Charles, and Benedek was counting on administering to him now the defeat he had hoped would occur earlier on the Iser or at Gitschin. He realized that the Prussian Crown Prince would seek to frustrate this plan, but here again he was optimistic. Intelligence reports indicated that the Prussian Second Army was too far away to intervene in the battle at an early hour, and Benedek believed that, when it did arrive, it could be held by Festetics and Thun while he did his work.

Certainly there was nothing in his demeanor to suggest irresolution as he rode forward with his staff from Königgrätz to his chosen command post at Lipa early on the morning of July 3. The forward units of the army were already in position, and the reserves had been moving westward since before 8 A.M. The special correspondent for *The Times*, W. H. Russell, watched them from Königgrätz tower, and saw the advancing brigades forming "squares and parallelograms of snowy white, dark green, azure, and blue on the cornfields like the checker work of a patchwork quilt."[8] As their commander-in-chief passed through their ranks on his way forward, sitting erectly but easily in the saddle, his bright eyes darting from face to face as he shouted greetings and rough witticisms to the regimental officers and the long troop columns, the bands played and the men cheered. It was a moving scene and one the like of which the world would not see again, for the warriors of the future would be drably costumed and monotonous masses, whereas here blazed all the splendor and variety of the old Empire—the infantry with its white coats and blue trousers, green-clad Jaeger wearing cross-belted greatcoats and broad-brimmed hats decked with caper-cailzie feathers, hussars with yellow-trimmed *tschakos*, and uhlans with red-bordered *schapkas* and gaily-flagged lances, brown-coated artillerists and high-booted cuirassiers with crested helmets—all shouting together as the staff with its gold-laced cocked hats and light green plumes rode by. Despite the rawness of the day and the cold rain that fell on the already sodden fields, Benedek's progress toward the front brought color, music, and a momentary gaiety to the army as if a festival were anticipated rather than a battle.[9]

Benedek reached Lipa before nine o'clock, received Pidoll's report, talked with his light cavalry commanders and, in the brush with Edelsheim that has already been alluded to (see above, page 10 and the authorities cited) warned them that the army was going to do its business "plainly and solidly" and warned them against "hussar comedies." He then learned of two changes in the troop dispositions he had ordered earlier. A Saxon officer from Crown Prince Albert's headquarters came to ask for his approval of the positioning of the Saxon corps, not on the heights of Popowitz and Tresowitz as originally planned, but at Problus-Prim, where it could more effectively dominate an enemy approach by way of Nechanitz. This Benedek approved without question, remarking that he had complete confidence in the Crown Prince's military judgment. The change was in fact a good one and greatly strengthened the army's left wing, where the Saxons held their own until late in the day.[10]

The second change had graver consequences. When IV Corps had moved into position along the line between Chlum and Nedelist, its chief of staff, Colonel von Görz, pointed out that the position was overlooked by the height of Maslowed and would be untenable if the enemy took that point. He urged his commanding officer, Count Festetics, to move the corps forward to occupy Maslowed, arguing that the orders from headquarters must be based on faulty terrain appreciation. Festetics was a man of limited military talents who had risen to his position because he belonged to one of the oldest feudal families in the Empire. He yielded to Görz's pleas, which were supported by his own second in command, Major General Anton Freiherr Mollinary, an unreflective soldier of the "up and at them" school. Indeed, Festetics not only ordered the forward movement, but authorized Görz to get in touch with the *chef* of Count Thun's II Corps and to persuade him to move forward also. Görz had no difficulty in carrying out this assignment, since Thun's orders from headquarters were somewhat ambiguous, commanding II Corps merely to keep in line beside IV Corps. The result was that the two corps left their prepared positions and moved forward to the line Maslowed–Horenowes. By the time this movement was complete, the greater part of their forces were facing, not northward as planned, but to the west; and the only troops left to guard the vital northern flank were the Brigade Henriquez of Thun's corps, on the heights north of Sendrasitz, the Sixth Uhlan Regiment at Trotina, and, farther back, the 2nd Light Cavalry Division at Nedelist. This was a screen that was not only weak but filled with inviting gaps.[11]

This significant change, upon which the issue of the battle

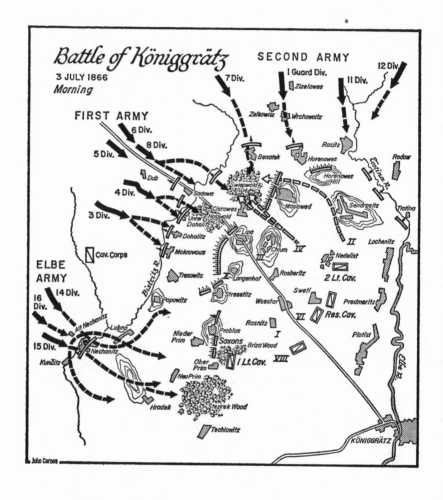

Battle of Königgrätz

3 JULY 1866
Morning

SECOND ARMY

7 Div.

I Guard Div.

II Div.

12 Div.

Zizelowes

Zelkowitz
Wrchownitz

FIRST ARMY

6 Div.

8 Div.

5 Div.

Benatek
Horenowes

Racitz

Radaw

Dub

Trotinka R.

Swiepwald

Horenowes
Hill

4 Div.

Sadowa

Cistowes

3 Div.

Unter
Dohalit

Maslowed

Sendrasitz

Trotina

Ober
Dohalit

Lipa

Cav. Corps

Mokrowous

Chlum

IV

II

Lochenitz

Bistritz R.

III

ELBE
ARMY

Tresowitz

Langenhof

Rosberitz

Nedelist

14 Div.

Popowitz

Stresetitz

Swet

2 Lt. Cav.

16
Div.

Wsestar

Predmaritz

15 Div.

Alt Nechanitz
Lubno

Nieder
Prim

Problus

Rosnitz

Saxons
Briza Wood

I

VI

Res. Cav.

Kunčitz

Nechanitz

Ober
Prim

Neu Prim

I Lt. Cav.

VIII

Plotist

Stezirek Wood

Hradek

Techlowitz

Elbe R.

KÖNIGGRÄTZ

John Carnes

was to turn, was not corrected immediately after Benedek's arrival at Lipa. This was due partly to the confusion caused at headquarters by the belated announcement to Krismanic that he was no longer chief of staff but had been superseded by Major General Alois von Baumgarten, who made his first appearance on the scene at this late hour. Since in addition, Henikstein, despite his recall, had remained with Benedek, headquarters was served on this fateful morning by three chiefs of staff, one inexperienced, one resentful, and the third—Henikstein—as sarcastic and unhelpful as usual. This did not make for clear lines of authority or speedy correction of mistakes.

In the second place, there were now other pressing matters to concern the staff. The cannonade that had accompanied their ride to the front had redoubled in volume, and along the Bistritz, where the first shots had been exchanged at about 7:30 A.M., a formidable Prussian offensive was developing. The first phase of the battle was about to open.

There had been activity in the divisional headquarters of the Prussian First Army from midnight onward, and by four o'clock the troops were on the move to their forward positions. On the left Fransecky's 7th Division advanced to Cerekwitz; in the center, Horn's 8th Division moved down the Gitschin-Königgrätz road to Klenitz; to its right the 3rd and 4th Divisions advanced on Dohalitz and Mokrowous; and further still to the right the three divisions of Herwarth's Elbe Army began the march toward Nechanitz. All of the troops were short of sleep and few had had breakfast; and the driving rain that began at dawn did not help their mood. The casual observer would have been hard put to it to assess their spirit as they slogged forward. Certainly there was nothing in their appearance to indicate dash or inspiration. The color of the Austrian regiments found no counterpart in these uniformly gray-green masses, nor was there anything particularly martial about them, for most of the infantry had laid aside the *Pickelhaube* with its shiny spike and wore instead the untheatrical field cap.[12] Under the rain the corn lay heavy and matted in the fields, and the battalions toiled heavily through it. The artillery horses had to strain to pull the gun carriages through the sticky soil. But everything went forward methodically without hitch or confusion and with a minimum of noise, and before six o'clock the forward divisions were in position and the reserves (5th and 6th Divisions and the cavalry corps) were close behind the front.

This advance was unimpeded, for the enemy had withdrawn from the area in which Major von Unger had found them the day before, a circumstance that aroused some concern among Prince Frederick Charles's staff as they moved toward Dub. The Prince was riding beside Unger as they approached the village and he said, half to himself, "I hope they haven't withdrawn." About six o'clock, as they ascended Dub hill, their doubts were put to rest and the Prince wrung Unger's hand warmly.[13]

In a notable journalistic achievement, that enterprising newspaper, The Times, had three reporters at the front, one with each of the opposing headquarters and the dean of war correspondents, Russell, in the Königgrätz tower.[14] The correspondent attached to the headquarters of the First Army has left a good description of the scene that opened on Frederick Charles's vision as he looked down from the height of Dub. "A person standing this morning on top of the ridge," he wrote, "saw Sadowa below him, built of wooden cottages, surrounded by orchards, and could distinguish among its houses several water mills; but these were not at work, for all the inhabitants of the village had been sent away, and a white coat here and there among the cottages was not a peasant's blouse, but was the uniform of an Austrian soldier; three quarters of a mile down the Bistritz a big red house, with a high brick chimney beside it, looked like a manufactory, and some large wooden buildings alongside it were unmistakably warehouses; close to these a few wooden cottages, probably meant for the workers employed at the manufactory, completed the village of Dohalitz. A little more than a mile still further down the Bistritz stood the village of Mokrowous, like most Bohemian villages, built of pinewood cottages enclustered in orchard trees. . . . Behind Dohalitz and between that village and the high road which runs through Sadowa, there lies a large thick wood; many of the trees had been cut down about ten feet above the ground and the cut-down branches had been twisted together between the standing trunks of the trees that were nearest the river to make an entrance into the wood from the front extremely difficult. On the open slope (behind Dohalitz) there seemed to run a dark dotted line of stumpy bushes, but the telescope showed that these were guns, and that this battery alone contained twelve pieces. Looking to the left, up the course of the Bistritz, the ground was open between the orchards of Sadowa and the trees that grow round Benatek, a little village about two miles above Sadowa, which marked the extreme right of the Austrian position, except where, midway between these villages, a broad belt of firewood runs for three quarters of a mile. Above and beyond these villages and woods the spire of Lipa was seen . . ." and above that waited the massed power of Austria.[15] Altogether a formidable prospect!

Both Prince Frederick Charles and his chief of staff were to claim later that they were completely undaunted by what they saw from Dub.[16] Even so, the commander of the First Army had some compunction about launching an attack at once, in view of the fatigue and hunger of his troops. He decided not to make too great a commitment at the outset, hoping to have a little time in which to rest his troops and give them a good meal.[17] At about 7 A.M., therefore, when he began his action, he pushed forward only his cavalry and horse artillery. The *Times* observer saw them move down the slope toward the Bistritz "at a gentle trot, slipping about on the greasy ground, but keeping most beautiful lines, the lance flags of the uhlans wet with the rain, flapping heavily against the staves. At the bottom of the hill the trumpets sounded and in making their movements to gain the bridge the squadrons began wheeling and hovering about the side of the river, as if they courted the fire of the enemy. Then the Austrian guns opened upon them from a battery placed in a field near the village at which the main road crosses the Bistritz, and the battle of Sadowa began." The first shots were fired at half past seven. The Prussian horse artillery close to the river replied to the Austrian batteries, but there was no heavy firing, and for half an hour the exchanges were confined to single shots.[18]

At about a quarter before eight King William and his suite arrived at Dub. The sovereign had left Gitschin at five o'clock and, with a cavalry escort, driven in an open carriage to Klenitz, where horses were waiting. As he mounted, it was noticed that he was wearing no spurs, a circumstance that struck a few of those present as constituting an omen, although whether good or evil was a matter of conjecture. In any event the omission was rectified, and the King rode on to Dub accompanied by Bismarck—who, as a major in the *Landwehr* cavalry, was wearing a cuirassier's helmet and a long grey coat and was mounted on a large fox-red horse—and Moltke, who had a cold and was making frequent use of a red silk handkerchief.[19] As the King reached the height with his rather too numerous staff a shell from an Austrian battery fell and exploded twenty paces from him. The King said calmly: "I owe that one to you, gentlemen," as the horses reared. A second shell landed amid a squadron of uhlans, causing heavy casualties, and anxious staff officers urged the suite to disperse out of consideration for the King's safety.[20]

The haze now obscured the view across the valley, although the flashes of the guns could be seen. Bismarck spurred his horse over to Moltke and asked: "Do you know how long this towel is whose corner we have grabbed here?" "No," answered the Chief of Staff, "we don't know exactly; only that it is at least three corps, and that it is perhaps the whole Austrian Army."[21] The answer has been often quoted; it is less often pointed out that Moltke, who was not averse to mystifying nonprofessionals, was being unresponsive. Ever since he had drafted his battle order the night before, he had operated on the assumption that the whole of Benedek's force was before him; and in the orders which he issued now he showed that he had not changed his mind. For shortly after eight o'clock, Frederick Charles was ordered to attack along the whole Bistritz line.

This was a disagreeable surprise to the First Army commander. He had hoped to be able to delay any major attack until about ten o'clock; and, by making this impossible, Moltke's orders meant that many men had to go into battle with empty stomachs. Moreover, the order revealed that Moltke had a different conception of the role of the First Army than had its commander. Frederick Charles had believed from the beginning that his forces would play the decisive part in the battle and would have the honor and glory of smashing the Austrian center and routing Benedek's army. It was clear now that Moltke believed that the battle would be decided on the flanks, by the concentric movements of Herwarth's Elbe Army on the right and the Second Army on the left. In the eyes of the Chief of Staff, the First Army's task was to attack and pin the enemy, so that he could not escape the pincers when they closed.[22] Moltke admitted as much to Bismarck later in the day, when casualty figures began to reach headquarters. The Minister President was worried, and he asked whether it might not be possible that the First Army's commitment was too great and that more could be achieved by pulling back and enticing the enemy down from his strong defensive position. Moltke denied this and said that "the important thing was to hold the enemy for a battle of the whole (*Gesamtschlacht*)."[23] The Chief of Staff recognized that the First Army would suffer heavy losses; he did not believe, on the other hand, that the Austrians would be capable of going over to the offensive themselves and defeating the First Army after its energies had been drained away.[24] His real concern, he told an Italian observer, was lest the enemy escape altogether. This the First Army had to prevent, by holding on, despite the hammering it would have to take, until the Crown Prince arrived on Benedek's right flank.[25]

This diminution of role was disappointing to Prince Frederick Charles, and it was to leave him with a lasting feeling of resentment which he sought, not entirely successfully, to control.[26] But he knew how to obey orders, and he did so now. For the last hour the artillery duel had been mounting in intensity. The guns of the 7th Division were now shelling the town of Benatek, and Horn's batteries were exchanging shot for shot with the Austrian 8-pounders behind Sadowa. Now, at about 8:30 A.M., came the first serious commitment of infantry; and all along the river from Nechanitz to Benatek the Prussian riflemen attacked the bridges and the wooded slopes that lay beyond.

Despite prodigies of valor, the tangible gains made by this offensive were for long hours negligible.

On the extreme right the three divisions of Herwarth von Bittenfeld's Elbe Army were in position before 8 A.M., and at about half past that hour the advance guard, seven battalions strong, led by Major General von Schöler, began the attack on the river line. Schöler's objective was Nechanitz bridge, the only solid crossing on this stretch of the river; the others in the vicinity—at Lubno to the left and at Kunčitz to the right— being wooden foot bridges which would not be able to support an army and its artillery. Schöler made a frontal attack on Alt-Nechanitz, on the west side of the Bistritz, sending the fusilier battalion of the Twenty-eighth Regiment forward, while supporting its advance by simultaneous attacks on Lubno by the fusiliers of the Seventeenth and on Kunčitz by the 2nd Battalion of the Thirty-third. Kunčitz fell without difficulty, and the Thirty-third turned left along the stream toward Alt-Nechanitz. The defenders —the 7th and 8th Battalions of the Saxon Division Schimpff— retired in a spirited rear-guard action during which they almost succeeded in destroying the bridge, by ripping off its flooring and setting fire to its frame. The Rhinelanders of the Twenty-eighth, however, disregarding heavy fire from the Saxon Battery Zenker, put out the fire with their field kettles and effected temporary repairs by throwing spars, fence posts, and the wings of a large courtyard gate across the holes. They then pressed on into Nechanitz. With their supporting cavalry and guns, the defenders withdrew to the heights of Problus and Prim, going— as Crown Prince Albert said later—"with the greatest calm and in strict accordance with the orders given them, as if they were on the drill ground."[27]

Schöler's seven battalions followed the Saxons and, at about ten o'clock in the morning, took up a position on the ridge between Lubno and Hradek. An artillery duel now began that was to last until the middle of the afternoon. In the late morning, the Prussian advance guard tried to improve their position by a three column attack against the woods of Nieder Prim. But they had not been reinforced and did not have the weight to consolidate the gains they made; thus, between noon and one o'clock, the Saxon Life Brigade cleared them out of all the woods except for the pheasantry between Jehlitz and Nieder Prim and pressed them back to the Lubno–Hradek ridge.

The failure of this drive to develop more strength and speed must be attributed equally to the skill of Crown Prince Albert's defense and to the caution displayed by his antagonist; and there is a strong intimation in the Prussian staff work that the latter was the more important. Frederick Charles wrote later that Herwarth was "an obedient, easy-going subordinate, who doesn't make trouble," but one who always preferred to work under direct orders than to be on his own. At Nechanitz he showed neither urgency nor imagination. He waited patiently but over-long for the 8th Engineer Battalion to repair the bridge that the Saxons had damaged, without attempting to throw pontoons across the river at other points; and, in consequence, his reliance on a single crossing created a traffic problem of serious proportions. The 15th Division (Lieutenant General Philipp Karl Freiherr von Canstein) didn't start across the bridge until ten o'clock; the movement of the 14th (Lieutenant General von Münster-Meinhövel) was delayed until after 11:15 A.M. In the meantime, Herwarth refused to consider launching any serious attack, apparently desiring to wait until the bulk of his forces were deployed across the river. Requests from Frederick Charles's headquarters for action that might reduce the pressure on the center had no effect upon him; and when, around eleven o'clock, Colonel Karl Gustav von Doering came from the King's headquarters to ask him to attack the Austro-Saxon left wing, by sending Division Canstein and Count Goltz's cavalry brigade against Ober and Nieder Prim, while Division Münster crossed the river at Lubno and enveloped the enemy right, Herwarth demurred and said that this would be possible only if he were given more cavalry. By devious ways, this request or evasion led to the transfer of the Cavalry Division Alvensleben from the First Army's reserve to Herwarth, without Frederick Charles's knowledge or permission, an eventuality that infuriated that commander, the more so because Herwarth made no use of the additional horse assigned to him.

There is reason to suppose, indeed, that the real cause of the delay on the right wing was that Herwarth did not believe very strongly in victory and was constantly expecting a collapse of the Prussian center which would leave him isolated and open to destruction. He was therefore more intent than he should have been upon keeping a line of retreat open; and lack of imagination prevented him from seeing that a little daring might relieve his fears and bring him profit and, indeed, glory. For these reasons, no progress was made on his front until after two o'clock in the afternoon.[28]

This was true also of the center, although this was not for want of energy. At about 8:30 A.M. Horn's 8th Division began an attack on Sadowa, while to the right the 4th Division marched against Unter-Dohalitz and the 3rd Division against Mokrowous. The Austrian tactics were much like those of the Saxons at Nechanitz: a stubborn defense at the river line, followed by an orderly retirement toward the heights. It was not, however, a mere token resistance that they offered at the crossings. For once, the needle gun was at a disadvantage, for the haze and smoke obscured Prussian targets, whereas the defending Jaeger battalions, with good cover, fired blindly at the sound of the advancing company columns and inflicted heavy losses upon them. To help the infantry, Prussian batteries opened heavy fire upon the villages and started fires in Sadowa, Mokrowous and Dohalitz. These events were seen by W. H. Russell in his eyrie at Königgrätz, and he wrote: "It looked as if the Prussians had attacked the position almost simultaneously from left to right, for no sooner had the action developed itself on the center than it rolled back from Nechanitz on the left, and before 9:30 the whole range of hills and valleys and slopes, for nine miles and more, was as if the earth had been turned into snow wreaths agitated in a wintry gale. Before ten o'clock a thicker and darker cloud rose from the trees and the village on the right." It was soon discerned that Sadowa was in flames, and Russell was inspired to a flight of sentimentality that was doubtless appreciated by his readers. "That pleasant little village, snug church, hospitable mill —all were burning. It was with surer divination of the coming woe than we had that the poor people had fled in tears, or remained in hopeless sorrow in their homes. The heat of this great battle burnt up whatever it touched, and sent forth the lava which destroyed as it flowed on all sides." The Austrian officials who watched with Russell from the tower were less obviously moved by what they saw. "They said, 'Ja so!' and 'Hem!' and uttered various other sounds of varied import possibly, smoked their cigars and looked on."[29]

Mokrowous and Dohalitz were cleared of defenders shortly before ten o'clock, thanks to the courage and dash of the

Fourteenth and Fifty-fourth Regiments and the support afforded by the guns. But this ended the forward progress of the Prussian 3rd Division for the next four hours, for behind the villages it had captured the ground rose in a long open slope to the heights of Lipa and Langenhof, between which were concentrated the seventeen batteries of the Austrian III and X Corps, a total of 136 guns. These kept up such a continuous fire upon the woods and slopes before them that before eleven o'clock in the morning three of X Corps's batteries had shot themselves out, and the corps commander, Lieutenant Field Marshal von Gablenz, had to request replacements from the reserve 3rd Cavalry Division and the army's artillery reserve. Six new batteries were sent to the lines at Langenhof, and the disabled ones retired, so that, soon after eleven o'clock, 160 Austrian guns were ranged in tiers between Langenhof and Lipa.[30]

Only part of their fire was directed against the Prussian 3rd Division, but this was enough to pin it down. Exercising the most rigid discipline, General von Werder forbade all forward movement and told his troops to take what cover they could find until an opportunity presented itself to outflank the guns. No other course of action was possible. If Werder made no progress, he at least kept casualties in his sector at a minimum.[31]

Meanwhile, with admirably precise co-ordination, the Prussian 4th and 8th Divisions had enveloped Sadowa; and while the advance guard of the 8th engaged the Brigade Prohaska, which was holding the town, in frontal fire, its main body (or *Gros*) and the advance guard of the 4th Division were ordered to advance from the north into the wood that lies behind Sadowa, in order to cut off the Austrian defenders. This maneuver almost worked, but the danger was recognized by the Austrians in time. Brigade Prohaska withdrew swiftly from the town and fell back on Lipa, covered by the 34th Jaeger and the Regiment Roman-Banat, which held the woods until the retirement was complete, and then withdrew themselves.

Having got this far without excessive trouble, the forward battalions of the 4th and 8th Divisions, and the regiments that stood behind them in the village of Ober-Dohalitz, found themselves in a position much like that of Werder, for a good proportion of the artillery massed on the heights was now turned against them. Neither the wood nor the village offered much cover. The so-called *Holawald* was not extensive, measuring only about 1,600 square yards; it lay along the southern rim of the high road, so that its position could be calculated with exactitude ("The dogs! They're using measured ranges!" the Prussian troops cursed) and it was composed of young trees, thick enough to splinter, but too thin to afford much concealment. The town was small, and its houses flimsy. "We looked for cover," one soldier wrote later, "but where was one to find it in this kind of fire! The bombshells crashed through the clay walls as if through cardboard; and, finally, raking fire set the village on fire. We withdrew to the left, into the woods, but it was no better there. Jagged hunks of wood and big tree splinters flew around our heads. At last a kind of apathy came over us. We pulled out our watches and kept count. I was standing by the flag. Inside of ten seconds, four bombshells and one shrapnel shell exploded right in front of us. When shrapnel explodes in the air, it rattles down on the ground like hailstones, and in the sky a beautiful smoke ring rises, getting bigger all the time, till it disappears. I saw all that. We all felt we were in God's hand."[32]

Under this kind of bombardment, and the hellish noise that goes with it, troops tend to seek relief in irrational or desperate action. The two divisions had to take this shelling for four long hours, and during that time the officers had difficulty in restraining aimless movements from the woods to the village and back again, and suicidal assaults upon the gun-studded heights whence their torment came.[33] A member of the Order of the Knights of St. John, riding over the battlefield the next day, saw pathetic signs of these convulsive movements inside the *Holawald* and in the cleared area beyond its farther edge. "The grain fields and the great stretches of sugar beets were trampled and covered with the dead," he wrote. "One saw Prussian corpses lying within three hundred paces of the battery position."[34] The whims of war left some units virtually untouched, while decimating others and leaving them leaderless and in a state of shock. Sometimes companies and battalions reached the end of their endurance, and staggered out of the woods, with torn uniforms and unbound wounds. One observer saw the wreck of a battalion stumble to the rear, led by a sergeant and the battalion mascot, a Newfoundland dog whose left hind leg had been shot away but which limped along beside the battalion colors.[35]

Sometimes, when such retirements occurred, the King caused painful scenes. Shortly after the beginning of the infantry advance, he had moved with his staff from Dub to the Roskosberg, which was immediately behind Sadowa; and from here he could see what was going forward in the woods, although without having to suffer the heavy pounding the troops were taking. Perhaps this led him, rather too easily, to impute cowardice to units which could take no more. At about noon, when the wounded Lieutenant Colonel Heinrich von Valentini came out of the *Holawald*, leading some shattered battalions of the Thirty-first and Seventy-first Regiments, which had led the way into the wood at 8:30 A.M. and had stood under heavy fire ever since, the King spurred angrily toward them and, reproaching Valentini, said to the weary files: "I'm going to send you forward again! Let's see you fight like brave Prussians!"[36]

Prince Frederick Charles, who was much given to orotundities about the martial virtues and the spirit of sacrifice, once said, "There is no question that the presence of the King in battle has the most inspiring influence upon officers and men. Beneath the King's eyes, the Prussian soldier goes towards death more happily than usually."[37] During this uncomfortable incident, the Prince may have begun to entertain some doubts about the advantages of the royal presence. He had already discovered that he had lost half of his carefully hoarded cavalry because of the generosity of one of the King's staff in the matter of Herwarth's request for support. Now the sovereign himself was being less than generous to troops who had fought well; and no man was more jealous of the reputation of his command than Frederick Charles. He remonstrated with the King, pointing out that the Thirty-first and Seventy-first had more than done their duty, and assuring him that he had reserves enough to hold the contested wood.

As the morning wore on, some relief had been brought to the hard-pressed infantrymen by Horn's success in bringing artillery up to the saddle between Ober-Dohalitz and Dohalitzka. By noon, seventeen Prussian batteries had come into action. Some of these were smooth-bore 12-pounders, whose ineffectiveness became

rapidly apparent and led to their removal; but the rest responded
stoutly to the Austrian fire, as did eight additional batteries
brought up to the north side of the *Holawald* from the 8th
Division and from the army's artillery reserve. Even so, by noon
there was no burking the fact that casualties in the wood had
already been very heavy and that this expenditure of Prussian
blood had made not the slightest impression, as far as anyone
could see, upon the Austrian lines. This was the more worrying in
view of the punishment that Fransecky's 7th Division was taking
on the left.

Eduard Friedrich Karl von Fransecky was known in the
Prussian Army not as a combat soldier but as an intellectual. He
had received his commission in 1825, been seconded to the
General Staff in 1843, and spent most of his career since in
administrative, instructional or scholarly work. An inspiring
lecturer on tactics in the *Allgemeine Kriegsschule* in the years
1845–48, he had served on Wrangel's staff in Denmark in
1848–49, and for years thereafter had directed the historical
section of the General Staff, where he had written a life of
Gneisenau, a history of the operations of the Silesian Army in
1813, and numerous articles which were published in the
Militärwochenblatt. In 1860 he had been transferred to the War
Ministry in order to work on aspects of the Roon army reform;
but he acceded in the same year to the pressing request of the
Grand Duke of Oldenburg and entered his service, spending the
next four years reforming the Oldenburg army and its staff and
school system. In November 1864 he returned to the Prussian
Army and received command of the 7th Division in Magdeburg.
It was generally acknowledged that his career had been distinguished, but it was nevertheless true that he had had very little
experience with problems of command—he had never, for
instance, been either a company or a battalion commander—
and until the fight at München grätz on 28 June 1866 he had
never led troops in battle.[38] Yet at Königgrätz, despite his inexpe-
rience, he played a crucial role—in a sense, the whole battle turned
upon the action of his division—and no troop leader came out of
that battle with greater honor.

It was perhaps because, or partly because, Fransecky was an intellectual that this was so. No general officer in the Prussian Army sensed the spirit of Moltke's battle plan as accurately as he, or understood better the necessity of keeping the enemy pinned down until the Crown Prince's army should arrive on the flank. When he left Cerekwitz some time after seven o'clock on the morning of the battle, he had sent his ordnance officer, Lieutenant Count von Hohenthal, to seek contact with the nearest unit of the Second Army and to tell its commander that he was probably going to attack Benatek. About an hour later, he received orders to co-ordinate his movements with those of the 8th Division and to enter the fight when and how it seemed best to him; and as soon as he heard Horn's guns firing at Sadowa he despatched another message to the Second Army, saying this time that he was attacking, that his left flank would be exposed, and that he would need support. This message reached Division Alvensleben, the point of the Guard Corps, whose commander ordered an immediate advance towards Fransecky's position.[39]

Before that had happened, however, the 7th Division was involved in what was to be, for both sides, the bloodiest fighting of the day. The four battalions of its advance guard, led by Colonel von Zychlinski, who had shared with Major von Unger the honor of discovering the whereabouts of the Austrian Army on the previous day, advanced on the village of Benatek and after a brief fire fight occupied it at about eight o'clock. As they sought to push on from the village, however, they became aware of heavy enemy concentrations in the woods on their left flank. Fransecky called a halt until the Twenty-sixth and Sixty-sixth Regiments had had a chance to come up and then ordered the 14th Brigade to advance into the wood.

This wood, called the *Swiepwald*, covered an area 2,000 yards long and 1,200 yards broad, and was of mingled firs and oaks, older and more thickly planted than the trees of the *Holawald*. It began at the edge of a meadow which extended for 500 yards south of Benatek, mounted steeply up to a saddle behind which ran a bushy ravine, and then climbed again and reached its widest extent on a higher ridge, some 900 feet in elevation, which was situated about 500 yards from the limits of the village of Cistowes to the south. Off to the east, some 700 yards from the

Swiepwald's eastern border, was the height of Maslowed. At the time of the Prussian attack, the wood was occupied by the 27th Jaeger Battalion (Steiermärker), two Venetian battalions from Grand Duke Michael's regiment, and a Hungarian battalion from the Regiment Erzherzog Wilhelm—all of which belonged to Major General von Brandenstein's brigade from Festetics's IV Corps. In addition, the wood was covered by almost four full batteries of 4-pounders and 8-pounders from Brigade Appiano at Cistowes and some forty more guns which were emplaced at Maslowed.[40]

The Prussians burst into the woods at 8:30 A.M. with Major General Helmuth von Gordon leading the two musketeer battalions of the Twenty-seventh Regiment on the left, Zychlinski commanding the fusilier battalions of the Twenty-seventh and the Sixty-seventh Regiments on the right. Before starting, Zychlinski had heartened his men by shouting, " '*Vorwärts!*' as Father Blücher used to say! '*Drauf!*' as Father Wrangel used to say! '*Durch!*' as the poet of the liberation, Körner, has sung!"[41] Gordon was apparently content to spur his men on with boisterous cries of "Fresh fish! Good fish!"[42] They pressed the Austrians back without much trouble; and Zychlinski, joined now by the 2nd Battalion of the Twenty-seventh Regiment, attacked Cistowes. This village proved to be strongly held by Appiano's brigade, and after directing a punishing fire against Zychlinski's force which wounded that doughty commander and killed the leader of the 1st Battalion of the Twenty-seventh Regiment, Lieutenant Colonel von Sommerfeld, the 4th Jaeger Battalion and two battalions from Archduke Henry's regiment charged the faltering Prussians and drove them back. The badly mangled Twenty-seventh received support now, however, from the Sixty-sixth Regiment and renewed the fight; and despite the tactics of the Steiermark Jaeger, who used the tree cover as skilfully as had their ancestors in fighting with Andreas Hofer, and the commitment of fresh battalions from the Austrian IV Corps, they gradually cleared the woods and occupied the village of Cistowes. In about an hour's fighting, six Prussian battalions had knocked out more than ten Austrian battalions, destroyed Brigade Brandenstein as a fighting force, and killed its commanding officer.[43]

Zychlinski wrote later that it was the kind of fight in which a commanding officer's authority was dissipated, the tactical units becoming progressively smaller, until in the end every man seemed to be fighting his own hand. One of his noncommissioned officers agreed, adding: "It was hardly possible for the officers to hold their columns together . . . but the rain of shells [from Maslowed] which came down on us and the boughs and tree splinters that flew at us from all sides drove us instinctively forward, in the sheer hope that, by pressing further ahead, we could get out of our critical position. . . . Our higher officers (since there was nothing for them to command) could only influence the men around them by the example of their personal bravery. And this example was not in vain. I can remember no case in which I saw an unwounded man give up the fight."[44] In this kind of warfare the losses were heavy. Wherever there were clearings, heaps of Austrian bodies gave mute testimony to the needle gun's effectiveness when it had a good field of fire. But the Austrian Jaeger had taken their toll too. The Prussian Twenty-seventh Regiment had been hit particularly hard, and many of its officers killed; and its victory over Brandenstein was only the beginning of a long day's work, for the Austrians were already coming back in force.

In fact, the near destruction of one of his brigades had infuriated Festetics, and by doing so it started the process by which his corps and the neighboring II Corps of Count Thun were sucked down into the *Swiepwald*, with fateful strategical consequences. At 9:30 A.M., the IV Corps commander ordered two more brigades, those of Poeckh and Fleischhacker, to get ready to clear the wood and, to prepare the way for them, laid on a barrage of 80 guns from Maslowed height. As this artillery preparation got under way, the Prussians replied in kind, and a bomb shell burst in Festetics's headquarters post, killing his *chef* Görz, who had been the guiding spirit in turning the corps in this direction in the first place, and blowing off part of the corps commander's foot. Festetics was forced to turn the command over to his deputy, Major General Mollinary, who was, if anything, more intent than he upon driving the Prussians out of the *Swiepwald*. Mollinary not only confirmed the orders for the new attack but sent a message to Lieutenant Field Marshal Count Thun, asking that II Corps lend him some support.[45]

In the second phase of the *Swiepwald* fight, the Austrians reverted to the tactics that had cost them so dearly at Podol and Nachod. Brigade Fleischhacker charged into the woods with horns blowing and drums beating and tried to clear it by sheer impetus. But Fransecky had now committed his four reserve battalions and was soon to get two more from the 8th Division; and the needle guns of the 1st and Fusilier Battalions of the Twenty-sixth Regiment were able to blunt the first assault by the Austrian brigade and to press it back slowly toward the southern edge of the wood. Mollinary then threw in a second brigade. Led by the Fifty-first Regiment (Rumanians and Magyars), with the hard-driving Colonel von Poeckh at their head, it smashed into the Prussian front and left flank and drove the stubborn Magdeburgers before it to the farthest limits of the wood. Poeckh had all but carried the day. But now, in the words of the Austrian battle report, "suddenly, on a tree-covered rising on the right flank, masses of Prussians were seen, and they opened a murderous fire on the more deeply vulnerable brigade. It was here that it suffered its greatest losses. The brigade commander and all of the staff officers save one fell; General Staff Captain von Klobus, who raced back to get support, had to break out through the enemy's lines and lost his horse. Meanwhile, the situation in this corner of the wood became intolerable. Encircled on all sides, the troops had no alternative to fighting their way out. Grappling at times hand-to-hand with the enemy, as their contusions and bayonet wounds showed, only a small remnant made good their escape."[46] The losses of the Fifty-first and the 8th Jaeger Battalion which had supported them were terrible. The first line of Brigade Poeckh was nearly wiped out. Out of 4,000 men committed to the charge, only 1,800 returned,[47] and these were wounded in body and shaken in morale. No more striking evidence could be given of the failure of Austrian tactics. Even if it were necessary to win back the wood—and the Austrian General Staff work on the war denied this[48]—one wonders, as Fransecky did,[49] why it never occurred to the IV Corps commander that the 7th Division had an open flank and might have been pinned frontally and attacked circuitously by way of Benatek, with fewer losses.

It was now eleven o'clock in the morning and however gratifying the results of the fighting may have appeared to Fransecky, his casualties were mounting and the Austrians were obviously determined to press the attack. At about this time, one of the King's adjutants, Lieutenant Colonel Karl Walther Freiherr von Loë, came to him, and the commander of the 7th Division made it clear that his resources were running low, although he insisted that he would fight to the last man. Loë rode back to headquarters and expressed the opinion that Fransecky should be sent some fresh infantry. While the King was considering this, Moltke interjected and in firm tones said: "I must seriously advise Your Majesty to send General von Fransecky not a single man of infantry support. Until the Crown Prince has begun his attack, which is the only thing that can bring help to the general, we must be on the look-out for an Austrian offensive. We will beat it off as long as we have III Army Corps [this was the reserve] at our disposal. We have already sent Count Bismarck's Cavalry Brigade to help him, and Lieutenant Colonel von Loë must have seen it. In any case, I know General von Fransecky, and I know that he will stand firm."[50] The King followed the advice of his Chief of Staff.

On the Austrian side Count Thun had by now acceded to Mollinary's request and placed two fresh brigades—those of Major General von Saffran and the Duke of Württemberg—at his disposal. The IV Corps commander had also received a message from Benedek, telling him that he should remain in line with III Corps on his left until the proper moment for an offensive arrived. Intent on the business before him, Mollinary returned an ambiguous answer, intimating that the projected attack by the brigades of II Corps was intended to enable his own troops to withdraw.[51] He then sent the fresh brigades into the wood. They comprised fourteen battalions, led by the Steiermärker of the Forty-seventh Regiment and the Poles of the Fifty-seventh, and they had an *élan* that the defenders could hardly match. There was a note of desperation in Fransecky's response to a new enquiry from the King's headquarters: "Tell His Majesty that the division is suffering heavily but will hold fast." This was close to being wishful thinking, for once more the dwindling battalions of the 7th Division had been pushed back to the fringes of the *Swiepwald*. For hours now their officers had been pleading, "Just half an hour more! The Crown Prince is coming!"

But the Crown Prince hadn't come, and human endurance has its limits. Fransecky's nineteen battalions had stood off fifty, but they had now lost 84 officers and more than 2,100 men, and the enemy showed no sign of stopping his attacks. In the 1st Battalion of the Prussian Sixty-sixth Regiment almost all the officers had been wounded; and although this led one of the infantrymen to say, "*Na*, we'll come out of this in fine shape. The dogs are aiming only at first lieutenants!" no one thought this very funny.[52] It was now noon, and morale was beginning to falter. At the very moment that King William, on the Roskosberg, was upbraiding Valentini's shattered command and sending it back into the *Holawald*, Fransecky was saying to his weary troops, "Hold on, *Leute!* Hold on! We've got to stand here or die!" And to an officer from the Second Army staff who had come to tell him that Alvensleben's troops were really on their way, he said somberly, "In school we learned the saying: 'I wish the night would come, or Blücher.' We are no Wellingtons here, but that's exactly how we feel!"[53]

This was the high tide of Austrian fortunes. After a long morning's fighting their lines were still undented, and their guns had inflicted heavy losses on Frederick Charles's army. In the woods of Maslowed and Sadowa the Prussian battalions were growing weaker; there was no sign of progress on Herwarth's front; and there was no evidence to indicate that the Crown Prince's forces were close enough to bring any kind of relief in the foreseeable future. In view of all this, it was understandable that at royal headquarters on the Roskosberg tempers should have become uncertain and nerves tightly strung. Only Moltke retained his calm and seemed sanguine about the outcome; and although those who shared the *Feldherrnhügel* with him on the day of Königgrätz later remembered all of his reassuring gestures in the hours of uncertainty, it is a sign of their own tension on that morning that they could never agree as to when he made them. A hundred years later, we can only guess about this, while reciting the incidents that have over the years become honored with the telling. At some time in the late morning, the King—disturbed by withdrawals from the *Holawald*—asked Moltke's opinion of how things were going and received the answer: "Your Majesty will today win not only the battle but the campaign."[54] At some time before or after noon, Bismarck, worried about the outcome, offered Moltke his cigar case and was reassured to see the Chief of Staff choose the best of the cigars contained in it.[55] At some time, perhaps in the early afternoon, when the King asked about preparations made for possible withdrawal, Moltke is reported to have answered, "Here there will be no retreat. Here we are fighting for the very existence of Prussia. [*Hier geht es um Preussen.*]"[56] Whether true or apocryphal, the anecdotes indicate that the Chief of Staff sought to combat pessimism and the kind of irrational activity that is likely to be prompted by it.

Moltke also tried to prevent gestures of impatience from disturbing his battle plan. Shortly before noon, he rode from the Roskosberg in the direction of Lipa and admired an ox which he found grazing calmly among the sounds of battle and the falling shells. When he got back to the King's headquarters, he found that Prince Frederick Charles had profited from his absence to order Lieutenant General Albrecht Gustav von Manstein to lead the 6th Division across the Bistritz, so that it would be prepared to go forward as soon as the Crown Prince arrived. With bands playing "Heil dir im Siegerkranz," the division had paraded before the King and then crossed the Bistritz, where it had to stand for hours exposed to enemy fire.[57] This was the sort of thing that Moltke had tried to prevent by impressing upon his associates that the only virtue needed here was patience and that action was pointless until the Crown Prince arrived on the scene. As long as there was no evidence of the approach of the Second Army, however, the King's nervousness and that of his staff continued to grow.

The fears that plagued the King of Prussia might have been relieved had he known what was now, shortly after noon, known in Benedek's headquarters at Lipa and what results were already flowing from it. To the Austrian commander, well satisfied with the morning's work and speculating upon the moment at which he might launch a major assault against Frederick Charles, there had come at about 11:30 A.M. a telegram from Josephstadt with the shattering intelligence that the Prussian Crown Prince— fondly imagined or wishfully hoped as remote as Chimborazu—

had for some hours been moving rapidly toward the scene of the battle and could be expected, if not momentarily, at least reasonably soon.[58] This news for the first time made abundantly clear the seriousness of the commitment made by Festetics, Mollinary, and Thun in the *Swiepwald*. The question now was whether, and how, the vulnerable Austrian right flank could be shored up before the Prussian Second Army threw its weight against it.

6

THE BATTLE:
The Advance of the Prussian Second Army

Viktoria hat heute Dienst am Tor:
"Garde, zeig deine Karte vor,
Preußische Garde, willkommen
    am Ort,
Aber erst das Losungswort."

"Wir bringen gute Losung heim,
Und als Parole 'nen neuen Reim,
Einen neuen preußischen Reim
    auf Ruhm."

"Nenn' ihn, Garde!"
        "Die Höhe von Chlum."[1]
    —THEODOR FONTANE,
    "Einzug, 20. September 1866"

(Victoria is on duty at the gate
    today.
"Guard, show me your pass!
Prussian Guard, welcome here,
But first the password!"

"We bring home a good rallying
    cry
And, for a password, a new
    rhyme,
A new Prussian rhyme for glory."

"Tell me it, Guard!"
        "The heights of Chlum!")

O<small>N THE MORNING</small> of July 3 the Prussian Second Army was concentrated around Königinhof, all of its components bivouacked on the far side of the upper Elbe with the exception of units of I Army Corps, which were pushed forward toward Praussnitz, and the advance guard of the 1st Guard Division which was at

Dobrawitz. The morning dawned cold and grey and with a light driving rain, but the men rose in good spirits and gathered around their campfires for coffee. There was little awareness of an impending battle, and even the sound of distant guns, which was heard from seven-thirty onward, attracted little attention around the fires. None of the men knew of the feverish activity that had followed Count Finckenstein's arrival at army headquarters during the night with orders for a speedy advance against the enemy's flank. Shortly after eight o'clock, when the call came to break camp, there was no great excitement. An officer of the 2nd Battalion of the Third Guard Regiment wrote later that no one really expected to get to where the guns were until the Austrians had withdrawn; this would just be another day of marching.[2] The men got their gear in order, rolled and folded their coats, and packed them, with their mess kits and knapsacks, into the baggage wagons, and then—having accomplished all that with despatch—did what soldiers have done in similar circumstances in every army since the invention of the art of war: they waited.

The waiting varied in duration from unit to unit, according to the temperament of the commander. At Dobrawitz, where Fransecky's messenger came pelting in at about 8:30 A.M. to say that the 7th Division, with one flank resting on nothing but air, was already engaged against superior numbers and wanted support, Major General Konstantin von Alvensleben ordered an immediate advance toward Jericek, without bothering to seek authorization from army headquarters. At Praussnitz, on the other hand, where General Bonin was still in command of the East Prussian Corps (despite Blumenthal's view that he should have been replaced for his conduct after Trautenau),[3] no urgency was apparent. Moltke had given I Corps freedom to act in accordance with the developing situation, but its commander refused to stir until he had explicit instructions from the Crown Prince, and, even after he had them, moved with undue circumspection. The East Prussians did not move out of their bivouac area until well after nine o'clock, and they were not to reach their first objective, Groß Burglitz, until after eleven. The other two corps were moving out a good hour before I Corps got started: VI Corps (11th and 12th Divisions) from Gradlitz in the direction of Welchow; the Guard

Corps from Königinhof in the direction of Chotoborek and Jericek.

At Königinhof, the commanders and staff of the Guard Corps assembled at the railroad station shortly after eight o'clock to receive marching orders. The commander of the reserve artillery, Hohenlohe, was in a touchy mood, because he had so far seen no action during the campaign, generally arriving with his guns after the issue had been decided, as he had done in the case of the fight at Soor. He was tired of the good-natured gibes of his friends in the other arms and disgusted with what appeared to be a disposition on the part of the staff to treat his artillery as baggage. Now, when the corps chief of staff, Colonel Ferdinand Franz von Dannenberg, handed out the orders, Hohenlohe discovered with indignation that he was to be frustrated again, for the reserve artillery was instructed to start for Chotoborek only after the 1st and 2nd Guard Divisions had begun to march. He remonstrated furiously, but Dannenberg was in no mood for argument. He had just learned of Alvensleben's headlong departure from Dobrawitz. This appeared to worry him, and he silenced Hohenlohe curtly. The artillery commander flung himself across the room and began glumly filling his pockets with sandwiches from a large pile on a nearby table, doubtless cursing infantry-minded brass hats as he did so. Then suddenly Dannenberg appeared to relent. "Just to be nice to you," he called across the room, "the Reserve Artillery is to follow the First Guard Division, and the Second Division follows you. Can you arrange that?" "Gladly," answered Hohenlohe with relief. He despatched a lieutenant to his second in command, ordering him to bring the guns into line. This took some doing, for the 1st Division was already on the move, and the 2nd Division was preparing to follow; but it was accomplished successfully, and the guns rumbled off towards Chotoborek. Both this change of disposition and the pause that preceded it were to have significant results. Thanks to the first, the Guards had enough guns in line at crucial points in the battle. Thanks to the second, Hohenlohe's pockets were padded in such a way as to save him from a nasty wound at the height of the fighting.[4]

Even for the divisions that moved out early, the going proved to be difficult and slow. Major von Verdy of the Crown Prince's staff, which moved forward with the main body of the 1st Guard

Division, later described the rigors of the morning's march. "The infantry, closed up in section columns as long as we could use the broad highway, had to shift to files when it became necessary to leave the high road for the by-ways; and it wasn't long before the difficulties caused by the unfavorable weather and the condition of the soil made themselves felt. The cold rain, which had streamed down almost without interruption during the night, held on throughout the whole course of the forenoon and not only made the march more difficult for the individual soldier but also helped soften the ground in such a way that the troops were able to move ahead on the uphill, downdale paths only with the utmost exertion." All efforts to keep them closed up failed; the columns got longer, and ever-widening gaps appeared between the regiments and the battalions.[5] For the artillery the going was even rougher. To get around straggling infantry units, the batteries sometimes had to leave the roads and use the fields, where the grain caught in the carriage wheel spokes and had to be chopped away with sabers, and the wheels sank to their hubs in the soft ground, causing the teams to strain and, on more than one occasion, to die in the traces.[6]

If the Second Army's progress was slower than the First Army staff had hoped, these conditions of weather and terrain were responsible, rather than any dilatoriness on the part of Crown Prince Frederick William and General Blumenthal, as Prince Frederick Charles later charged.[7] It is nevertheless true that, although they urged their troops on with commendable energy, the Crown Prince and his *chef* were no more expecting a major battle than their foot soldiers. This was doubtless partly due to Blumenthal's skepticism with respect to assessments of the situation made by staffs other than his own; but it was caused more by the fact that the wretched visibility concealed any evidence of the impending encounter. Even at Dobrawitz, which they reached some time after nine o'clock, there was nothing much to go on but the continuing sound of the guns, now somewhat louder, and columns of smoke in the western sky that might denote burning villages. Thus, it was not until eleven o'clock, when the Crown Prince and Blumenthal reined in at Chotoborek, that a sense of what was really impending broke upon them. From the height on which they stood, they looked down into a shallow valley through which ran a stream called the Trotina. On its banks below them was the village of Jericek, then farther to the left, Luzan, and farther left and just out of sight, Trotina village—the last two in the line of march of VI Corps. Beyond Jericek, on the other side of the stream, the ground rose in a series of flat ridges to the hill of Horenowes, which cut off their view toward the Bistritz valley, which lay beyond. Along the height of Horenowes they could see the flashes from Austrian batteries—eight of them, it was learned later—firing westward; and the volume of smoke and the mingled sound of artillery and small arms made it clear that no chance encounter or rear-guard action was in progress, but that the First Army must be engaged heavily along its whole front. Blumenthal turned to the Crown Prince. "This is the decisive battle," he said, and Frederick William silently agreed.[8]

At this point, Hohenlohe reached Chotoborek, having wrangled his guns up the hills and around and through the infantry of the 1st Guard Division, and reported to his corps commander, the Prince of Württemberg. Through his telescope, he studied the valley floor and with practiced eye calculated the Austrian artillery strength. "Things don't look good for the First Army," he said. "That's right," a voice said behind him, and Hohenlohe turned to find that the Crown Prince had ridden up. "Things aren't going well for my cousin Fritz Karl. I've got two choices: I can march to join him, but it's too far and I'd get there too late, or I can go straight ahead and take them in the flank and rear. Take a look at that big tree! That's the Austrian right flank. Keep that on your right! And bang away smartly, so that Fritz Karl will know I'm here!"[9]

The tree in question—Russell had noticed it when he mounted to his tower at nine o'clock and had called it "the only remarkable object" on the ridge—was in fact two linden trees, standing on either side of a large crucifix. By taking this point as the goal of the Guard Corps advance, the Crown Prince was shifting his line of march about twenty-five degrees to the left; for up to this point he had been moving in the general direction of Benatek and the fight in the *Swiepwald,* and his advance guard under General von Alvensleben had, as we have already seen (see above, pp. 105, 114), started in that direction at 8:30 in the morning in the hope of relieving Fransecky's beleaguered division. Alvensleben's forces were by now at Zizelowes, Zelkowitz and Wrchownitz, and at 11:30 A.M. Colonel Alexander Wilhelm von Pape had actually reached Benatek with the 2nd Battalion of the Second Guard Regiment and the Third Guard Jaeger Company. But before they could be put into action, Pape was ordered to turn back and, with the rest of Alvensleben's brigade, to lead the advance towards "the tree" at Horenowes.[10]

At Chotoborek the main body of the 1st Guard Division began to move in the same direction, going down the slope past the Crown Prince and his staff and cheering as they did so. Their commander urged them on, pointing towards the heights of Horenowes and shouting, "You've got to go that way! That's the place where it's happening!" Verdy was so struck by the scene that he later sketched it from memory and gave it to the staff artist of the *Illustrated London News;* and anyone who cares to take down the appropriate volume of that paper can see the march of the Guard as it appeared that morning, the men waving their caps as they passed their commander and went down the slope, the rectangular columns crossing the Trotina, their flags flying, the gun carriages jolting in their wake.[11] It was a brave sight, and Verdy shyly asked the British observer, a Colonel Walker, what he thought of the troops. Walker was a veteran of the Crimea and the Indian Mutiny; he had seen more war than anyone else at Chotoborek, and his opinion was valued. He did not disappoint his hosts now. If these troops had been going into battle for the first time, with no idea of the danger that awaited them, there would be nothing remarkable about their appearance, he said. But, he added, "I have never seen troops going into the danger of death for the second time looking like this." The Crown Prince and his staff glowed with satisfaction.[12]

Meanwhile, farther east, the two divisions of General von Mutius's VI Corps were also moving forward. These were Silesian troops, as yet untried in battle, for they had been in reserve behind Steinmetz when the "lion of Nachod" had won his victories in the mountain passes. Now the roles were reversed, and, while V Corps brought up the rear, the eager Silesian divisions pressed forward toward the Trotina River. Originally the mission of the 12th Division had been to keep Josephstadt under observation, but by ten in the morning the divisional commander, Lieutenant General Conrad Wilhelm von Prondzynski, received a penciled note from his superior: "Keep the enemy in view. Maintain contact with 11th Division, which is directing itself toward the sound of the cannon." "Break out the flags!" Prondzynski ordered, and as the standards flapped heavily in the rain, the division began to wheel toward the west and, leaving Josephstadt to its left, to move toward Trotina.[13] On its right, Lieutenant General Alexander Friedrich von Zastrow's 11th Division was racing toward Racitz, and at just about the same time the Crown Prince saw his troops pass in review at Chotoborek and start for Horenowes its advance guard bore down upon the river crossing at that point. Thus, without waste of motion or of time, two of the Crown Prince's corps were in line for the assault upon the enemy's weak flank. Absent were General Bonin, the prey of doubts and hesitations at Groß Burglitz, and the Second Army's cavalry division, commanded by Major General Julius Hartwig Freiherr von Hartmann, which, according to Blumenthal, "seemed to disappear from the face of the earth" at about noon and wasn't heard from again until four o'clock in the afternoon.[14]

While these forces had been gathering for their push, desperate fighting had continued in the *Holawald* and the *Swiepwald*, to the increasing gloom of the Prussian royal headquarters. On Lipa, on the other hand, there was general satisfaction with the course of the battle, and the volatile Benedek was once more entertaining visions of victory. Evidence of his mounting confidence were his messages to his reserves in the rear, ordering them to close up on Lipa, and the additional fact that he asked one of his cavalry commanders, Lieutenant Field Marshal Wilhelm Prince Schleswig-Holstein, to look over the terrain for a likely place to launch the decisive blow westward. It was probably Benedek's preoccupation with the coming thrust to the west that led him also to reverse an earlier decision—taken at Baumgarten's insistence—to fill the gap on his right flank by ordering Ramming's corps to take position there. This, he convinced himself, would be unnecessary, and the deposed Krismanic agreed with him. It was too soon to commit reserves, and, in any case, in a little while there would be more satisfactory work for Ramming in the shallows of the Bistritz.[15]

This euphoric mood was shattered, at least momentarily, by the arrival at about 11:30 A.M. of the telegram already alluded to (see above, page 111), saying that Crown Prince Frederick William was on his way. On the heels of this wire, Baumgarten, who had been inspecting the left wing of the army, returned to Lipa to find that Ramming's corps had not moved. He said later: "I was terrified by this [discovery], because I was afraid for the right wing. The blood drained from my face, and if anyone had lanced one of my veins, he would have got not one single drop." Baumgarten rode over to Benedek to demand an explanation; and, without answering, the commander-in-chief pulled the telegram from his pocket in his balled fist. The chief of staff knew then that the countermanding of his order was even more serious than he had thought, and he reproached Benedek for having changed his mind. Rather clumsily, Benedek answered that the order could always be reissued. The *chef* answered despairingly, "You can't move fifty battalions as easily as pieces on a chess board. It's too late!"[16]

At this critical moment in his fortunes, Benedek might—and some thought he should—have thrown discretion to the winds and launched his long-planned attack against Frederick Charles or, alternatively, against Herwarth, simultaneously ordering part of his reserve to move into defensive positions on the right flank as fast as possible. But he could not persuade himself to do this, apparently believing that the moment for the offensive stroke would come later, and that when it did he would need all his reserves to support it. He decided, therefore, to return to his original battle plan. He now sent urgent orders to IV and II Corps, instructing them to detach their troops from the *Swiepwald* without further delay and to return to the prepared positions between Chlum, Nedelist and Sendrasitz which had been assigned to them at the beginning of the day.

This order Mollinary and Thun resisted and carried out slowly and imperfectly. The former commander, indeed, refused to make any retrograde movement until he had ridden back to Lipa to argue the toss with Benedek.[17] In the end he gave in, after Benedek had ordered him flatly to obey, and he passed the word down the line to his subordinates. But what had been proven at Gitschin was shown to be true here also: it was difficult to pull the troops back either quickly or safely. It was one o'clock before any appreciable number had started back; and, when they had, they were tired and—because of being forced to retreat from a fight they had hoped they were winning—dispirited.[18] They were hardly in a condition, either physical or psychological, to withstand the powerful thrust that the Prussian Crown Prince was now preparing all along the Trotina River. Nor were there many fresh troops in line to bear the brunt of that attack. Of the 59 infantry battalions originally deployed on the right flank between the Bistritz and the Trotina, 46 had been involved in the *Swiepwald*, and three more, from Brigade Thom, had had to be invested at the very end in order to help detach the others. The only unblooded troops on the vulnerable flank were ten battalions of II Corps, and these were strung too loosely across too great a distance.[19]

In obedience to the Crown Prince's instructions, Hohenlohe led the reserve artillery down the slope to Jericek village shortly after 11:30 A.M. The village was under fire, for the Prussian movements had by now been detected by enemy artillery observers on the heights. The narrow streets were filled with wounded from the advance units, and around the wooden bridge the Austrian shells were falling with depressing accuracy. The thought of taking guns over this rickety crossing was not pleasant, but the stream was swollen and turbulent from the rains and there was no alternative. Forcing his way through the marching battalions of the 1st Guard Division, Hohenlohe got his four batteries across and spurred up the slope to a flat ridge about 2,500 yards from the Austrian position. Here two batteries of the 1st Guard Division were already firing, and Hohenlohe fell in beside them.[20] An artillery duel began that continued for about an hour, during which time the Prussian batteries gradually increased in number, for in midmorning the Crown Prince had ordered VI Corps to send its guns forward in the direction of Horenowes, and General von Zastrow of the 11th Division had despatched six batteries without delay. By 12:30 the Prussians had about 78 guns firing at the 40-odd Austrian guns on the height, and after a time the Austrians limbered up and began to move out.[21]

It is doubtful whether Hohenlohe and his companions effected this result by themselves. Guns which are not well protected by infantry are in a highly vulnerable position, and this was true of the Austrian batteries, whose gunners had to worry not only about the Prussian bombardment but about the needle guns of the 1st Battalion of the Second Guard Regiment which led the attack now launched by Alvensleben's brigade. Concealed by the tall grain, the Guards maneuvered their way up and around the slope to take the batteries in enfilading fire. The Austrians fought back with grape and canister and held their own until fresh battalions joined the fight against them shortly after one o'clock. Then they retired, with a loss of five guns. A Prussian attempt at pursuit by three squadrons of the Second Dragoons was beaten off with heavy losses by the rear guard, the 3rd Battalion of the Regiment Sachsen Weimar.[22]

At just about this time, two observers eight miles apart saw things that interested them. From Königgrätz tower, W. H. Russell saw Austrian artillery falling back over the brow of the hill "near the big tree" and noticed signs of enemy activity there. This appeared to him to be "inexplicable and very serious, for although on the left and center the Austrians might be victorious, this movement threatened, by forcing back their right, to cut them off from Königgrätz. . . . A general who saw what was visible to those in the tower would have felt uneasiness and have turned his attention to fill the gap in his line at the center, and to drive back the Prussians who were doubling up his right."[23]

From another vantage point, on the Roskosberg, Count Bismarck trained his telescope on the same ridge that was attracting Russell's attention and noticed that something he had thought was a line of trees was actually moving and that Austrian guns seemed to be firing toward it. He handed his glass to Moltke, who took a long look and then put away his red handkerchief with a decisive flourish. He spurred his horse over to the King and said, "The campaign is decided and in accordance with Your Majesty's desires!" The King, who was suffering under the pressure of anxiety and doubt, looked annoyed at this, and said that he didn't know what Moltke was talking about, and that they had better keep their minds on what was happening today. "No," the Chief of Staff answered, "the success is complete. Vienna lies at Your Majesty's feet."[24]

This Olympian utterance did not succeed in overcoming the

King's skepticism. It would probably have struck others as unconvincing also. The weary troops along the Bistritz, still subjected to Austrian gunfire, would not have been impressed by it. At Chotoborek, the Crown Prince would have been surprised, because, when the Austrian guns retired from Horenowes, he thought that the fighting was probably over for the day,[25] and he had no idea that the momentum of his own troops was about to prove this false. And, on Lipa, Benedek would have found Moltke's statement preposterous. As Friedjung has written, the Austrian commander lived from moment to moment, intent upon what was happening in front of him. An inspection of his right wing had convinced him that II and IV Corps were getting back to their original positions with all due promptitude and that consequently he had reasonable security against the Crown Prince's advance. Once more his mind was playing upon the idea of a frontal assault against Frederick Charles. Some time after one o'clock he muttered, "Now is the time to carry out the stroke," only to relax, as one of his aides suggested it might be better to wait until the smoke and fog lifted a bit, with the words, "*Nun, meinetwegen*" ("All right as far as I'm concerned").[26] His indecisiveness was as palpable as ever, but it still seemed untinged by premonitions of defeat.

Moltke's eyes were fixed, however, not on the fighting at his feet or even on the present situation of the battle as a whole, but rather on what it would be like in two hours' time. As new evidence began to come in of the Crown Prince's arrival on the flank—Voigts-Rhetz returned from a ride to the 7th Division front and said that units of the Second Army had apparently been engaged in fire-fights since noon—the Chief of Staff's first concern was to prevent overhasty action on the part of the Prussian center. Prince Frederick Charles was now burning with impatience, and on his own initiative he sent orders to General von Manstein to begin the commitment of III Corps, the army's reserve. This Moltke had to veto, pointing out that the important thing was to hold the enemy, not to push him back out of the vise that was closing on him.[27] At the same time, Moltke sought to galvanize the Elbe Army into more activity on the right flank. At a quarter to two, he sent a message to Herwarth which read: "Crown Prince at Zizelowes. Retreat of Austrians to Josephstadt cut off. It is of greatest importance that corps of General von Herwarth advance against the wing opposed to it while the Austrians are still making a stand in the center."[28]

When this message reached him, Herwarth's forward battalions were heavily engaged. The Austro-Saxons had been emboldened by their first counterattack, in which, as we have seen (see above, page 98), the Saxon Life Brigade had all but driven the Prussians back to the bridgehead at Nechanitz, and Crown Prince Albert had resolved to mount a more elaborate drive, using almost four full brigades and supporting troops. Consequently, he requested the Austrian VIII Corps to send two brigades to take position at Ober Prim, in front of the wood of Stezirek, where they could protect his left flank, while he sent the Saxon Second Brigade forward to renew the attack of the Life Brigade in the center. Once the Prussians began to yield under this pressure in the center, it was intended that the Second Mounted Brigade and the 1st Horse Battery, supported by Edelsheim's Light Cavalry Division, would attack south of Stezirek wood, by way of Techlowitz, hitting the Prussian right flank and rolling up the line of artillery on the height of Hradek. It was a well-conceived plan, and it might have succeeded had it not been for a series of bizarre accidents.[29]

The Second Saxon Brigade moved down from the heart of the Saxon position at Problus toward Neu Prim, and at about 1:30 P.M. began to push forward across the wavy ground between that village and the pheasantry. Led by the 6th Battalion, they made good progress and were beginning to creep around the left flank of the Prussian artillery position when disaster struck. To their consternation, they were hit and overrun not by Prussian troops but by a wildly fleeing horde of Austrians.

In fact, the whole left wing of Prince Albert's projected operation had collapsed. When he had requested support from the Austrian VIII Corps, its commander, Archduke Ernest, had sent Brigade Schulz and Brigade Roth to form the screen along the edge of the wood at Stezirek. The first of these fell into position smartly; the second was late and in a state of some tactical disorganization when it followed—the 5th Jaeger Battalion having become mixed up with elements of the Nassau Regiment. Troops were trying to sort themselves out and to find their own officers, and the brigade as a whole was still attempting to form a firm connection with Brigade Schulz on its right when the Prussian Sixty-eighth Regiment burst out of the woods and fell upon the straggling Austrian line.

Prince Albert was unfortunate in having launched his second attack about half an hour too late. Despite Herwarth's hesitations, he had gotten the rest of the 15th Division across the river by one o'clock. Its commander, General von Canstein, had orders to mount an attack over Hradek against Neu and Nieder Prim, and he had done so by sending the Twenty-ninth Brigade (Major General von Stückradt) into the woods that separated those villages from Hradek, simultaneously ordering the Thirtieth Brigade (Major General von Glasenapp) to make a looping movement to the right over Techlowitz and through Stezirek wood against the Austrian left wing.

It was this latter movement that ruined all of Prince Albert's plans. Led by the fusilier battalion of the Sixty-eighth Regiment, Brigade Glasenapp hit the Austrian line, which buckled and then broke. The collapse came first in Brigade Schulz, which had been hard hit at Skalitz and seemed, indeed, still to be suffering from the traumatic effects of that fight. Panic broke out among the Czech battalions of Regiment Nobili as they found themselves being raked once more by Prussian needle guns, and they broke and fled, carrying the battalions of Regiment Gerstner with them. Half of Brigade Schulz, together with its commander, and the confused units of Brigade Roth were hurled back upon Ober Prim; the other half was driven to the left, toward Neu Prim, precisely at the moment when the Second Saxon Brigade's advance from that village toward Hradek was picking up momentum. The fleeing troops hit the Saxons like a thunderbolt, and the struggling mass rolled westward, right into the guns of the Prussian Twenty-ninth Brigade. This completed the collapse of Austrian morale, and a rout might well have followed had it not been for the behavior of the Saxons. Although their two leading battalions had suffered heavy losses under the Prussian fire, they manfully preserved a semblance of order in the center, while their brigade's second wave, led by the 2nd Jaeger Battalion, ad-

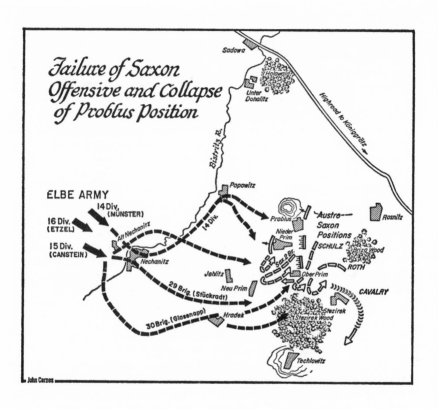

Failure of Saxon
Offensive and Collapse
of Problus Position

Sadowa

Holawald

Unter
Dohalitz

Bistritz R.

Highroad to Königgrätz

Popowitz

Problus

Rosnitz

ELBE ARMY

14 Div.
(MÜNSTER)

16 Div.
(ETZEL)

15 Div.
(CANSTEIN)

Alt Nechanitz

14 Div.

Nieder
Prim

Austro-
Saxon
Positions

SCHULZ

Briza Wood

Nechanitz

Sax.2 Br.

ROTH

Jehlitz

Ober Prim

Neu Prim

CAVALRY

29 Brig. (Stückradt)

30 Brig. (Glasenapp)

Hradek

Stezirek
Stezirek Wood

Techlowitz

John Carnes

vanced in ordered ranks and with music playing against the threatened flank, opening their files to let the last of the fugitives through, and then closing up and opening fire on the on-pressing Prussians. Under their protection, the remnants of the Austrian brigades—they had lost a thousand men—tried desperately to re-form at Ober Prim, while the Saxons fell back methodically toward Problus.[30]

The Austrian attempt to hold at Ober Prim was in vain. Although the 3rd Infantry Battalion of Colonel von Gerstner's regiment conducted a stubborn defense against the Prussian Sixty-eighth, it was compelled to give way when a concentric attack by the Twenty-eighth Regiment threatened to cut its line of retreat. As the last Austrians withdrew, dashing in small groups across the grain-covered fields that separated the village from the relative safety of the Briza wood, Major General Schulz, who had seen his whole brigade smashed despite his own strenuous attempts to hold it together, fell from his horse with two Prussian bullets in his breast. He lay for some time under the heavy fire of his own guns, which were seeking now to stem the Prussian advance, and although he was finally rescued by a patrol of the Prussian Twenty-eighth Regiment, led by a Captain Perizonius and a Lieutenant Tempel, he died as they carried him back to the village.[31]

Prince Albert's position was now in the gravest jeopardy. It was 2:30 in the afternoon. The Prussian Thirtieth Brigade at Ober Prim was in position to outflank his forces at Problus by advancing through the Briza wood, which was held only by two battalions of the Brigade Wöber. Nieder Prim was already in flames and was under heavy attack by the Prussian Twenty-ninth Brigade; and if it fell the 46 Austro-Saxon guns on Problus height would soon be exposed to infantry attack. Even more serious was the fact that, in response to Moltke's order of 1:45 P.M., Herwarth had ordered General von Münster's 14th Division to launch a major assault upon the Problus position, and, with their banners flying and their bands playing, Münster's two brigades were now attacking along the whole Problus–Stresetitz line. The Saxon Crown Prince had committed the First Saxon Brigade in an attempt to repair the damage done during the last hour. But now, as he watched, that brigade was hit by heavy fire from Münster's guns and began to retire from Nieder Prim to the Briza wood, only to come under the needle guns of the forward units of the Thirtieth Brigade. The First Saxons had fought valiantly since the beginning of the war, but they had been hard hit at Gitschin, and their spirit was not what it had once been. Signs began to multiply that the brigade was beginning, although not quickly, to come to pieces.[32]

The danger of being outflanked was, therefore, all too clear, and Prince Albert drew the only possible conclusion. He resolved to retire. Indeed, if he had any doubts on this score, they were removed by intimations that the Austrian X Corps on his right was preparing to do the same.[33] Prince Albert, therefore, sent his cavalry to the flanks and ordered the Third Infantry Brigade to hold the line between Nieder Prim and Problus, while the bulk of his forces fell back to Briza. The Third Brigade performed this mission with skill and fortitude, holding on grimly until after three o'clock, despite mounting losses which included the brigade commander, Major General von Carlowitz, and the commander of the 3rd Jaeger Battalion, Lieutenant Colonel von der Mosel. By that time, most of Prince Albert's forces had made good their withdrawal. Even so, the rear guard was reluctant to break off the fight. The 1st Jaeger Battalion was still holding on at three-thirty, when Prince Albert and his staff rode wearily up to them at the edge of the wood of Bor. They greeted their prince with cheers, and he answered them by praising their valor and giving them the honor of protecting his headquarters as they retreated.[34]

Problus was in Prussian hands shortly after three o'clock; the left wing of the Austrian array was broken and its defenders were retreating; and the first part of Herwarth's task was accomplished. But only the first. In Moltke's view, it was now his duty to press on, harrying the retreating foe and driving him into the ranks of those Austrian corps which were beginning to fall back in the center, so that encirclement must be the inevitable result. A vigorous pursuit by his own cavalry and the Alvensleben cavalry division, which he had borrowed from Frederick Charles, and by his uncommitted 16th Division offered great opportunities and might have given Herwarth a decisive role in the last part of the battle.[35] This chance was let slip. Herwarth had not even ordered the 16th Division to start crossing the Bistritz until after two o'clock, and the cavalry was still on the farther bank at that time also. His forward divisions were too done up to undertake pursuit themselves; they had lost 71 officers and 1,557 men, and were physically exhausted.[36] With the fall of Problus and the occupation of Briza wood a little later, the momentum of the Elbe Army slackened and stopped. It was not Herwarth who was going to deliver the decisive blow to Benedek's army, but the Prussian Crown Prince.

As we have seen (see above, page 119), two of the Crown Prince's three corps had been moving in a co-ordinated wheeling advance toward the weak Austrian flank ever since ten o'clock. On the extreme left, Prondzynski's 12th Division had made speedy progress and by two o'clock was advancing up the eastern bank of the Trotina River toward the village of that name. On its right, Zastrow's 11th Division had crossed the Trotina an hour earlier at the village of Racitz further upstream. There was enemy resistance here, but it was brief. Racitz bridge was held by a battalion of Italians from the Austrian Division Holstein. They had been involved in the fight in the *Swiepwald* and had suffered casualties, and had then been pulled out and rushed to the east to try to plug one of the many gaps in the line. Their morale had trickled away in the process, and after the briefest exchange of fire with the 1st Battalion of the Fiftieth Prussian Regiment they yielded their position and fled.[37] The 11th Division pushed across the stream and at two o'clock was nearing Sendrasitz. Its real objective lay beyond that village, however, at Nedelist, possession of which would place it at the flank and rear of the strong Austrian position at Chlum, the key to Benedek's defense. The 12th Division was aiming at Lochenitz, whence it could go on to cut the Sadowa–Königgrätz road and prevent an Austrian retreat. Between the two divisions and their ultimate objectives, there was as yet no very considerable Austrian force. Behind Trotina, the Brigade Henriquez—nicknamed "the black and yellows" and renowned for their exploits in Denmark—could be expected to put up a stiff defense, but in front of Sendrasitz there were no more than two Hungarian battalions, and these were backed up only by two battalions and a company from Brigade Thom, plus the cavalry division of Prince Taxis, whose two batteries were already laying down a pattern of fire across the approaches to the village.[38] This was hardly a force big enough to defend the eastern end of the Austrian flank, but at two o'clock the 11th and 12th Divisions had not yet developed their attack, and there was presumably still time for additional Austrian battalions retiring from the *Swiepwald* to strengthen the line, provided nothing happened farther to the west.

For a time it appeared that there was little chance of this. Although the Prussian 1st Guard Division took Horenowes shortly after one o'clock and was followed closely by the corps artillery reserve, the Guard Corps commander hesitated to authorize a further advance, at least until the 2nd Guard Division had come up in reserve and the 11th Division had taken Sendrasitz and diminished the possibility of an Austrian flanking movement against the Guards. Colonel von Dannenberg, the corps chief of staff, rode over to Horenowes and told the divisional commander, Hiller von Gärtringen, to remain where he was until further orders.[39]

Hiller was a thruster who would probably have objected in any circumstances to a voluntary surrender of the initiative. In the present case, he sensed instinctively that any slackening of the advance would give the Austrians time to strengthen their lines. Dannenberg had hardly left his command post, therefore, before Hiller had committed what could fairly be described as an act of insubordination, for which he would probably have been disciplined if it had not been successful and if he had not paid with his life to make it so. He made some brief obeisance to the orders given him by calling back the battalions of Alvensleben's brigade, which had paced the whole advance from Königinhof and had led the way up to Horenowes, and ordering them to take up the position of a reserve to the east of Maslowed. But simultaneously he ordered his other forces forward against the gun-crested ridge in front of them. Thus began the Prussian assault on Chlum.

As the First Guard Infantry Brigade, led by Colonels von Obernitz and von Knappe and followed closely by the three battalions of Colonel von Kessel, passed through Alvensleben's battalions, it was about 2:30 in the afternoon. Hohenlohe watched the *tirailleurs* moving across the swelling ground under heavy fire and remarked to Major General Louis Max Napoleon von Colomier, the corps artillery commander, that they wouldn't get far without artillery support. Where were Hiller's batteries? Colomier answered that he guessed they were back in Zizelowes where Hiller had left them, and that it looked as if he had simply forgotten to order them up. Hohenlohe watched the shells bursting in the ranks of the infantry for a moment or so and then, after the briefest of struggles, surrendered to his own first impulse. He would give the necessary support himself. Colomier seemed to have no objection; so Hohenlohe limbered up and careened down the slope with his own batteries and those he had borrowed earlier from Zastrow's 11th Division. He pushed forward to a point about 1,300 paces from the ridge, in plain view of the Austrians, and opened fire in the hope of attracting their attention. He was badly outgunned, for there were 108 cannon on the ridge between Chlum and Nedelist; but he figured that, by utilizing every fold of the terrain and by changing his position frequently, he might make the Austrians overshoot him.[40]

These methods had some success for, by three o'clock, without serious casualties, Hohenlohe's batteries had diverted Austrian fire, and this was precisely the time when Obernitz's *tirailleurs* were passing through the danger zone between Maslowed and Chlum. The riflemen probably never fully appreciated the assistance they were getting. Amid the deafening din of artillery fire, they had no time for thought, let alone gratitude. With their drums beating—*Tambour battant*—they stumbled up the slope through the tall grain at a half run, instinctively keeping their loose lines and moving fast to get under the curtain of fire and onto the heights.[41]

Chlum was a pretty little village which lay athwart the height of the same name. It was divided by a cross street into northern and southern halves—the latter, which included a church that was visible for miles, situated on the highest point of the ridge; the former lying somewhat lower, at the top of the downhill slope. The village was built in such a way that it was impossible from any point inside it to get a clear view of what was happening on the approaches from the valley below or in the trenches and earthworks that had been built on the ridge to the left and right of the village. Even when one went to its northern limits, one's view was obstructed by the height of Maslowed, and between that hill and the foot of Chlum the ground rose and fell in waves and was covered for the most part with grain standing five feet high. All this made ready detection of an approaching enemy difficult.[42]

The defense of Chlum had been entrusted to the brigade of Major General von Appiano. This officer was one of those stern disciplinarians who, after the suppression of the Hungarian revolution, had administered the severe punishment meted out to the regiments that had defected. It was Hungarians who constituted the bulk of his command now—the Regiments Sachsen Meiningen (Forty-sixth) and Erzherzog Heinrich (Sixty-second)—although these were supplemented by the 4th Jaeger Battalion from Moravia. Earlier in the day, some of Appiano's battalions had been stationed at Cistowes and had participated in the fight against Fransecky, and this had left an indelible impression upon their commander, even after his troops were ordered back to the trenches on Chlum. He was singularly inattentive to any threat from the north; his troops were still facing west; and he himself remained intent on the possibility of smiting Frederick Charles hip and thigh before the day was done. This, as Friedjung says quite properly,[43] is inexplicable, since Appiano's forces had been subjected to the fire of the Crown Prince's guns on Horenowes from one o'clock onward, but it is no harder to explain than his further conduct. In order to protect his troops from that fire, and from the shells of Frederick Charles's batteries as well, Appiano withdrew the greater part of his force to a point 800 yards south of Chlum which had the advantage of cover but from which the village could not be seen. In Chlum itself he left only the 2nd and 3rd Battalions of the Forty-sixth Regiment, keeping the 1st Battalion at his command post. The result of this was that none of the Sachsen Meiningen battalions could see either of the others, which promised to make mutual support difficult, if not impossible.

In Chlum itself, a certain nervousness reigned and rumors spread that the Prussians were on their way. This aroused only derisive laughter from the regimental commander, Colonel von Slaveczi, who had set up his command post with the 3rd Battalion in the southeastern corner of the village. "You are all seeing phantoms!" he said, when his officers expressed their concern, and later, when it was reported to him that troops wearing what appeared to be Prussian Guard helmets were developing an attack against the lines of Archduke Joseph's brigade between Chlum and Nedelist, he said confidently (but in words which betrayed a complete ignorance of the battle order of his own army): "Those are Saxons!"[44]

All in all, the Austrian behavior at this vitally important point at the hinge of their line invited disaster, and such invitations rarely go unanswered. While Slaveczi was finding amusement in the apprehensions of his junior officers, battalions of the First and Third Guard Regiments and the Guard Jaeger rose up like specters out of the smoke and fog and fell upon the gun positions just east of Chlum. These were protected by the Sixty-seventh and Sixty-eighth Regiments, Slovaks and Magyars of Archduke Joseph's brigade. They had seen no action this day, and now, when it came upon them so suddenly, they panicked. The captain of the first Prussian company to swarm into the guns wrote later, "Instead of fighting back with determination, they stood undecided and without firing a shot, and then turned and struggled away in every direction under our murderous fire."[45] In vain did their officers beat them with the flats of their swords, shouting, "Oh, you cowards! Stand there, you yellow dogs!" In vain did their brigade commander, Archduke Joseph, who had three horses killed under him this day, cry out, "Children, don't leave me in the lurch!" Deaf to all appeals, they fled, abandoning sixteen guns as they did so. Their ugly rush to the rear, moreover, swept away the troops standing behind them—remnants of that unfortunate brigade of Brandenstein which had been so roughly treated by Zychlinski in the *Swiepwald* earlier in the day. Despite the determined efforts of their officers, these troops also streamed away. In an attempt to stem the torrent flowing toward the rear, Lieutenant Colonel von Hofbauer, the commander of 64 guns of the army's artillery reserve, which were stationed behind Archduke Joseph's brigade, brought his batteries forward to the abandoned earthworks; but, instead of standing, the panic-stricken troops swept over and through his guns, and he had to pull back again. He did so with great courage and skill, extricating his guns with minor losses and re-forming his lines on the height before Sweti to the south, where he was to go on fighting for some hours.[46]

But the main line was breached, and Brigade Obernitz, followed by Kessel's three battalions, swept through the gap and on in the direction of Rosberitz village. Now, however, they noticed some firing from Chlum village, which they had thought unoccupied and had bypassed. Immediately, the 1st Battalion and the Fusiliers of the First Guard Regiment turned to the right and burst into the village on top of the unsuspecting 3rd Battalion of the Sachsen Meiningen, just as its commander was saying, confidently but for the last time, "You are seeing phantoms!" Slaveczi died with these words on his lips, and with him fell scores of his command, for the needle guns were firing from every direction into the hollow way where the 3rd Battalion had taken its position, and within five minutes it was virtually destroyed. The Guards then cut the village in two and sealed off the 2nd Battalion. Led by Lieutenant Colonel Freiherr von Schimmelpenning, the Austrians tried to cut their way out, only to lose their commander and more than a hundred others in a matter of minutes. The remaining 600 men surrendered.[47]

The other battalion of the Austrian Forty-sixth was stationed, as we have seen, south of the village, and for it was reserved the kind of disastrous accident that had been suffered by the Second Saxon Brigade during their advance on Hradek an hour earlier (see above, page 124). Alerted by the sound of infantry fire in the village, Major von Noack ordered his battalion to attack, confident that Appiano would support him with his other regiment. With great bravery the 1st Battalion marched toward Chlum, despite withering Prussian infantry fire, and they had covered half the distance to their goal when a troop of wildly galloping Austrian horsemen appeared from nowhere, smashed into their flank, and threw them into complete disorder and headlong retreat.

Once more the sins of Festetics, Görz and Mollinary were being visited on the army. To break off the commitment which they had made to the fight in the *Swiepwald* was difficult, as we have already seen; and it had not been completed before the Prussian Second Army's attack began. At that time, what was left of Colonel Emerich von Fleischhacker's brigade was still at Cistowes, and so were the Seventh Hussars. The hussars tried to extricate themselves from their predicament by riding toward Maslowed, but they attracted the attention of Hohenlohe's batteries, which opened fire upon them with effect and drove them off toward Chlum. Their heedless flight brought them down like a cyclone upon Noack's battalion. They struggled through the frantic and cursing infantry into a wall of fire from the guns of the Prussian Guard Jaeger, reeled and broke away once more toward Horenowes where—in full view of the Crown Prince's staff—they were raked by massed fire from riflemen of the Second Guard Regiment and the Guard Hussars. With shattering losses, they limped to the south and made good their escape, but at Chlum they left chaos in their wake.[48]

It was a chaos that Appiano did not try very hard to repair. During the first stages of the attack on Chlum heights, he had remained in the position he had chosen south of the village and had apparently seen or heard nothing that alarmed him. It was only after the destruction of his Sachsen-Meiningen Regiment— and the term is chosen deliberately, since this fine regiment, which had distinguished itself in Italy and Denmark, had casualties exceeding 2,000 and more than 400 dead[49]—that Appiano made a halfhearted probe toward Chlum with units of Regiment Erzherzog Heinrich (Sixty-second). He did not like what he found there and, without more ado, turned and marched off toward Sweti and Königgrätz.[50]

Not all of the Austrian troops on Chlum showed this kind of spiritless behavior. A single cavalry battery commanded by Captain von der Groeben, which was stationed in the earthworks to the northwest of the village, tried to prevent the Guards from exploiting their victory, and also to cover the withdrawal of Austrian troops, by bombarding Chlum's southern exit. Its first salvos were answered by such a volume of rifle fire that within five minutes Groeben, another officer, 52 men and 68 horses were killed, their bravery having succeeded only in winning a monument on the spot where they fell and the pathetic title "the Battery of the Dead."[51]

With equal gallantry, six squadrons of the Cavalry Division Holstein tried to stem the onward rush of Kessel's battalions toward the village of Rosberitz. As they charged the Prussian lines, however, their first wave plunged into a concealed ditch. While they tried to control their terrified horses and to extricate themselves before they were overrun by the squadrons behind them, the Franz Joseph Cuirassiers were almost wiped out, and the uhlans of the same name suffered grievously. Under the protection of their own guns, their remnants reformed and made their way to Langenhof, while Kessel's infantry occupied the northern half of Rosberitz.[52]

Meanwhile, on either side of Chlum, the Prussian Second Army methodically improved its positions. To the west, Alvensleben's brigade had moved into the wood at Lipa, and had occupied it after a sharp brush with what was left of Fleischhacker's shattered columns, which were still making their painful withdrawal from Cistowes and now barely managed to escape before the trap was sprung. The occupation of the wood opened the way for an attack upon Lipa village, which was almost immediately launched by the advance guard of the 2nd Guard Division.[53] Further to the east, the 11th and 12th Divisions had continued their co-ordinated movement over Sendrasitz and Trotina, aided by an Austrian defection that was even more difficult to justify than Appiano's. The commander of the Austrian II Corps, Count Thun, had had more success than Mollinary in withdrawing his forces from the *Swiepwald;* and by the time the Prussians were over the Trotina and on their way toward Nedelist and Lochenitz, he had more than one-and-a-half fresh brigades at his disposal, in addition to the cavalry of Prince Thurn und Taxis. But Thun had no stomach for a fight, and, to the dismay of many of his officers, decided to seek safety on the other side of the upper Elbe. Despite his later attempts to prove that his withdrawal started only after the general retreat of the army had begun, it seems incontrovertible that Thun ordered the unblooded Brigade Henriquez to proceed to the crossing at Predmeritz half an hour before the Guards took Chlum; and the retirement of his other forces followed without delay, the cavalry supplying the necessary protection. Without being given an opportunity to prove themselves, some 25,000 men left the battlefield; and, in ordering them to do so, Thun exposed the only line of retreat available to the rest of Benedek's army to grave danger. Thus, against only minimal resistance, Zastrow's 11th Division moved into Nedelist and Prondzynski's battalions occupied Lochenitz.[54]

It was now three o'clock, and the Second Army had won at least a temporary foothold on the line Chlum–Nedelist–Lochenitz. The capture of the ridge by the Prussian infantry had been accomplished with style and with speed, and it was perhaps well for the cause of Prussia that they had done their job with such despatch. For at just about the same time as the Guards were materializing like wraiths out of the soon-to-be-celebrated "fog of Chlum"[55] and overwhelming the terrified Slovaks in the outer defenses, the first serious signs of a crack in Prussian morale was discernible on the *Holawald* front. Shortly before three o'clock the commander of II Army Corps, Lieutenant General von Schmidt, decided that the battle was lost. He had just committed the last reserves of the 4th Division to secure the road on the north side of the *Holawald;* he had nothing left, and he told General von Manstein, the commander of III Corps, standing in reserve, that he was going to begin a retirement and that Manstein would be wise to think of doing the same. Manstein rode forward and pleaded with Schmidt to hold on, saying that he intended to do so himself in any case; and he placed his Twelfth Brigade at Schmidt's disposal. Schmidt did not, in the end, retire, but the fact that he considered doing so perhaps indicates that there were possibilities of panic on the Prussian side also, and that the Guards' blow at the heart of the Austrian position came not a moment too soon. It became customary after the war to describe Schmidt's behavior as the onset of the mental disorders to which he succumbed a little later.[56] But the military historian Lettow-Vorbeck, a careful and judicious student of the war, convinced himself that this was an inadequate explanation, since Schmidt's chief of staff was as firmly convinced as his commanding officer that the end of Prussian endurance in the *Holawald* had been reached.[57]

The capture of Chlum was achieved with such bewildering rapidity that some time elapsed before its effect was communicated to the headquarters of the opposing armies or to the bulk of the forces engaged in this great battle. Minutes after the heights were secured, Hohenlohe rode up the slope and joined Hiller von Gärtringen and Colomier on the ridge. He wrote later: "I was astonished by the view which opened before me. The height upon which we had stopped is the most dominant in the whole area. In front of us, at the foot of the hill, extended a magnificent valley, in which the villages of Langenhof, Stresetitz, Rosberitz, Wsestar lay, and on the other side of this rose the the heights of Rosnitz and Problus. On the right, the hills of Lipa stretched toward Tresowitz; ahead, down to the left, one saw the towers of Königgrätz, toward which ran the *chaussée* that came out of that valley and along the foot of our hill. The unique feature of the view was that the whole valley for about a quarter of a mile in length and breadth was completely filled with Austrians." These were the I and VI Infantry Corps, drawn up in beautiful order, with cavalry on their wings and their supporting artillery behind them, and all facing to the west. "From our bird's-eye perspective we looked down on them, and they looked like beautiful white stones with which children play. . . . In peacetime it is seldom that one has an opportunity to survey more than two army corps with one look. The view surprised me so that, forgetting everything else, I cried out: 'God! How beautiful that looks!' But Colomier pulled me up and said: 'This is no time for admiring pretty things. Get your batteries up here!' "[58]

7

THE BATTLE:
The Stricken Field

Dringend wiederholten Streichen
Müssen unsre Feinde weichen,
Und mit ungewissem Fechten
Drängen sie nach ihrer Rechten
Und verwirren so im Streite
Ihrer Hauptmacht linke Seite.
Unsers Phalanx feste Spitze
Zieht sich rechts, und gleich dem
    Blitze
Fährt sie in die schwache Stelle.
Nun, wie sturmerregte Welle
Sprühend, wüten gleiche Mächte
Wild in doppeltem Gefechte;
Herrlichers ist nichts ersonnen,
Uns ist diese Schlacht gewonnen![1]
            —Faust, Pt. II, Act IV

(Under repeated hammer blows
Our foe has to give way
And, in a confused melee,
Falls back toward the right,
Throwing the left wing of his
    battle line
Into confusion as he struggles on.
The firm point of our phalanx
Turns to the right and, like
    lightning,
Thrusts itself against the weak
    point.
Now, foaming like storm-whipped
    waves,
The well-matched powers rage
Wildly in twofold conflict.
Nothing grander was ever
    conceived!
Ours is the victory in this battle!)

Sʜᴏʀᴛʟʏ ᴀғᴛᴇʀ ᴛʜʀᴇᴇ ᴏ'ᴄʟᴏᴄᴋ, Colonel von Neuber of Benedek's staff thought he'd better get a fresh horse and ride over to
the village of Chlum. There, to his surprise, he saw Austrian cavalry fleeing from its blazing streets under a hail of enemy bullets.

Neuber was thunderstruck and galloped back to the command post. He didn't want to blurt out his news, fearing to cause a general panic, and tried to draw his commander apart. "We have no secrets here," Benedek said. "Very well," Neuber answered, "then I have to report that the Prussians have taken Chlum!" "Nonsense!" Benedek said shortly, and started to dictate an order to an aide. Then, more vehemently, "*Plauschen's nicht!*" he repeated. Neuber shook his head and insisted that what he had said was true. Benedek eyed him narrowly and then turned to Baumgarten, asking him to go and investigate the situation at Chlum. But then he seemed to change his mind, and, spurring his horse abruptly, he galloped off with his whole staff to see for himself.[2]

The military correspondent for *The Times*, who had stuck close to the commander-in-chief all day, watched his impetuous flight and its sequel. The needle gun was no respecter of persons. "More quickly than I can fairly tell," he wrote the next day, "Prince Esterhazy was down, his horse shot under him; Count Grünne was wounded, it is said, mortally[3]; Baron Henikstein's English mare was severely wounded, and there were many casualties among the men. I saw young Prince Esterhazy, his face covered with mud, stagger to his feet, and, taking a horse from a dragoon, who was instantly supplied with another, ride, as did all the rest, to seek a safer position; not, however, before they had rallied the men, who, startled by the suddenness of the attack, were breaking their ranks. The key of the position was in the hands of the enemy, and consternation was on every face. No one was cooler than Benedek himself as, attended by all who caught sight of him, he rode off to bring up some of the reserves and to retake the position. The bullets still fell thickly, as the Staff galloped after their chief; and on their approaching a small farm with outhouses, which should have sheltered them, they were saluted with a fresh volley of balls from the Prussian tenants, one of which wounded the Archduke Wilhelm in the head, but not, I believe, seriously. It is not surprising," *The Times* correspondent added, with the understatement admired by his countrymen, "that this unexpected apparition of the enemy in our very midst, when the Austrian army seemed on the point of victory, should have created some confusion."[4]

In similar circumstances, Appiano and Thun had succumbed

to discouragement and abandoned the field. Benedek's reaction seems to have been one of rage. At this moment, when the tide of fortune had turned against him, all of the Hamletlike vacillations and all of the incipient defeatism that appear between the lines in his letters to his wife dropped away and the hero of Solferino appeared, fighting with cunning and fortitude against forbidding odds. Whatever may be said of Benedek's conduct of operations since the beginning of the campaign or of his fateful procrastination on the morning of Königgrätz, his leadership of the fight during the late afternoon was masterly, and to his skill thousands of men were to owe their lives.

Benedek's first impulse was to hurl the Prussians out of Chlum by his own efforts. Riding forward to the area of the Fifty-second Regiment, he placed himself at the head of some Hungarian battalions and, flogging them on with floods of rhetoric and showing a complete disregard for danger, led them to the very edge of Chlum village and actually penetrated the Prussian lines. But the Guards had been reinforced now by fresh troops from the 2nd Division and against their fire the Fifty-second was unable to hold its own. All of Benedek's eloquence was powerless to prevent a retreat to its original position.

Moreover, as the attack of the Fifty-second broke upon Prussian strength, so did one mounted by Colonel von Catty, the chief of staff of III Corps, in Lipa wood. One of the ablest officers in the Austrian Army, Catty had throughout the long day resisted attempts made by neighboring commanders to drain his strength away, harboring it jealously for the stroke that would be delivered, he hoped, against Frederick Charles when the right moment came. There was little hope of that now, but he had managed at least to keep all of his corps together, with the exception of Appiano's brigade, and he directed it now against the wood of Lipa, hoping to retake Lipa village, which had just been lost to the Garde-Schützen of the 2nd Division, and to threaten the Prussian flank at Chlum. In the interest of control and mass, unfortunately, Catty launched his attack in closed columns, and once more these tactics proved disastrous. The Prussians waited cold-bloodedly until his Croats and Magyars were under the very muzzles of their guns, and then mowed them down with rapid fire. Catty himself was badly wounded; his troops broke and retired; and the Prussians pushed through the woods in the direction of the Sadowa–Königgrätz road.[5]

It was this threat, at about 3:30 P.M., that forced Gablenz's X Corps, which had for some time been apprehensive about its line of communications to the rear, to begin a retirement (see above, page 128). And it was the general pressure upon the Königgrätz road that was, from this point onward, Benedek's main preoccupation. To remove the threat to the highroad, he now made up his mind, at long last, to commit his reserve, and he ordered the commander of VI Corps, General von Ramming, to mount a massive attack and throw the Prussians out of Rosberitz and Chlum.

To the successes won up to this point by its divisions, the headquarters of the Prussian Second Army had contributed little in the way of guidance or advice; and for the past two hours it had had, indeed, a very imperfect knowledge of the progress of the battle. This was partly due to the fact that the Crown Prince's staff, too small to begin with, had been left even more short-handed by the necessity of assigning staff officers to corps commands, and it was simply incapable of doing everything that a staff should do in time of battle. But this is hardly an adequate excuse, and when one considers that the royal headquarters on the Roskosberg, with two hundred riders at its disposal, also spent much of the battle in ignorance of what was happening on its left and right wings, it appears clear that the much-vaunted efficiency of the Prussian staff system was less than perfect. If the battle had ever started to swing the other way, this deficiency of intelligence might have had the most serious results.

When the Prussian Crown Prince and his staff reached Maslowed at about 3:30 P.M., they had only the foggiest notion of the situation of their forward units, and what they could see from Maslowed didn't help them much. To their right the fighting in the *Swiepwald* seemed to have stopped; at least, there were less obvious signs of activity in that direction. Over Lipa and Chlum there was a heavy pall of smoke; the church tower in the latter village was in flames; and an artillery duel was in progress. To the left they could dimly discern Nedelist, where some kind of a fight seemed to be raging; but in the smoke and fog one could not distinguish units or guess at the way the tide of battle was flowing.

The headquarters staff was so numerous that it attracted artillery fire, and shells began to burst uncomfortably close to the Crown Prince. Captain Mischke, concerned for the prince's safety, urged Quartermaster General Stosch to find a pretext for drawing Frederick William out of danger. "Yes, you're right," Stosch said. "But this is the first time that I have actually been under fire. Why don't you speak to Blumenthal? He's been in lots of battles." Whether Stosch would have been quite as exhilarated had he suspected that the bombs bursting around him came from Prussian guns in Lipa wood is questionable; but if Verdy was correct in concluding from his later study of regimental accounts that this was so, it may be taken as another indication of the breakdown of communications between headquarters and its subordinate commands.[6]

A few moments later, the situation received some clarification, for Major von Gravenitz of the Eighth Hussars rode into Maslowed with the news that the Guards had taken Chlum. There was a burst of cheering. If this were true, then the Crown Prince had played the part of Blücher at Waterloo, and the battle was decided. The mood of the staff turned from anxiety to a heady excitement. They were, Stosch wrote later, "drunk with victory." It is understandable, therefore, that there should have been general astonishment when another rider panted into the command post, this time General von Boyen from royal headquarters, his face dark with foreboding. The situation was desperate, he said; and the King urged the Crown Prince to speed his advance lest the battle be lost. He intimated further that the sovereign had been playing with historical parallels too, but that the battle he kept muttering about was not Waterloo but Auerstedt,[7] and the visions that he saw were not of victory but of retreat.[8] It was only with difficulty that the Crown Prince persuaded Boyen that so much had happened since he had left the Roskosberg that even the King must know by now that his fears were groundless. Chlum had fallen, and the battle was as good as won.[9]

But was it? The next hour was to see some of the fiercest fighting of the day, and there were moments when commanders closer to the front than Stosch and the Crown Prince feared that the wheel of fortune might even now turn against them.

Ramming was meanwhile preparing his assault on Rosberitz and Chlum—somewhat too slowly for the impatient Benedek, who sent repeated messages to hurry him on, but carefully and methodically, as was his way. He had given responsibility for the first attack to the brigade of Major General von Rosenzweig, and in order to soften up the defenders had opened up a massive cannonade upon the two villages. The volume of fire was so intense that it soon reduced them to rubble and—as the Crown Prince had noticed when he reached Maslowed—set the Chlum church tower afire.

At the receiving end of this terrific barrage on Chlum height, Hohenlohe was still trying to carry out Colomier's orders and bring his batteries up to the ridge. Once more he was heavily outgunned, and once more he resorted to trickiness, ordering his batteries to expose themselves to Austrian fire until the enemy had calculated their range and then to rush the guns forward some 300 paces to the lip of Chlum plateau so that the Austrians would overshoot. The maneuver was less successful than it had been during the advance towards Chlum. The gunners of the first battery over the ridge lost their heads and began to fire canister wildly, a procedure which could do no possible harm to the Austrians, but which threatened to kill Hohenlohe and his staff. With some difficulty he stopped this senseless behavior, and the battery moved forward as instructed; but it was hit almost immediately by accurate Austrian fire and lost a large part of its crews and all of its horses. Hohenlohe got his other batteries in line in front of the southern exit from Chlum village, but it seemed likely that their fate would not be different, for they were standing in a veritable inferno of fire. Hohenlohe rode over to Colomier and said that, as far as he could judge, about 120 guns must be trained on them. "They're not all firing at us," Colomier answered, "and even if they are, as long as we hold this hill, the battle is won." At this moment, a shell burrowed its way into the ground between them and exploded, showering them with dirt. Colomier took a small whisk broom from his pocket and brushed off his coat carefully. His companion was delighted. "Even though this general was always good-natured toward me," he wrote later, "I had felt until now a certain antipathy toward him, because his pedantry was contrary to my nature. But from this moment on I liked him and put up with his fussiness with patience."[10]

The Austrian infantry attack had now begun. It was originally intended as a two-pronged advance, with the first wave of Rosenzweig's brigade cleaning out Rosberitz, while the second moved up toward Chlum. But the resistance in the former village proved so strong that the whole of Rosenzweig's brigade had to be deployed against it before the Prussians could be dislodged. The attack began at the southern end of the sprawling village and was launched by the 17th Jaeger Battalion and the Deutschmeister Regiment of Vienna, one of the crack units of the imperial army. They advanced with great spirit, the Jaeger horns sounding the charge and the Deutschmeister bands intoning the strains of "Gott erhalte Franz den Kaiser," while the infantry moved ponderously forward in massed columns behind a thin line of *tirailleurs*. The defenders—three companies of the Second Guard Regiment, commanded by Major von Erckert—were dispersed among the flimsy houses and behind the walls and the courtyards of the village, whence they directed their fire. The forward ranks of the Austrians staggered and fell, but the white-and-green lines pressed on, bayonets fixed, without faltering, until they were in among houses and at close quarters with their antagonists.

By this time the southern half of Rosberitz was a shambles. A Guards officer wrote later: "The air was literally filled with shells, shrapnel and canister; branches of trees, stones, splinters flew around our ears and wounded many, and for extra measure, Prussian shells landed not infrequently also. The shells crashed through the buildings; walls collapsed and buried the sound and the wounded; big clouds of dust rose in the air, made up of pulverized plaster and bricks and mingled with the smoke of the powder. It was as if the world were coming to an end. But nothing could make the brave fusiliers quail; they fell in rows, but they were worthy of the old breed, the fusilier battalion of Schill,[11] and they didn't waver a foot's breadth."[12]

Erckert inspired the defense, riding from platoon to platoon under the very muzzles of the Austrian guns, and leading charges against the advancing Jaeger. His prominence in the fight invited death, and he came close to achieving it; for, as the intensity of the fire increased, his horse was hit in the neck and, when he leaned forward to inspect the wound, he was hit twice in the upper arm and side, while a third bullet passed through his throat. He slid heavily from the saddle. Two of his men rushed forward and picked him up and then carried him to the relative safety of the cornfields to the east of the town. Placing their commander carefully in a furrow, they tried to make their way back, but were cut off and taken prisoner by Austrian Jaeger advancing on Chlum. Erckert lay quietly in the grain while the battle raged round him, and two Austrian battalions advanced, and later retreated, over his apparently lifeless body. Although unable to move, he was in fact in full command of his senses and had the curious experience of watching the fight as if it were a play put on for his private entertainment. He later remembered that for what seemed an intolerably long time an Austrian general stood close by him, watching the assault and repulse of his troops with an impassive face. Erckert was finally rescued after the last Austrian charge on Chlum had failed, and he later recovered from his wounds.[13]

Inside Rosberitz, the loss of their commander had shaken the fusiliers. Captain von Kropff rallied them and the fight went on; but their ammunition was running low, and they were having to detach men to collect unexpended ammunition from the dead and the wounded. The Austrians were not long in seizing this opportunity. As the Prussian fire slackened, the Deutschmeister delivered a mass bayonet charge and drove the shattered defenders down the village street. They fought back furiously. Of the Eleventh Company only twenty men were still standing, but under the leadership of a Sergeant Gursch, who was carrying the colors, they charged the Austrians repeatedly and escaped with their standard to the high ground above the village. The remnants of the other two companies had already preceded them.[14]

The Austrians then pressed from the south and west into the center of Rosberitz, which was somewhat more weakly held by three companies under the command of Lieutenant Colonel von Helldorf. In the bitter hand-to-hand fighting that took place here, there were no recognizable tactics—the bayonet and the butt being the preferred weapons. Helldorf was killed by a shell splinter at the outset of the fight; and shortly afterward Prince Anton of Hohenzollern, the son of Prince Charles, the cavalry commander in Frederick Charles's First Army, was wounded three times, so seriously that he died soon afterwards. In the Fourth Company of the First Guard Regiment all of the officers but one were killed; and casualties in general were so high that this part of town had to be evacuated also, the retreat being covered by parts of two companies of the Third Guard Regiment which entered the village from the east at the height of the fighting. With them was a young lieutenant named Paul von Hindenburg, who only a few minutes earlier in a confused fight between Chlum and Nedelist had captured a battery of five guns, nearly being killed in the process when an enemy bullet pierced his helmet and grazed his skull. None of the battles which he fought in the First World War weakened Hindenburg's memory of his baptism of fire; and when the Field Marshal wrote his memoirs, he recalled the fight inside Rosberitz vividly: the murderous struggle among the burning houses, in which "there was no longer any question of fighting in ordered formations but everyone fired and hacked around him as well as he could"; the growing fear that they would be cut off; the collapse of a flaming thatched roof which covered the village street with fire and smoke and enabled the defenders to retire under its cover to the slope north of the village.[15]

There seemed at this point to be no denying the Austrians. While the Jaeger and the Deutschmeister mopped up in the middle and lower parts of the village, the second wave of Rosenzweig's brigade, the Regiment Gondrecourt, smashed into the northern end of Rosberitz from the west. This part of the village was held by five companies of the Guard Fusilier and Second Guard Foot Regiments, commanded by Lt. Colonel Count von Waldersee, who was to survive the perils of this day but to fall before the gates of Paris in 1870. Waldersee was a stubborn fighter, who exploited every chance he had to hold on in a position which he recognized as essentially untenable, but he was also cunning

enough to withdraw before his command was destroyed as a
fighting force. As the Austrian weight began to tell, therefore,
he led his men out the northern exit of the village and up the
slope behind it. This was furrowed by paths with high banks—
hollow ways or defiles, almost like narrow ravines—which
meandered up toward Chlum, and well up the long incline there
were diagonal paths of the same description. Bringing his companies into this broken terrain, Waldersee sought a position
which would afford cover and a clear field of fire and enable him
to continue the fight.

Rosberitz was now completely in Austrian hands. The recapture of the village was an undeniable victory, and it brought a
thrill of hope to Benedek's reserve corps. By itself, of course, the
success was incomplete. Colomier was right when he told Hohenlohe that the key to victory was the possession of Chlum, and
Ramming was well aware of this. Most of his corps was still uncommitted, and behind it were the unused resources of I Corps—
all in all, eight fresh brigades. Ramming buckled down to the
job of retaking the heights.

It was just as well for the Prussians that their enemy had
neither the time nor the space to develop a concentric attack with
two or three brigades on a wide front. Perhaps because he was
impressed with the urgent necessity of throwing the Prussians off
Chlum before they were able to bring up more strength, Ramming sought to accomplish his purpose by the most direct method,
by repeated frontal attacks by his separate units. VI Corps made
four such attempts. After clearing the northern part of Rosberitz,
Rosenzweig led his Ruthenians, closely supported by the Deutschmeister, to the very edge of Chlum village where, after a frantic
fight in the light of the blazing church, they were finally forced
to retire. This first attempt was followed by assaults by the
Wasa Regiment, led personally by Ramming, the Regiment
Kronprinz von Preussen, led by Colonel von Jonak, and the
Brigade Hertwek. Each of these was launched in storm columns,
moving swiftly on a two-battalion front. None of them, after
the Ruthenians, got more than halfway to Chlum. On their
right flank Waldersee had found what he was looking for and
had re-formed his companies in a defile that cut diagonally across
the slope. Here, with the words "This far and no further!" he

planted his colors. His fire and that of four companies of the Third Guard Foot Regiment, which Major Rudolf Wilhelm von Barby had brought into the hollow ways in front of Chlum, inflicted grievous losses on the successive Austrian waves, which were punished hard also by the fire of a battery of 4-pounders, commanded by Lieutenant Colonel von Eltester of the 1st Guard Division, which avoided all attempts to capture it and continued to pour canister into the close-formed Austrian ranks.[16]

How much longer this defence would be effective was questionable. On Chlum heights, Hohenlohe reflected that the Austrians were seeking "with a mad bravery and a madder formation to force what could be won more cheaply and with a little reflection"[17]; but, as the hands of the clock passed four, he began to feel that there might be method in the Austrian madness. On the slope below, Prussian strength was being chipped away, and the lines were creeping back toward the village; and no infantry reserves seemed likely to be available in the near future. Shortly before four o'clock, Captain von Kaltenborn, from VI Corps headquarters, had arrived on the hill with the news that the 11th and 12th Divisions were reorganizing near Nedelist and that General von Mutius wanted to know where they were needed most. Hiller von Gärtringen had requested that he march toward Rosberitz and take the Austrians in the flank and rear, and Kaltenborn had raced off to Nedelist with this message. But no one on Chlum height expected effective aid from Mutius's corps before another hour had passed.

More critical was the fact that the reserve artillery, which had done more than its share to break up the successive enemy assaults, was beginning to falter. When one battery chief pleaded that his gunners could fight no longer, Hohenlohe had told him that none of them was going to get off the hill alive and that they might as well resign themselves to that fact and be glad that they had contributed to a victory that was now inevitable. Speeches like this could sometimes check deterioration of morale; they were less effective in stopping depletion of ammunition. By 4:15 P.M. Hohenlohe had had to allow one of his batteries to retire because it had nothing more to shoot; and he soon discovered that three others were getting close to rock bottom also. He prowled up and down his lines, trying to keep the gunners' spirits up and to encourage the most economical expenditure of ammunition that was consistent with effective defense. It was an insoluble problem, made doubly unpleasant by the volume of Austrian fire crashing around his ears, which made it appear as if the enemy's resources were inexhaustible.

A man who loved his work, Hohenlohe was able to detach himself sufficiently from his cares to admire the art of his opponents. It was while he was noting the action of the Saxon Battery Heydenreich, which had been firing all day with great calmness and effect (and with guns constructed in Prussia, Hohenlohe remembered wryly) that he came close to being a victim of its accuracy. An Austrian bomb burst almost under his horse's hoofs, and he felt a heavy blow in the neighborhood of his groin. When the first shock passed and he found himself still in the saddle, he saw that he had reason to to be thankful that his preoccupation had allowed him no time to eat. The bomb splinter that hit him had spent its force on the sandwiches with which he had filled his pockets in the station at Königinhof eight hours earlier and had left him with nothing worse than a bad bruise.[18] This didn't improve his temper. With heavy heart, he now saw that he was going to have to pull his batteries back before all their ammunition was gone. He took what comfort he could from the fact that most of the infantry of the 1st Guard Division had now fallen back upon Chlum, so that a withdrawal would not deprive them of support. At four-thirty he ordered his gunners to limber up and retreat to the next ridge and then to prepare to repel new Austrian assaults with what little ammunition they had left.

During all this time, the commander of the 1st Guard Division, Hiller von Gärtringen, had been sitting on a height at the southwest exit of Chlum, where he could watch and control the actions of his dispersed units. His adjutants rode ceaselessly back and forth with his orders, and one of them, the young Lieutenant The Losen, for whom Hiller had a great affection, had not long before been killed by an Austrian grenade near the northern exit of the village. Hiller's father had been commander of the Sixteenth Brigade in Blücher's army and on 18 June 1815, at the critical moment in the battle of Waterloo, had stormed Planchenoit, wrested it from the Imperial Guard, and by threatening Bonaparte's rear assured the success of Blücher's flank attack. The parallel between his father's action and his own was obvious; but as Hiller watched the fight raging in and above Rosberitz and his troops being forced to fall back up the slope, he may have wondered whether he was going to be able to make the parallel actual or whether this was going to be a Waterloo *manqué*. By four-thirty, as he saw Hohenlohe's batteries preparing to withdraw, the latter may have appeared to him to be the more likely. If he thought so, he was wrong. In his anxiety, he rode a bit to the north and saw, less than a mile away, grey columns of marching men. A moment later, Major von Sommerfeld, the commander of the East Prussian Jaeger, who were assigned to Bonin's I Corps, rode into his command post. The general's face lighted up, and he rode eagerly towards the newcomer. "*Gott sei dank!*" he cried. "There you are! What have you got for me?" "My battalion," Sommerfeld answered, "and, right behind us, the whole *Avantgarde* of the I Army Corps!" "Now everything will be all right!" Hiller cried with burning eyes. Then he reeled in his saddle and put his hand to his breast. "Help me, comrade," he murmured, "I'm wounded," and he slipped to the ground. He had been hit by a shell splinter and died almost immediately.[19]

Hiller died knowing that the Prussian possession of Chlum was now secure. Within a quarter of an hour, five battalions of fresh infantry were taking up their positions behind and between the weary units of the Guard, and new guns, with something to shoot, were moving in also. The last assault of Ramming's VI Corps beat in vain against these new forces and then reeled back. The Prussians began to gather for another drive on Rosberitz; and the vital escape route was once more placed in jeopardy.

Half an hour earlier, on the Roskosberg, King William finally gave the command that Frederick Charles had been waiting for and began an advance along the whole line. From the *Swiepwald* and the *Holawald* and Mokrowous, the battered divisions of the First Army moved eastward, the batteries rumbling along the highroad toward the heights of Lipa and Langenhof. Behind them, crossing the Bistritz at Dohalitz and Mokrowous, came the 5th and 6th Divisions, which had until now been held in reserve.

Gablenz's Austrian X Corps had already withdrawn, hurrying to get through the narrowing gap to safety. His rearmost units could barely be seen as the First Army advanced, although the fire of his artillery continued.

In about half an hour's time, the royal staff, led by the King, reached Lipa. The fire was now more intense, and Bismarck, who was never far from his sovereign's side on this day, was once more terrified lest William be hit, and furious because none of the soldiers would urge the monarch to withdraw. "The king rides where he will," one staff officer told the Minister President frostily. Bismarck was in no mood to tolerate feudal etiquette. He confronted the King himself. "As a major I have no advice to give to Your Majesty in time of battle," he said, "but as Minister President it is my duty to beg Your Majesty not to expose yourself to danger in this way."[20] The story that he punctuated this speech by hitting the King's horse on the haunch so that it moved away from the heavy fire is almost certainly apocryphal. Bismarck did not permit himself such liberties. But he was probably as firm in his demeanor as he later said he was and the King yielded to his urgency, although not without some grumbling and some later gibes about "the place in which I must ride in accordance with supreme command (*allerhöchsten Befehl*)."[21]

The rain had stopped and the sky was brightening, and those on Lipa were now granted a spectacle that moved even the least romantic among them. Colonel von Zychlinski wrote later: "The fog, which had until now hung heavily over the bloody field of honor, suddenly parted and, almost abruptly, one saw at a distance the whole Prussian army, marching into the curve that opened towards the southeast, brigade after brigade, battalion after battalion. Tears of gratitude sprang to my eyes for having been permitted to experience this moment. . . . Ever onward, without pause, the Prussian formations pressed towards Problus and Königgrätz, the Guards and the I and VI Corps on the left, on the right Herwarth with Rheinland and Westphalia."[22]

But before these converging forces closed upon his retreating army, Benedek had one more throw to make. The battle was still not over, and the watchers on Lipa were now privileged to watch a final dramatic act.

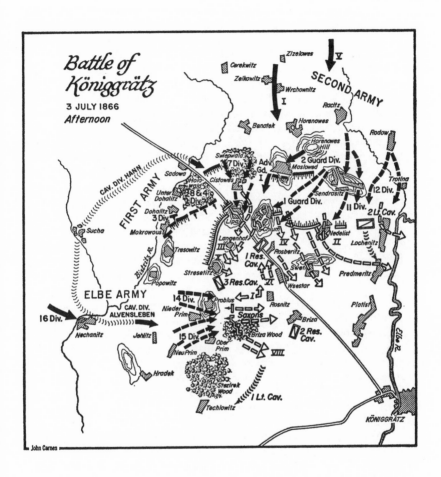

Battle of
Königgrätz

3 JULY 1866
Afternoon

SECOND ARMY

V

Zizelowes

Cerekwitz

Zelkowitz

Wrchownitz

I

Racitz

Rodow

Benatek

Horenowes

Horenowes
Hill

CAV. DIV. HANN

Swiepwald

7 Div.

Adv.
Gd.
I.

2 Guard Div.

Maslowed

Trotina

12 Div.

Sadowa

Holawald

Cistowes

FIRST ARMY

Unter
Dohalitz

8 & 4
Div.

I Guard Div.

Sendrasitz

II Div.

2 Lt. Cav.

Dohalitz

3 Div.

Lipa

Chlum

Nedelist

II

Lochenitz

Mokrowous

Langenhof

III

IV

Rosberitz

Predmeritz

Tresowitz

I Res.
Cav.

Swer

Bistritz R.

Stresetitz

VI

Wsestar

Sucha

Popowitz

ELBE ARMY

3 Res. Cav.

Plotist

CAV. DIV.
ALVENSLEBEN

14 Div.

Problus

I

Rosnitz

16 Div.

Nieder
Prim

Saxons

Briza

2 Res.
Cav.

Nechanitz

Jehlitz

15 Div.

Ober
Prim

Briza Wood

Neu Prim

VIII

Hradek

Stezirek
Wood

I Lt. Cav.

Elbe R.

KÖNIGGRÄTZ

Techlowitz

John Carnes

To the despair of his staff, Benedek had spent the last half hour dashing from point to point within the shrinking area in which the Austrians still had freedom of action, exposing himself recklessly to enemy fire as he encouraged and cajoled and threatened his troops. To some it appeared that he was seeking death, and an occasional remark of his seemed to corroborate this. At about 4:30 P.M. his ordnance officer, Captain von Wersebe, was thrown to the ground when his horse was killed. As he rose to his feet, Henikstein congratulated him on his narrow escape, and Wersebe said bitterly, "I wish the bullet had been a couple of feet higher." At this, Benedek embraced him, somewhat theatrically, and said, "That is true! Happy the man who needs no longer look upon this day!" But even in moments of bitter earnestness Benedek was always a bit of a play actor, and these words need not be taken too seriously. Certainly there was no resignation or flagging of determination in his behavior at this critical juncture. He was still intent on keeping his escape route free, and after his melodramatic scene with Wersebe he snapped out a series of orders which sent his aides flying to every corner of the field. Ramming was to call off his piecemeal assaults on Chlum. The I Corps of General Gondrecourt was to attack that height with three brigades and force the Prussians well away from the highroad. Major General von Piret's brigade, which had done so well at Gitschin, was to make a push toward Problus to hold up a possible advance of Herwarth's divisions. And the cavalry divisions of the Prince of Holstein and Major General Karl Maria Count Coudenove were to attack towards the west, breaking up any pursuit intended by Prince Frederick Charles's forces.[23]

And so at last came the hour of that cavalry which had so impressed W. H. Russell as he watched it during the morning hours from the tower at Königgrätz—"a force of horse," he felt, "with which a Murat or a Kellerman or a Seidlitz could have won a battle and saved an empire."[24] It was late in the day for that kind of victory now, but in the fight that followed—which Friedjung has called the greatest cavalry fight in Europe since Liebertwolkwitz on 14 October 1813[25]—the Austrian horse served its comrades well.

Even to the trained eyes watching from the hills, this phase of the battle, which involved 39½ Austrian squadrons and 31 Prussian, was complicated, and it is difficult to describe it without a dangerous degree of oversimplification. Two separate but related engagements were fought: one between Rosberitz and Langenhof, the other in the area between Stresetitz and Problus. The first of these began when the Prussian cavalry brigade of Major General Georg Reinhold Count von der Groeben, leading the advance of Frederick Charles's horse from the other side of the Bistritz, reached Lipa and received orders to proceed towards Rosberitz and attack as opportunity offered. Perhaps because the long ride had led the squadrons to spread out a bit, this order did not reach the whole force; and when Groeben turned towards Rosberitz with his two regiments—the Thuringian Hussars Nr. 12 and the Neumark Dragoons Nr. 3—three squadrons of dragoons failed to get the word and went off in the direction of Langenhof. A little later, Colonel Albert Freiherr von Barnekow of the Thuringians saw three infantry battalions pulling out of Rosberitz with their artillery, and without a moment's hesitation ordered the gallop and then the charge. The hussars were met with canister and infantry fire, but despite losses got in among the guns and the infantry and were engaged in hand-to-hand fighting when they were themselves hit in the flank by a strong body of horse.

This force was the Stadion and Kaiser Franz-Joseph Cuirassiers, part of the Prince of Holstein's division which Benedek had, minutes earlier, ordered to advance to the west. With beautiful precision, they swept the two squadrons of Prussian dragoons out of their path and came down upon the hussars, who were by now in a state of some disorder. The shock threw the Prussians backward, and under the momentum of the Austrian charge and the flailing blows of the heavy cuirassier sabers, both hussars and dragoons were forced in a disordered struggling mass toward Langenhof.[26]

From this critical situation the Prussian horse was saved by the intervention of three squadrons of Pomeranian Uhlans under the command of Colonel von Kleist, who charged with their lances couched against the Austrian flank and harassed them until their comrades had extricated themselves. The two forces then separated to re-form.

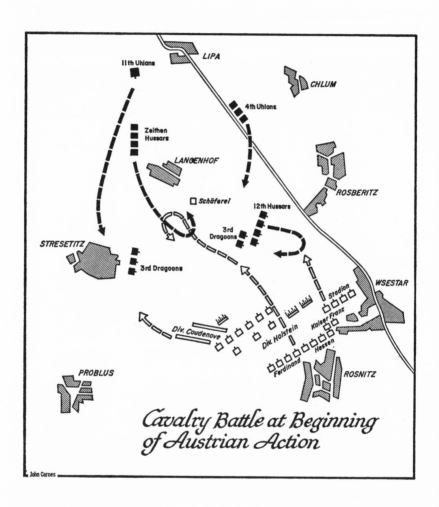

Cavalry Battle at Beginning
of Austrian Action

John Carnes

Meanwhile, the Prince of Holstein's second brigade—the Ferdinand Cuirassiers, the Hessen-Cuirassiers, and the Kaiser Max Uhlans—was bearing down on Langenhof, where there was every indication that it would sweep the field of the few squadrons of Prussian horse available there. As the brigade passed a sheep-farm (*Schäferei*) to the east of Langenhof, however, it came under the guns of the infantry Regiment Colberg and received such withering fire that it turned back with crippling casualties. Seeing the brigade's shaken state, four squadrons from the Ziethen Hussars and the Fourth Uhlans charged the Hessen Cuirassiers. These Pappenheimers (see above, page 61), how-ever, gave back as good as they got until the fight came again within rifle range of the *Schäferei* and renewed infantry fire per-suaded them to break off. Both sides retired, the bulk of the Prince of Holstein's division withdrawing to Rosnitz, where it re-formed and some time after five o'clock was ordered to leave the battlefield in the direction of Pardubitz.[27]

During the fight of the Hessen Cuirassiers, the Austrian di-vision of Count Coudenove had advanced toward Stresetitz, with Major General Prince Windischgrätz's brigade in the van. Here they found the three squadrons of Prussian dragoons who had become detached from Groeben's command during the fight-ing at Rosberitz. The Preussen Cuirassiers and the Wrangel Cuirassiers attacked them forthwith and, in a fight that was wit-nessed from afar by the King of Prussia and his staff, inflicted heavier losses on them than were suffered by any other single Prussian unit of comparable size on the field this day. The rem-nants of the dragoons were hurled by the force of the cuirassiers' attack into the ranks of their own Eleventh Uhlans; and once more things might have gone badly for the Prussians if the fight had not rolled within range of Prussian artillery and infantry fire. The Austrian heavy cavalry was proving itself superior to any horse the enemy could send against it, but the power to exploit this advantage was negated by the steady encroachment of Prussian infantry upon the arena in which it was fighting. In this instance, the Austrian cavalry, in swinging back from Stresetitz in two columns, was hit from the *Schäferei* at Langen-hof and by Prussian infantry north of Problus, and the Preussen Cuirassiers lost 21 officers and 269 men before they got out of the field of fire.

The main purpose of the Austrian cavalry action was to destroy the possibility of Prussian pursuit. Its effectiveness in accomplishing this was nowhere more effectively demonstrated than in the area north of Problus, where the Alexander Uhlans of Coudenove's second brigade surprised the First Guard Dragoon Regiment, which had just crossed the Bistritz, broke its right wing and center, smashed into two squadrons of the Fifth Hussars, and caused such confusion before they were compelled to retire that the Guard Dragoons and the Blücher Hussars became embroiled in a fight against each other. Once more, Prussian infantry and artillery drove the Austrians off, the fire being so heavy that the Bavaria and Neipperg Cuirassiers maintained their order with difficulty as they withdrew. The Alexander Uhlans, however, trotted back to the rear in fine fettle and in perfect order.[28]

Indeed, the Austrian cavalry as a whole had every reason to be satisfied with itself. Its casualties had been heavy—64 officers had fallen, 1,094 men and 1,681 horses—but this had been largely due to infantry and artillery fire. For its part, it had inflicted losses of 31 officers, 409 men and 246 horses upon the enemy. More important, it had thrown his cavalry into disarray, made pursuit by the horse unlikely, and delayed the advance of the Prussian infantry from the west by at least half an hour. This was not only precious time for the Austrian infantry retiring from the Bistritz front; it also gave the Austrian artillery an opportunity to construct the line of guns which was to hold up the Prussian advance after the cavalry had retired, and thus further to discourage pursuit.[29]

Meanwhile, Benedek's order to Brigade Piret to make a thrust toward Problus had, although at a very heavy cost to the infantry, discouraged Herwarth from seeking to push beyond Problus and seems actually to have persuaded the commander that it would be wise to pull back some of his artillery.[30] This relieved some of the pressure on the southern side of the Sadowa–Königgrätz road and supplemented the work done by the cavalry. The attempt to keep the Prussians away from the right side of the road was also successful, although at frightful cost.

After Ramming's failure to take Chlum, Benedek had decided to throw the last of his reserves, the I Corps, against the same objective, not any longer in the hope of capturing it, but to keep the Prussians from cutting the line to the rear. General von Gondrecourt had three brigades at hand but little room to deploy them, and in any event he was, as his record in Denmark showed, a believer in shock tactics. In the last Austrian infantry attack of the day, therefore, the Austrians gave another demonstration of the inadequacy of their tactical doctrine; and Poschacher's brigade, which had learned something of the efficiency of the needle gun at Podol, learned more now. The Prussian infantry lay in the defiles that crisscross the slope below Chlum and waited calmly until the advancing foe was within 300 yards. Then the old story repeated itself. Poschacher's "Iron Brigade" now lost all its mounted officers, including its commander, and hundreds of men. The Ringelsheim Brigade, which had fought so valiantly at Gitschin, and Leiningen's brigade fared no better. Some 150 officers and 5,800 men fell on the slopes in this last Austrian assault, and 2,800 more gave up the fight and delivered themselves into the hands of the Prussians. Before the corps had gotten back to Wsestar, its losses had risen to 279 officers, 10,000 men, and 23 guns. One fourth of the casualties of the Austrian Army on the day of Königgrätz were suffered by I Corps, in Benedek's last attempt to keep the gate ajar while his forces moved toward the Elbe.[31]

But that effort had now been successful. By the time that the last of I Corp's efforts had been repelled and the Guards had begun to move again toward the much fought over village of Rosberitz, the greater part of Benedek's retreating forces were past that point and were moving as rapidly as they could toward the Elbe. Their retreat was covered by Colonel von Abele's brigade of I Corps and by the reserve artillery which Lt. Colonel von Hofbauer had led back to Sweti when he was abandoned by the infantry on Chlum earlier in the day (see above, page 133). In a fleeting meeting in the turmoil of the late afternoon, Hofbauer promised Benedek that he would fight to the last gunner. He made good his pledge, and the 60 to 70 guns which he drew up between Sweti and Wsestar—what was left of his own strength plus the remaining guns of IV and VI Corps—kept up a continuous cannonade throughout the last hours of this great battle. Hofbauer's position was constantly threatened by the advance of Zastrow's 11th Division on his flank, and after the Fifty-first Regiment had forced its way into Wsestar and the Tenth Grenadiers into Sweti, he was forced to withdraw at heavy cost. But he re-formed and went on firing, and as he retreated, he was joined by other batteries from units whose infantry had gone ahead toward Königgrätz. Not the least of the reasons why this battle was not a Sedan is the courage and skill displayed by the gunners, who kept their lines until night had fallen and the remnants of the army were over the Elbe. The last shot was fired by Prince Albrecht zu Solms at nine o'clock in the night.[32]

A Prussian General Staff study was later to state that the heroic resistance of the enemy until the very end prevented the Prussians from realizing the true dimensions of their victory.[33] Neither Moltke nor any of his subordinate commanders had any idea that Benedek no longer possessed a brigade, let alone a corps, that was capable of combat, and that if caught and hit hard his retreating army would probably have dissolved in panic. Benedek and the cavalry, Poschacher and the guns had created an illusion of strength that discouraged pursuit. There were, to be sure, other reasons for this. Although half an hour too late, Moltke's trap did close: the wings of his army joined behind the beaten foe, and when they did confusion and delay resulted. At six o'clock, Hohenlohe, trying to find the headquarters of the Guard Corps, came to the hill of Rosnitz and, looking down, saw "a mixture of the whole army"—artillery from the 2nd Guard Division, infantry from every corps which had been engaged, and cavalry of every description, all muddling around in an unsorted mass.[34] In the circumstances, it was virtually impossible to get things straightened out in time to pursue an enemy effectively; and there was hesitation about sending unprotected cavalry into the dusk against a strong artillery force with a clear field of fire, particularly when most of the available cavalry had already suffered heavily.[35] Finally, there was no energetic attempt at pursuit because, in the exhilaration of victory, the King had ridden off to sprinkle congratulations and decorations among the various formations of his army, and Moltke could not find him to get his assent to a plan of procedure.[36] Thus, it was not until 6:30 P.M. that the Chief of Staff directed to the commands of the First and Second Armies an order which said that the following day would, in general, be a day of rest, with marching confined to what was needed for the reassembling and quartering of troops, that the Second Army should put out advance posts toward Josephstadt and the First Army toward Königgrätz, and that Herwarth's infantry should pursue the enemy forces withdrawing toward Pardubitz "as far as possible."[37] For Moltke this was a curiously ambiguous document—it has been suggested that his cold was worse and that he was tired and feverish[38]—and its effect was negative.[39]

Thus, Benedek was able to extricate 180,000 of his troops, an achievement that should serve to mitigate some of the faults of his conduct of the campaign. It is nevertheless unfortunate that the strenuous activity that characterized his conduct of the last phase of the battle and his frequent separation from his staff prevented him from dictating a systematic set of instructions with respect to the crossing of the Elbe. The different corps were not told where to march or how to make their way across the river, and although Krismanic, in the absence of both Benedek and Baumgarten, tried to remedy the lack by drafting some orders on his own initiative, he was not entirely successful. The result was confusion and, when the river was reached, a not inconsiderable amount of panic in some units. The crossings on the upper Elbe had been lost, thanks to Thun's defection earlier in the afternoon. There were not enough fixed bridges lower down to accommodate an army of this size, and no one had thought to throw more pontoons across the river.

Moreover, although the more disciplined formations—like the Saxon brigade—left the highroad and moved toward the lower river where there were two fixed and two military bridges available in the neighborhood of Pardubitz, most of the retreating forces, more than 100,000 of them, pressed frantically toward Königgrätz, doubtless expecting to find protection in that fortress at the confluence of the Elbe and the Adler Rivers. This was a mistake. Königgrätz was protected not only by its walls but by the area outside its glacis, which could be inundated by the opening of sluices along the river. Even before four o'clock, the

Times correspondent Russell had been advised to leave the town, and shortly thereafter the commandant, Major General Weigl, who seemed to expect a Prussian attack before nightfall, closed the town gates and opened the sluices.[40] Across the broad morass thus created stretched a few narrow causeways, and onto these, in their panic, crowded 50,000 to 60,000 troops, together with guns and wagons. The fall of night caught them in this precarious situation. Some sought to wade through the water to their goal; others pushed ahead, trampling over fallen comrades; guns and even wagons full of wounded were shoved off the causeways into the black waters. The chaos was described by a soldier who had been marching toward the citadel at the time that the sluices did their work. "The waterworks were opened," he wrote, "and the soldiers who were crossing . . . found themselves suddenly in a sea of water that grew deeper and deeper. Hundreds drowned. On the narrow ways everyone shoved together, gun carriages overturned, the fleeing soldiers of the Italian regiments fired off their weapons: in short, it was like the crossing of the Berezina."[41] Those who managed to get to the end of the causeways clambered over the palisades and began firing their guns against the town walls. Attempts by their officers to restrain them and restore order were fruitless. The senseless fear that the Prussians were on their heels had destroyed morale and added significantly to the day's casualties. It was not until 10:30 P.M. that the fortress commandant made up his mind that Austrians rather than the enemy were hammering at his walls and opened the gates to the broken fragments of the imperial army.[42]

Meanwhile, in the victorious camp, the army commanders had met and exchanged the kind of remarks appropriate to the occasion, attributing the victory first to each other and then, privately, to their own chiefs of staff.[43] The King had had an affecting reunion with his son and had awarded him the *pour le mérite*.[44] The army leaders then separated and sought quarters for the night. The Crown Prince and his staff rode back to Horenowes, arriving there at about ten o'clock. The castle had been turned into a hospital, and there were about three thousand prisoners of war in the courtyard, so the Crown Prince's party had to commandeer a not very pretentious inn. Their baggage had not arrived from Königinhof, and the inn was provided with neither bedding nor food for a large staff. Someone managed to buy a loaf of black bread from a sutler, half of which was given to the Crown Prince and his personal aides, and the rest shared out among the staff. Everyone then found a bed where he could. Blumenthal and Stosch shared a room, while the junior members were forced to doss down in an empty *boutique*, where the fumes from old wine barrels helped put them to sleep.[45]

The King, after leaving his son, rode with his personal attendants toward Sadowa. He dismounted there after having spent almost thirteen hours in the saddle, with the words, "One feels that one's youthful years are over." He then visited a lazaret tended by the Knights of St. John and sought to comfort the wounded.[46] At Prince Frederick Charles's urging, he gave up the idea of returning to Gitschin and instead drove in a carriage to Horitz, a little town that normally housed less than 4,000 persons but was now filled to overflowing with 20,000 troops. At Frederick Charles's headquarters, the King had a cup of hot tea and a frugal supper, while he dictated a telegram to his wife: "Complete victory over the Austrian army won today in eight-hour battle fought near the fortress of Königgrätz between Elbe and Bistritz. Losses of enemy and trophies not yet counted, but significant, including 20 cannon. All eight corps fought, but losses painfully heavy. I praise God for his mercy; we are all well. William. (For publication: the governor is to fire a victory salute!)" The King then retired, on a bed improvised from a sofa, two chairs and a table.[47]

The man whose diplomacy had precipitated the war and who was to build a new Germany upon this victory rode back to Horitz after his sovereign. Throughout the day, Bismarck had felt, as he admitted later, that he was playing a game of cards with a million-dollar stake that he did not really possess. Now that the wager had been won, he felt depressed rather than elated, and as he rode through the fields filled with dead and wounded he wondered what his feelings would be if his eldest son were lying there. When he got to Horitz, he found that no quarters had been prepared for him, and while he was looking for a place to sleep he went through a doorway into an open court and slipped and fell into a manure pit. He finally made himself a bed under the colonnade of the market place where the rain couldn't reach him, using a carriage cushion, and dozed fitfully until the Grand Duke of Mecklenburg took pity on him and invited him to his quarters for the rest of the night.[48]

In the fields in which the bloody fight had been decided, the Prussian troops had set up their camps and lit their fires and made their suppers of whatever provisions they were able to find. Afterwards, regimental bands played concerts of marches associated with past victories: the Dessauer March, the Hohenfriedberg March, the Entrance into Paris March and others. The darkness deepened, and around the rim of the plain the glow of burning villages could be seen. Then came the time for *Zapfenstreich;* the bugles sounded the evening call; the drums beat for Prayers; and the bands played the chorale "Now thank we all our God," its solemn strains passing from battalion to battalion and echoing across the dark plain.[49]

The defeated Austrian commander, having done all he could to save his army, had crossed the Elbe with two officers and an escort of uhlans shortly after six, using the pontoon bridge at Bukowina, southeast of Opatowitz. He rested here for a while and then, unaware of the chaos that was raging at the gates of Königgrätz, rode through the darkness to Hohenmauth. Here his staff, who had been searching for him for hours, found him late in the evening. He was composed and apparently ready to start retrieving what could be retrieved from the catastrophe. His deeper feelings he kept to himself. Perhaps Helmuth von Moltke, going to bed in Horitz with a fever, had some idea of what they were like. He was later to say to a journalist: "A defeated *Feldherr!* Oh, if civilians had even the remotest idea of what that means! The evening of Königgrätz in Austrian headquarters! Oh, when I try to imagine it to myself! And such a meritorious, brave and prudent general as Benedek!"[50]

8

THE AFTERMATH

Gestern noch auf stolzen Rossen,
Heute durch die Brust geschossen,
Morgen in das kühle Grab.[1]
—W. HAUFF, "Morgenrot"

(Yesterday still on proud horses,
Today shot through the breast,
Tomorrow into the cold grave.)

ON THE AFTERNOON of July 4, the King of Prussia, who had spent the morning writing letters and drafting a proclamation to his army, drove with his suite from Horitz to Sadowa, to inspect the battlefield, visit the wounded, and attend the funeral services for Hiller von Gärtringen and Lt. Colonel von Helldorf, which were to be held on Chlum height. On the way he encountered another carriage bearing what appeared to be a wounded Austrian general, for his head was swathed in bandages and he was slumped in either pain or dejection. As the King drew near, he recognized Field Marshal Ludwig von Gablenz, and when they had exchanged greetings, he learned that Gablenz was not a wounded prisoner but an emissary from the Austrian high command seeking an armistice from the victors.

The King directed him to Horitz where, he informed him, he would find the Chief of the General Staff, and went on his way. So did Gablenz, arriving a little later at the headquarters of Prince Frederick Charles. That commander, who seems to have had no love for the ordinarily flamboyant Gablenz, was nevertheless shocked to see him so reduced. He looked shabby and broken and had none of his usual self-confidence as he spoke of the need for a cessation of hostilities. "Does your army *need* an armistice?" Frederick Charles asked. "My Emperor no longer has an army," Gablenz replied. "It is as good as destroyed."[2]

Looked at in terms of total figures, this was perhaps an exaggeration, but in its essentials it was true. The battle of Königgrätz broke the Austrian Army, and although the hostilities continued for another month there were few clashes of arms and no real doubt about the issue.

According to the Austrian General Staff's account of the war, Austrian casualties in the battle amounted to 1,313 officers, 41,499 men and 6,010 horses—of whom 330 officers and 5,328 men were dead, 431 officers and 7,143 men wounded, 43 officers and 7,367 men missing, and 509 officers and 21,661 men captured. The Saxons had casualties totaling 55 officers and 1,446 men—of whom 15 officers and 120 men were dead, 40 officers and 900 men wounded, and 426 men missing. Losses were heaviest in I Corps, which had made the last attempt to recapture Chlum, IV Corps, which had squandered itself in the brutal fighting in the *Swiepwald*, and III Corps, which had fought all day under heavy Prussian bombardment and then, in the afternoon, had been hit hard in Lipa wood. But all corps suffered heavily, and the army as a whole had lost more than a fifth of its effectives, including the cream of its troop leaders and noncommissioned officers, to say nothing of a high proportion of its guns, its transportation, and its supplies.[3]

Prussian losses were markedly lower. Total casualties for the day came to 359 officers, 8,794 men and 909 horses—of whom 99 officers and 1,830 men were killed, 260 officers and 6,688 men wounded, and 276 men missing. The First Army, which had had to hold on until the Crown Prince arrived, had more than twice as many casualties as the Second; and Fransecky's division and those of Schmidt, which had fought in the *Holawald*, had been hit particularly hard. For its great achievements on the enemy right flank, the Guard Corps had had to pay with the loss of 54 officers and 1,284 men. The losses in material were lower than in the case of the Austrian Army, and, except for horses, much that was lost could be either recovered or replaced, since the Prussians were left in possession of the field and everything on it.[4]

The wide discrepancy in losses was equaled by the differences of mood in the two armies after the battle. In the Prussian Army, eagerness to press on and strike the knockout blow was apparent at all levels, from the King, who was now in a state of stern rectitude and was apparently determined to march on Vienna and chastise his foe in his own capital, and Prince Frederick Charles, who longed for another battle to give him the glory he felt had been denied him in this one,[5] down to the youngest subalterns who still dreamed of stars to win. As for the men, Bismarck, who had a keener eye than most for the rigors of the common grenadier's lot, was moved to admiration by their spirit and their energy in the days following the grueling battle. "Our men are wonderful (*Unsre Leute sind zum Küssen*)," he wrote to his wife on July 9. "Every one of them so brave, so composed, so polite, despite empty stomachs, wet clothes, wet quarters, little sleep, the soles falling off their boots; friendly to everybody, indulging in no plundering or burning, paying what they can and eating moldy bread. Fear of God must be deeply imbedded in our common people or all this couldn't be."[6]

In the Austrian Army, this kind of determination and fortitude was conspicuous by its absence, and the heaviness of the losses in manpower is almost enough in itself to explain this. In addition, the fact that, in looking back over the past week, one could find only one encounter that could be described as a victory— Gablenz's costly fight with Bonin at Trautenau—left the officer corps discouraged and defeatist. In the ranks, this went even further and was coupled with breaches of order which in some units got completely out of hand. Even before the army had left the field of battle, there had been some cases of looting,[7] and these increased as the army went across the Elbe and started for Olmütz. Observers watching the retreat must have felt much as Gablenz did in his conversation with Frederick Charles: that there was no army any more. W. H. Russell, making his way slowly to Zwittau, passed through "wounded on all sides, fragments of regiments marching, the roadsides lined with weary soldiers asleep, dressing their wounds or cooling their feet; on both sides of us waggons, guns, cavalry of all kinds, Tyrolese Jägers, Hungarians, Croats, Italians. . . . The *débris* of the army."[8]

With the Northern Army in this state, there was little hope of achieving anything by continued resistance. When Gablenz's attempt to win an armistice failed—in the first instance because he was not provided with full powers, and in the second because the Prussians placed the price too high[9]—the Emperor ordered a continuation of the retreat and, as a means of defending his capital, summoned elements of his Southern Army from Italy. But meanwhile he took steps to secure peace, availing himself as early as July 5 of the good offices of the Emperor of the French for that purpose.

Thus, politics took precedence over military operations in the last three weeks of the Austro-Prussian war. This is not to say that there was no fighting. In the first days after the battle, the shattered Northern Army retreated towards Olmütz in three separate columns, moving by different routes.[10] They were slowed down by their baggage trains and by the lack of any tactical order—for the units were so mixed and the confusion so great that officers had to be stationed at crossroads to direct stragglers in the right direction—but they made good progress and were able to assemble in the vicinity of Olmütz on July 11 without having had more than a minor brush with an advance Prussian cavalry detachment. The Prussians had not started their pursuit until July 7, at which time the Crown Prince's army had been ordered to follow Benedek, while Frederick Charles and Herwarth had headed directly for Vienna by way of Brünn. The advantages Benedek gained by this Prussian delay he lost, however, by staying too long in Olmütz, in order to rest his men and issue them new weapons, and the Prussians closed in and cut the rail connection with Vienna so that it could not be used as an escape route. In the circumstances, the Austrian commander would have preferred to remain at Olmütz, but peremptory orders from Vienna compelled him to break out,[11] and, when he did so, he was caught on July 15 at Tobitschau by infantry of Bonin's I Corps and squadrons of the Fifth Cuirassiers, and lost 18 guns and was almost captured himself. His forces were so shaken by this and by another fight at Roketnitz on the same day, that he found it advisable to follow a circuitous route over the lesser Carpathians into Hungary and then, by way of Pressburg, to Vienna.[12] Only with the greatest difficulty was the harried commander able to elude the Second Army, to reach

Pressburg in time to help protect it from attack by advanced units of Frederick Charles's army, and, on July 22, to cross the Danube and join the forces of Archduke Albert, which had been brought north to defend the capital from Prussian attack.[13]

But there was to be no more fighting. Immediately after Königgrätz the Emperor of Austria had made it clear that he wanted to end the conflict; and for the past three weeks the man whose diplomacy had forced war on him in the first place had been doing everything he could to fulfill Francis Joseph's desire. Bismarck's task was not easy, for he had to make the kind of peace which he felt accorded with Prussian interest palatable to Napoleon III, on the one hand, and to King William and the generals on the other. In the end, he found it harder to win over his own compatriots than to persuade the Emperor of the French. In the post-Königgrätz euphoria, the King and his military advisers were dreaming of territorial annexations so extensive that any attempts to realize them would have frightened all Europe and possibly caused a war with France. At the same time they showed no desire to put an end to their career of conquest, at least until they had enjoyed a triumphal march into Vienna. Bismarck caused bitter resentment at one of the military councils held in the days following the battle by inquiring sarcastically why they should stop even in the Austrian capital. Why not pursue the Austrians into Hungary and, since it would then be difficult to maintain their communications with the rear, why not go on to Constantinople, establish a new Byzantium, and leave Prussia to its fate?[14] He refused to yield to the importunities of the soldiers and in the end his insistence that excessive demands would jeopardize the gains already made overcame his sovereign's stubbornness. William did not give in gracefully, but he gave in. On July 26 the preliminaries of peace were signed, and the victory of Königgrätz was confirmed.[15]

How great the political consequences of that victory were was realized when the peace terms were published. The Emperor of Austria recognized "the dissolution of the hitherto existing German Confederation and [gave] his assent to a new organization of Germany without the participation of the Austrian Imperial

State." He also agreed "to recognize the narrower federal relationship which His Majesty the King of Prussia [would] establish north of the line of the Main." He assented explicitly to the incorporation into the Prussian state of Schleswig and Holstein, the contested duchies of 1864–66, and tacitly accepted Prussia's acquisition of Hannover, Electoral Hesse, the Duchy of Nassau, and other territories as well. Finally, he agreed that the Kingdom of Saxony, while suffering no territorial loss, was to enter the new North German Confederation and to place its army under the command of the King of Prussia.[16]

These were provisions radical enough to justify the papal secretary of state Antonelli's horrified ejaculation, "*Casca il mondo!*" ("The world is collapsing!") Königgrätz had solved the long-vexed German question, but in such a way as to raise the most perplexing and dangerous problems for the future; problems, moreover, from which no European power was going to be permitted to detach itself. For Austria in particular, Königgrätz marked the end of an epoch and the opening of a new and troubled phase in its history. During the revolutionary days of 1848–49, when Austria's influence in Germany had been challenged, one of its leading statesmen had said: "Austria can exist only if it keeps a firm footing in Germany. If it is thrown out of Germany, it will dissolve itself." Now, after the first revelation of the conditions of peace and after it was seen that Austria's expulsion from Germany was unavoidable, a Viennese newspaper said: "The acceptance of the terms would involve an essential diminution (indeed, destruction) of Austria's Great Power status. Even though this state emerged from the peace conference with its territory undiminished . . . its German position, traditionally its pride and, when properly used, one of the most fertile sources of its strength, would be gone. Austria would then see beside it a great German Power whose influence would become increasingly impressive compared with our own because it would be superior to us in homogeneity of population and in intellectual and economic development. Prussia's word would be the decisive one in all central European questions, and the most Austria could hope for would be to make its influence felt in the east. The German nationality of Austria would henceforth be no more than a limb detached from its proper body; it would be handed over unconditionally as a victim to the brawling of the nationalities, which threatens to expose Austria to the fate of Turkey."[17]

These words were prophetic. It was no mere coincidence that, within six months of the signing of the peace, the imperial government was forced to accept the so-called *Ausgleich* of 1867, which transformed the old Habsburg empire into a dual monarchy. This "compromise," which made the Magyars equal partners with the Germans in a new Austria-Hungary, was the logical consequence of the blow struck against governmental authority by the defeat at Königgrätz. Nor did this concession restore the prestige of the monarchy or alleviate the troubles which threatened it. Distracted by the heightened ambitions of its subject nationalities, the Habsburg monarchy henceforth found it impossible to fulfill its old role as guarantor of order in Eastern Europe; and, to the extent that this was so, dangers were created for all members of the diplomatic community.[18]

The exclusion of Austria from German affairs made certain the creation of a centralized German state under Prussian domination. The peace treaty, to be sure, stipulated that Prussia's hegemony should extend only as far as the Main River, and that the German states that lay south of that stream should retain their independence. But few people of any political experience believed that this prohibition would long survive. Although Sedan was needed to confirm its results, Königgrätz had in all essentials created the future German national state.

This too was an event of epochal significance, for it involved not merely an adjustment of the territorial arrangements of *Mitteleuropa* but a change in the very nature of the existing balance of power. The old German Confederation had been established at the Congress of Vienna in the hope of diminishing interstate tension in the middle of the continent. This had been explicitly stated at Vienna by Wilhelm von Humboldt. "One must never forget," he had told his fellow delegates, "the true and actual purpose of the German Confederation insofar as it relates to European politics. Its intent is to secure peace, and its whole existence is therefore based upon a preservation of balance through an inherent force of gravity. This would be entirely counteracted if there were introduced into the ranks of European states, besides the larger German states considered as single units, a new collective state. . . . No one could then prevent Germany, as Germany, from becoming an aggressive state, which no good German can wish. For we know what great superiority in literary and scientific accomplishment the German nation has achieved in the absence of external political aims; but no one knows how such aims might affect our future progress in this respect."[19]

Now what Humboldt had said must not happen had done so, and it is not surprising that this should have aroused some concern for the future. "The most audacious man in Europe is in possession of its most effective weapon," one English journal noted with foreboding.[20] And indeed there was cause for alarm. Königgrätz had not merely driven Austria out of German affairs and established the centralized Prusso-German state; it had also gravely weakened those forces in Prussian politics which might have restrained irresponsible use of Germany's enhanced power in international affairs. Since 1860 Prussian liberalism had striven to introduce into the constitution of the state features which were by then taken for granted in other countries of the west: the right of elected representatives of the people to exercise a decent amount of control over the Crown and its instruments, the army and the ministry. But the surge of patriotism that was inspired by Königgrätz and the victories that preceded it swept away the popular support which the liberal parliamentarians had until then enjoyed and established royal absolutism as a *rocher de bronze* for another half century. Henceforth the prerogatives of the Crown were susceptible to no parliamentary limitation, and the foreign and military policies of Germany became matters which were determined by the King and his personal advisers. The dangers inherent in such a system were not wholly apparent while William I lived and while Bismarck remained as chief minister of state. With the coming of William II, they leaped to the eye, although too late to save Germany and Europe from calamity.

The political repercussions of Königgrätz were therefore profound, although not immediately perceptible. The military results, and the lessons to be drawn from the battle, seemed more obvious.

Even to the most superficial observer it was clear, for instance, that important changes had taken place in weaponry and that these would affect all arms of the service in future wars. The thing that impressed contemporary observers most—and the one thing that everyone still knows about Königgrätz and the war of 1866—was the needle gun. Its terrible effectiveness was described in detail by the front-line correspondents of *The Times* and *Le Siècle;* and their reports, sometimes rewritten in such a way as to exaggerate the power of the weapon, appeared in other daily newspapers and in the popular illustrated magazines, and even received attention in satirical papers like *Punch*. In countries which did not possess a similar weapon, the battle accounts were enough to prompt demands that it be procured. "Riflemen sent against men armed with breech-loaders," an English newspaper wrote, "might almost as well carry slings or bows and arrows, for all the harm they are likely to effect."[21]

Moreover, the experience of Königgrätz put to rest the doubts of those professionals who had argued that the ease with which the *Zündnadelgewehr* could be refired would lead troops to exhaust their ammunition too quickly. Studies released soon after the end of hostilities revealed that the Prussian infantry had fired about 200,000 bullets during the battle, slightly more than one shot per weapon, as compared to the ten to eleven shots fired by each French infantryman at Borodino (where, incidentally, the French were using muzzle-loaders).[22] This economy, of course, spoke highly for the discipline and training of the Prussian infantry, but it also showed that possession of the new weapon did not necessarily cause a high expenditure of ammunition, as the prewar critics had believed.

In addition to the needle gun, the effectiveness of the artillery on both sides, but particularly on the Austrian, invited attention. The very number of guns used and the volume of fire maintained by them (the Austrians employed 672 guns and fired 46,535 shots in the course of the day)[23] aroused the respect of a materialistic generation, while the fact that the defeated power made effective use of its guns to the bitter end made professionals revise their views about the role of massed guns during the defensive. It was also generally recognized that rifled cannon had now unquestionably proven their superiority, and the fact that one third of

Prussia's guns (the smooth-bore 12-pounders) had been unusable because of their inadequate range drove this lesson home. On the other hand, there was, even in professional circles, a tendency to underestimate the effectiveness of the Prussian cast-steel guns, which, generally operating at a disadvantage, had at times demonstrated a startling accuracy; while too much was made of the fact that some of the Prussian steel guns had exploded during the battle. Investigation revealed that this was due to imperfections in the breech mechanism rather than in the barrel, and the Prussian Army subsequently went over entirely to the Krupp cannon, completing the conversion before the war of 1870. Other countries failed to follow suit. The French, like the Austrians, remained faithful to brass guns, and the British to wrought iron strengthened by exterior coils.[24]

Aside from the attention paid to the new weaponry, and certain elementary conclusions about what effects increased firepower would have on infantry and cavalry tactics, postwar critiques contained little of interest, and the lessons drawn from the war were neither reflective nor profound, at least outside of Prussia. In general, the tendency was to attribute the Prussian victory to the army's possession of a superior infantry weapon. The British journal *Spectator*, critical of Moltke's battle plan, said flatly, "The breechloader more than made up for faulty strategy."[25] Friedrich Engels agreed. Having predicted an Austrian victory in the confident belief that crowned heads are too stupid to be good soldiers, he had the embarrassing task of explaining how the Crown Prince ever managed to arrive in time. He found the answer in the needle gun, explaining gravely that "it may be doubted whether without it the junction of the two Prussian armies could have been effected."[26]

From this tendency of foreign opinion to be fascinated by the new military hardware, there were some exceptions. The Russian observer at the battle, Major General Dragomirow, said later, "It wasn't the needle gun by itself that won the victories of 1866, but the men who carried it."[27] And the French military attaché in Berlin, Colonel Stoffel, wrote that, even if the Austrians had possessed breechloaders, it would not have changed the result in 1866: the war was won by the superiority of the Prussian high command.[28] These professional observers came closer to appreciating the true lessons of Königgrätz than most foreign newspaper and professional opinion. But even they did not push their analysis far enough, or appear to see what in retrospect can be seen easily.

If Königgrätz had anything to teach the military establishments of other powers, it was that, in an age in which industrial progress was making it possible to arm and transport armies which dwarfed those of antiquity, wars would be won by those nations which could raise, train, deploy and command large armies most effectively. The first lesson of the war was that the day of the small professional army was passing, if it was not, indeed, already past; and the second was that the efficiency of large armies would vary with the systems employed to raise them. The performance of Prussian troops throughout the war and especially in the culminating battle was a strong argument in favor of a system of conscription both universal and equitable and seemed to suggest that the way to avoid raising an army that was little more than an armed horde was, in the first place, to have a system which did not exempt the educated classes from service and, in the second, to have a training program that disciplined without destroying initiative.

With respect to this last point, the battle had also suggested that training programs should endeavor to inculcate mutual understanding between the different arms of the service in the interest of effective co-operation in the field. In a memorandum sent to the King in July 1868 concerning lessons that might be drawn from the war of 1866, Moltke noted that there were times in the campaign when it appeared that the different branches of the service were operating in complete disregard of each other. The infantry, he said, had "in every respect, in marching as well as in fighting, performed excellently," but there was no avoiding the fact that it had been supported "inadequately by the artillery, and by the cavalry as good as not at all."[29] With respect to the artillery, there had been a tendency to carry it too far back in the columns of march—here Moltke seemed to have come round to Hohenlohe's view—so that it often arrived at the scene of the battle after the fighting had begun.[30] This meant that infantry troops often had to attack without artillery preparation. They had done so "with a bravery which cannot be too highly praised, but which, against a better armed and more tenacious foe, can lead to some very serious situations." Moreover, artillery commanders often seemed to be unclear about the mission of the infantry, a state of mind that perhaps reflected a lack of co-ordination between arms in peacetime training, but was due in part also to failure of information during the battle itself. "It is urgently recommended," Moltke wrote, "that the higher troop leaders inform the artillery commanders attached to their staffs of the objective of the fight and the way in which they intend to achieve it and allow them to pass their orders on to the batteries."[31]

The campaign of 1866 and the battle of Königgrätz indicated that cavalry training had for some time past taken a false direction, with the result that the cavalry failed to give the kind of assistance to the other arms that it was capable of giving. Both armies had kept great masses of horse in the rear, waiting for that moment in the fight when it would strike the decisive offensive blow against the enemy; but in neither case had the reserve cavalry served the purpose for which it was so stubbornly hoarded. There was, indeed, good reason to believe that there never would be a time in the future when the cavalry could perform that kind of function. Moltke suggested that it was time to return to the Napoleonic emphasis upon the cavalry's duties of reconnoiter, intelligence, communication and pursuit—in all of which the Prussian horse, at least, had been woefully inadequate in the recent war.[32]

Even an army that is based upon an ideal system of recruitment and is excellently trained in the use of its weapons and in co-ordination of arms is useless unless it is brought to the scene of battle in time and in dispositions that will facilitate effective action against the enemy. The war of 1866 showed that the problems of mobilization and deployment had been enormously complicated by the increase in the size of modern armies, and that this would require from the commanders of the future the kind of fertility in expedients and daring of conception that Moltke had displayed, rather than the cautious conservatism that had characterized the leadership of Benedek and his advisers before Königgrätz.

This was not readily perceived by military critics in 1866. The unanimity with which they attributed the Prussian victory to weaponry, speed, luck, Austrian mistakes, and, indeed, anything but Moltke's operational plan and his strategical sense is a remarkable illustration of the conservatism of the military mind. In England, as we have seen (see above, pp. 45, 174.), Prussian operations before Königgrätz were considered foolhardy; in France, soldiers said patronizingly that Moltke had been protected by God and that if he ever followed a similar operational plan in a war against France they would make mincemeat of his armies; in Italy, General Giuseppe Govone, despite friendship with Moltke and long strategical discussions with him, disapproved entirely of his plan and believed that it had worked only because of Benedek's delays[33]; and in Austria *Feldzeugmeister* Ladislas Freiherr Nagy, in an article in the official military gazette in February 1867, described Moltke's strategy as "never rising above the level of mediocrity."[34] All of these critics repeated the time-honored shibboleths about the dangers of separation when confronting an enemy on interior lines and the sovereign excellence of concentration before battle.

Enough has been said above about the reasons for Moltke's adoption of the particular *modus operandi* employed in June 1866 to make a lengthy discussion here unnecessary (see above, pp. 33, 46). It is enough perhaps to point out that most of Moltke's critics were paying obeisance to principles which were impractical in the new conditions of warfare. The wars of the future were going to be won not by stereotyped formulas but by operational plans which took account of such things as time, space, the increased size of modern armies, the available methods of transportation, and the improved effectiveness of modern weaponry. In a particular situation, Moltke had given an impressive demonstration of how these factors must be related in an operational plan, separating his army to assure himself of the greatest possible speed in deployment, and concentrating it not before but during the battle, when concentration would have maximum effect.

Moltke himself always resisted any suggestion that Königgrätz could form the basis of a "system" of strategy. Circumstances alter cases, he believed, and there are too many variables in war to permit the simplification that systems call for. But he did commend to his critics a few rules of thumb. Against a *Feldherr* who knows how to avail himself of the means of modern transportation and is, in addition, willing to take reasonable risks, the occupation of interior lines is a shrinking asset. Aside from that, the separation of the army in the deployment phase, even when not required by delays in mobilization similar to those of 1866, will be made increasingly necessary by the size of modern armies. To move them with reasonable speed and to feed them while they are moving will be possible only if they are divided.[35] Similarly, the premature concentration of armies will become increasingly dangerous as firepower increases. In modern conditions, "any heaping up of great masses is in itself a calamity. . . . The heavy task of a good army command is to keep the masses separate without losing the possibility of uniting them at the right time."[36] Even concentration immediately before battle has its disadvantages now that firepower makes frontal attacks prohibitively costly and flanking and concentric movements mandatory. For these cannot be improvised by mere tactical shifts during a battle. They must be prepared in advance and started during the deployment phase. "If the forces can be brought from separate points and concentrated against the battlefield itself, if the operations can be directed in such a way that from different sides a last short march strikes simultaneously against the enemy's front and flank, then strategy has achieved the most that it can achieve, and great results must follow."[37]

Those observers who tended to overlook Moltke's distinctive contribution to strategy—his demonstration of how to control very large armies in such a way as to be able to shift them to meet any developing situation—and who emphasized instead the mistakes of leadership on the Austrian side were not, of course, entirely mistaken. Not the least important of the lessons of Königgrätz was the necessity of courage, determination, patience and discipline on the part of commanders at all levels. On both sides there had been costly instances of lack of restraint and disobedience; and if the premature crossing of the Bistritz by the Prussian 6th Division (see above, page 111) was of a different order from Mollinary's persistence in throwing troops into the *Swiepwald*, it too had resulted in unnecessary casualties. The problem of encouraging a healthy spirit of initiative among subordinate commanders while maintaining at the same time common purpose and co-ordination is one of the most difficult problems in the management of armies. Königgrätz did not provide a patent solution, but it at least gave new evidence of the results that can follow from failure to make earnest efforts to inform subordinate troop leaders of the battle plan and to impress on them the importance of co-operation in carrying out its objectives.[38]

With the signing of the preliminaries of peace, the captains and the kings departed for home—the victors to collect plaudits and decorations, the vanquished to receive public criticism and, in some cases, official censure. The two great artificers of the Prussian victory were well rewarded for their labors. Bismarck, who had been regarded by many in June as the gravedigger of Prussian power and honor, came back to Berlin in August as a hero and with a new reputation for political sagacity that greatly facilitated his future work. He also returned as a major general, a promotion which was regarded with mixed feelings by the soldiers. Henceforth, he generally wore a uniform, not, however, because of a sudden access of military feeling but rather because he discovered that the close-fitting tunic was useful in curbing his tendency to attacks of asthma and that, in addition, the King was generally more cordial and co-operative when his chief minister was uniformed than when he was in mufti. His military costume always tended, however, to be unconventional, and on warm days he would open his coat, revealing a black cloth vest, a habit which distressed Moltke, who used to talk of Bismarck's military *Dekolletierung*.[39]

To the Chief of Staff himself, the King expressed his gratitude by granting him the highest Prussian order, the Black Eagle, and, after the victorious army had returned to Berlin, by making him *chef* of the Ninth Infantry Regiment. This was a handsome gesture, for Gneisenau had once held that position, and the appointment was an intimation that Moltke's stature was equal to that of Blücher's chief of staff, who had, until now at least, been considered Prussia's greatest strategist.[40] In addition to this, Moltke, virtually unknown to the public before the war, returned home to be acclaimed and lionized and accorded a degree of veneration that was extraordinary and which grew with the years. Since he was a modest man, this did not particularly gratify him; and in the long run (although Moltke never realized it) it had unfortunate results for his country. The reputation for omniscience that Moltke acquired in 1866, and which was strengthened in 1870, came to attach itself to the so-called "Demi-Gods" who surrounded him and to the General Staff as an institution. Its prestige grew so enormously with the passage of the years that its advice came to be sought on other than military matters, and this led in time to a dangerous degree of military influence in the policy formation of the German Empire.

No such veneration attached itself to the defeated *Feldherr*. Benedek turned the command of his beaten army over to Arch-duke Albert on July 26, when he crossed the Danube at Press-burg. He had already been informed by the Emperor's Adjutant General, Count Crenneville, that his conduct of operations from the time of his assumption of command at Olmütz would be subjected to an official investigation,[41] and, on July 28, he went to Wiener Neustadt, where he had started his career in 1818 as a cadet, to submit himself to the court of inquiry. This body was composed of *Feldzeugmeister* Johann Count von Nobili, *Feldzeugmeister* Franz Ritter von Hauslab, *Feldzeugmeister* Nagy (who was later to describe Moltke's strategy as mediocre), and Auditor General Karl Ritter von Pfiffer, and they worked on the basis of a questionnaire which Archduke Albert had sent to subordinate commanders asking about the conduct of the campaign, the details of Königgrätz, and the responsibility for such critical setbacks as the fall of Chlum.

At the beginning of July, Benedek had written a series of letters to his wife in which he harked back to the time of his appointment and described those conversations with the Emperor in which he had warned Francis Joseph that the chances of victory in the war were minimal and his own competence for command in Bohemia slight, but had said that he was willing to serve if the Emperor insisted, even at the cost of his civil and military reputation. If he now had to stand trial because his fears had been realized, he told his wife, he would make no attempt to defend himself. He was willing to assume full responsibility for the debacle, but he would make no explanations to anyone but the Emperor himself.[42]

Benedek remained true to that promise during his trial, although he had the greatest difficulty in restraining his wife, who insisted that he was being made a scapegoat and urged him to speak up in his own behalf, and who threatened to publish details of his conversations with the Emperor if he did not. He silenced her with an eloquent letter in which he said: "Even though all the world around you curses and complains loudly and openly, the wife of *Feldzeugmeister* Benedek should mourn the misfortune that has befallen Austria and her husband quietly and with dignity. She should weigh her words, so that the evil tongues, the people who envy or hate her husband, and perhaps her too, should find no opportunity to twist this or that angry statement of Benedek's wife in a false way." No one, he said, could really hurt him but his wife. If his love were not enough for her, if she felt "a need to tear at my wounded heart and spirit, if you cannot keep my misfortune sacred, then it would be better for me to stay apart from you, to endure it alone, and to end it all in some obscure corner of the world."[43]

This, to modern ears, smacks of gaslight sentimentality, but Benedek was serious. He silenced his wife, and he remained silent himself, before the court of inquiry and later. Compared with his behavior, that of his government was undignified to the point of petty vengefulness. When Benedek submitted his resignation from the army in November, he had to give a formal promise to Archduke Albert that he would not write anything, or cause anything to be written, in which he attributed his misfortune to the mistakes of others.[44] Having exacted that pledge, the government proceeded to do what his wife had suspected they would do: they portrayed him as the author of all their woes and the sole begetter of their defeat at Königgrätz. The inquiry was quashed by imperial fiat on December 4, without any formal decision being released. But almost immediately the *Wiener Zeitung* printed an article in which it was argued that the hearings, which had involved Krismanic and Henikstein as well as Benedek, had been discontinued because those two officers were clearly innocent of the catastrophe, since they had been bound by Benedek's orders, and that in order to exculpate them it was necessary to stop proceedings against Benedek also. Those who felt that he deserved punishment for his mistakes could take comfort, the article intimated, in the fact that he had forfeited the confidence of his Emperor and had irretrievably lost his military reputation.[45]

In a private testament of June 1873, Benedek wrote that this article had been drafted in the General Staff and corrected by Lieutenant Field Marshal Franz Freiherr von John and Archduke Albert himself. For the government to have published this after it had his written promise not to reply was, he wrote, beyond his conception of "justice, fairness, and decency."[46] But he made no public protest and he remained mute in the fact of other injustices: the publication of the Austrian General Staff history of the war, which was even more critical of his actions than the article in the *Wiener Zeitung;* the handsome treatment accorded Clam-Gallas, who was cleared by a court inquiring into his behavior on the Iser and at Gitschin and who subsequently received an imperial letter of thanks for his services; the honors and promotions that came to men like Mollinary and Thun; and the rehabilitation of Krismanic, who was restored to active service in 1872.

Only Benedek remained outside the circle of official favor, a victim of reason of state, sacrificed to public opinion in order to draw attention away from those aspects of the imperial regime that were more responsible for the defeat at Königgrätz than he. There were moments when he rebelled against the tragic role in which he had been cast, but he always mastered his passions and remained, until his death in 1881 (and, indeed, afterward, since he burned all his papers dealing with the war), true to his pledged word. To speak out, even after years had relieved the popular bitterness of 1866, would, he once told his wife, "serve neither the Emperor nor the Army. A beaten *Feldherr* must bear his misfortune."

NOTES

1. Perhaps because so many people regarded it as a war of brothers, the Austro-Prussian war produced few songs and little good verse. These lines are part of a piece of anonymous doggerel that goes on to describe *Feldzeugmeister* von Benedek fleeing before the Prussian guns and crying, "My God! What will Franzel [Emperor Francis Joseph] say? He'll fire us all!" See Hans Ziegler, *Deutsche Soldaten- und Kriegslieder* (Leipzig, 1884), pp. 358 f.

2. *Illustrated London News,* XXIX, 25 (14 July 1866).

3. *The Spectator* (London), XXXIX, 737 (7 July 1866).

4. French writers, in 1866 and since, have generally preferred the name "Sadowa" to that of "Königgrätz," calling the battle after the village on the Bistritz where the first fighting took place on the morning of July 3. Other writers have pointed out that the most appropriate name would be "Chlum," since the capture of Chlum heights by the Prussian Guards was the decisive factor in the victory. But battles are named by the victors, and the name chosen by King William on the evening of his greatest success was "Königgrätz," although the fortress of that name lay some miles behind the Bistritz and did not figure in the fighting.

5. *Revue des deux mondes,* LXIV, 516 (14 July 1866).

6. Wilhelm Schüssler, in an interesting short political study, goes so far as to say that "a figure like Hitler is hardly to be explained without Königgrätz, for the result of that battle for Austria was an increasing decline of its German element, the rise of the Slavs, and the inflamed nationalism of the border struggles". *Königgrätz 1866: Bismarcks tragische Trennung von Oesterreich,* p. 8.

7. Estimates vary, but see Max Jähns, *Die Schlacht von Königgrätz,* pp. 484 f., and H. M. Hozier, *The Seven Weeks' War,* pp. 254 f., the latter with comparative tables.

8. *Oberst* Baron von Stoffel, *Militärische Berichte erstattet aus Berlin 1866–1870,* pp. 2 f.; *Generalfeldmarschall* Graf Alfred von Schlieffen, *Gesammelte Schriften,* I, 127.

9. For a discussion of this point, see Jähns, *op. cit.,* p. 489.

10. Werner Richter, *Bismarck,* p. 151.

CHAPTER I

1. A nineteenth-century song by F. W. Güll, called "The Little Recruit," which tells a rocking-horse soldier all the things he will need in order to look and act like the real thing. Ziegler, *op. cit.*, pp. 71 f.

2. In the sixth scene of *Wallenstein's Camp* by Schiller, a self-important sergeant-major speaks these words in reproof to a couple of boisterous Jaeger.

3. Helmuth von Moltke, *Gesammelte Schriften und Aufsätze*, III, 426–27.

4. Heinrich Friedjung, *Kampf um die Vorherrschaft in Deutschland*, I, 142.

5. See Hans Rothfels, ed. *Bismarck und der Staat: Ausgewählte Dokumente*, p. 113.

6. See W. H. Chaloner and W. O. Henderson, ed. *Engels as Military Critic*, pp. 121 ff.

7. Friedjung, *op. cit.*, II, 3.

8. Edmund von Glaise-Horstenau, *Franz Josephs Weggefährte*, p. 87.

9. A militia system had been established in 1809 by Archduke Charles but had long since been allowed to fall into disuse.

10. It was because the government knew that mobilization was bound to be slow that it was willing to accept the political onus of being the first to start mobilization.

11. For all this, see Friedjung, *op. cit.*, I, 351–53; Oscar von Lettow-Vorbeck, *Geschichte des Krieges von 1866*, II, 8–12; Freiherr von Freytag-Loringhoven, *Die Grundbedingungen kriegerischen Erfolges: Beiträge zur Psychologie des Krieges im 19. und 20. Jahrhundert*, pp. 108 f.; and, for his analysis of the financial aspects of the armament prob-

lem, Oskar Regele, *Feldzeugmeister Benedek: Der Weg nach Königgrätz*, especially pp. 311–384.

12. Lettow-Vorbeck, *op. cit.*, II, 16.

13. *The Times* (London), 11 July 1866, p. 9.

14. Lettow-Vorbeck, *op. cit.*, II, 17; Rittmeister Brix, *Das Oesterreichische Heer in seiner Organisation und Stärke, Uniformirung, Ausrüstung und Bewaffnung*, pp. 101–115.

15. Friedjung, *op. cit.*, I, 376, 379 f.; Brix, *op. cit.*, pp. 92 ff. Regele, *op. cit.*, pp. 358 ff. points out that by 1866 all important military agencies had been persuaded of the necessity of conversion, but that it was made impossible by the civil authorities' refusal to grant the necessary funds.

16. Friedjung, *op. cit.*, I, 358–377.

17. Glaise-Horstenau, *op. cit.*, p. 88. Cf. Regele, *op. cit.*, pp. 365 ff. It is worth noting that Prince Frederick Charles of Prussia, on the basis of observations in Denmark, thought Austrian tactics too costly in casualties. See Friedrich Karl, Prinz von Preussen, *Denkwürdigkeiten aus seinem Leben*, ed. by Wolfgang Förster, I, 112.

18. Freytag-Loringhoven, *op. cit.*, pp. 111 f.

19. "How could we prevail against the Prussians?" he said to a visitor. "We have learned little, and they are such studious people!" *Benedeks nachgelassene Papiere*, ed. by Heinrich Friedjung, p. 406.

20. Lettow-Vorbeck, *op. cit.*, II, 17; and, more dramatically, Carl Bleibtreu, *Königgrätz*, pp. 10 f.

21. Prinz Kraft zu Hohenlohe-Ingelfingen, *Aus meinem Leben, 1848–71*, I, 296.

22. Glaise-Horstenau, *op. cit.*, p. 31.

23. *Ibid.*, p. 71.

24. On Grünne's influence, see *inter alia* Josef Redlich, *Emperor Francis Joseph of Austria: A Biography*, pp. 43 ff., 88 f., 92; *Benedeks nachgelassene Papiere*, pp. 301, 311 ff., 320.

25. Beck, *op. cit.*, pp. 50, 53.

26. See Eugen von Frauenholz, "Feldmarschallleutnant Alfred Freiherr von Henikstein im Jahre 1866," *Münchener Historische Abhandlungen*, pp. 34 f.

27. On Benedek's early career, see especially *Benedeks nachgelassene Papiere*, pp. 1–250 *passim* and, on his popularity, pp. 63, 134, 175, 183, 265. See also Regele, *op. cit.*, pp. 261–289; Gustav von Hubka, "Ludwig Ritter von Benedek" in *Grosse Oesterreicher: Neue Oesterreichische Biographie ab 1815*, XII, 52. On Archduke Albert, see H. Ritter von Srbik, *Aus Oesterreichs Vergangenheit*, pp. 109 ff.

28. *Benedeks nachgelassene Papiere*, p. 353; William Alter, *Feldzeugmeister Benedek*, p. 137.

29. Glaise-Horstenau, *op. cit.*, pp. 94 f.

30. *Benedeks nachgelassene Papiere*, p. 76.

31. A better choice would have been Hess's most brilliant student, Lt. Field Marshal von John, but Archduke Albert kept him as *his* chief of staff.

32. This deficiency was corrected to some extent after operations began by a member of Adjutant General von Crenneville's staff, Lieutenant Colonel von Beck.

33. Henikstein bore some resemblance to those officers described by Helmuth von Moltke in his monograph on the Italian war, who "always know how to point out with great perception the difficulties in any proposed undertaking. ... They are always right, for they never propose anything positive themselves. ... These men of the negative are the bane of army commanders." *Moltkes Militärische Werke*, III. *Kriegsgeschichtliche Arbeiten*, Dritter Theil, pp. 10 f. For a defense of Henikstein, see Frauenholz, *loc. cit.*

34. Michael Howard, *The Franco-Prussian War*, p. 18.

35. On these, see Gordon A. Craig, *The Politics of the Prussian Army, 1640–1945*, chapter IV.

36. Chaloner and Henderson, *op. cit.*, p. 123.

37. Hohenlohe-Ingelfingen, *op. cit.*, III, p. 222.

38. On the reforms, see Craig, *op. cit.*, chapter IV.

39. See Lettow-Vorbeck, *op. cit.*, II, 1 ff.; Friedjung, *op. cit.*, I, 354–56.

40. See Friedrich Karl, *op. cit.*, II, 24 ff., 27; Lettow-Vorbeck, *op. cit.*, II, 2–3; Eberhard Kessel, *Moltke*, p. 28.

41. Hohenlohe-Ingelfingen, *op. cit.*, III, 243.

42. Stoffel, *op. cit.*, p. 60; Lettow-Vorbeck, *op. cit.*, II, 4–5; Wilhelm Berdrow, *The Krupps*, pp. 142 ff., 154, 160, 170 ff.; Norbert Muhlen, *The Incredible Krupps*, pp. 39 ff., 42 ff.

43. Hohenlohe-Ingelfingen, *op. cit.*, III, 217.

44. The only departure permitted was in the interest of education, and it was not a total exemption. Students above a certain grade in the Gymnasium could avoid service in the line by volunteering for a one-year officers' training course and, thereafter, standing in the active reserve. See Franz Schnabel, *Deutsche*

Geschichte im 19. Jahrhundert, II, 315 f.

45. *The Saturday Review* (London), XXII, 1 (7 July 1866).

46. Chaloner and Henderson, *op. cit.*, p. 61.

47. *Ibid.*, pp. 59 ff.

48. For technical details and information on the different models in use before 1866, see Werner Eckardt and Otto Morawietz, *Die Handwaffen des brandenburgisch-preussisch-deutschen Heeres 1640-1945*, pp. 101-130.

49. Glaise-Horstenau, *op. cit.*, p. 88; Chaloner and Henderson, *op. cit.*, p. 64.

50. Lettow-Vorbeck, *op. cit.*, II, 2. Helmuth von Moltke wrote three different memoranda on the effects of improved weapons upon infantry tactics—in 1858, in April 1861, and in 1865. See *Moltkes Militärische Werke*, II. *Die Thätigkeit als Chef des Generalstabes der Armee in Frieden*, Zweiter Theil, pp. 7-9, 29-41, 49-65. For his views on the use of company columns in the advance and on the proper use of the bayonet, see especially pp. 38, 59, 61 f.

51. Careful attention was paid to the selection of NCO's and to the kind of inducement that would keep them in the army. King William regarded them as the backbone of the military establishment in peacetime and war. For a memorandum of his on the subject, written in 1825, see *Geschichte des deutschen Unteroffiziers*, herausgegeben vom Reichstreubund ehemaliger Berufssoldaten (Berlin, 1939), pp. 250 ff.

52. Reyher, the son of a village organist, began his military career in 1802 as a regimental clerk. In 1809 he served with Schill and some time

later attracted the attention of General von Yorck, who encouraged him to take the officer candidates' examinations. He passed them and received his commission in 1810, and then rose rapidly in rank, thanks to meritorious service in the wars of 1813 and 1814 and to his success in a long series of staff and instructional assignments in the ensuing period of peace. He was ennobled by King Frederick William III in 1828 and reached the height of his career as Chief of the General Staff from 1848 to 1857. The brilliant staff officers of 1866—Moltke, Blumenthal, Voigts-Rhetz, Alvensleben, Goeben—were all, in a real sense, his students. *Ibid.*, pp. 257 ff., and Major Ollech, "Reyher," *Militärwochenblatt*, Beihefte, 1879, Nrs. 5-6.

53. See, *inter alia*, B. Schwertfeger, *Die Grossen Erzieher des deutschen Heeres: Aus der Geschichte der Kriegsakademie*, pp. 43 ff.; Karl Demeter, *Das deutsche Heer und seine Offiziere*, pp. 84-85; "Rühle von Lilienstern," *Militärwochenblatt*, Beihefte, Oct.-Dec., 1847.

54. Ollech, *loc. cit.*; *Von Scharnhorst zu Schlieffen*, ed. by F. von Cochenhausen, pp. 121 ff.; Paul Bronsart von Schellendorf, *Duties of the General Staff*, pp. 26 ff.

55. See Johannes Ziekursch, *Politische Geschichte des neuen deutschen Kaiserreiches*, I, 163; Rudolf Stadelmann, *Moltke und der Staat*, p. 32; *Von Scharnhorst zu Schlieffen*, p. 165.

56. Lettow-Vorbeck, *op. cit.*, I, 104.

57. *Moltkes Militärische Werke*, III. *Kriegsgeschichtliche Arbeiten*, Dritter Theil, p. 10.

58. Kessel, *op. cit.*, p. 444.

CHAPTER 2

1. A gay song from the last years of William I's reign, in which a recruit sings of having to leave the girls behind for three years. See Walther Werckmeister, ed. *Deutsches Lautenlied* (2. Auflage, Berlin, 1917), p. 436.

2. In Conrad Ferdinand Meyer's poem, the dying Ulrich von Hutten, fighting to hold on to his faith in the face of doubt and uncertainty, takes comfort in comparing himself with the common soldier who must execute commands without always knowing why, but who fights bravely because he has confidence in the supreme command and its plan.

3. "Über Strategie" (1871), reprinted in *Moltkes Militärische Werke*, II. *Die Thätigkeit als Chef des Generalstabes der Armee im Frieden*, Zweiter Theil, pp. 291 ff. On the similarity between these views and Bismarck's views on political strategy, see General von Schlichting, *Moltke und Benedek*, p. 13, and Bismarck, *Die gesammelten Werke*, IX, 49 f.

4. *Moltkes Militärische Werke*, I. *Militärische Korrespondenz*, Zweiter Theil, pp. 12–15.

5. *Ibid.*, p. 14.

6. *Ibid.*, pp. 18, 19.

7. *Ibid.*, pp. 36 ff., 40. See also W. Bigge, *Feldmarschall Graf Moltke: ein militärisches Lebensbild*, II, 153 ff.

8. Kessel, *op. cit.*, p. 441. Moltke was never averse to the idea of preventive war and was to demonstrate this on other occasions, notably in 1867 and 1887.

9. Friedrich Karl, *op. cit.*, I, 317.

10. Hans Delbrück, the historian of war and a very critical judge of commanding generals, had a high opinion of his qualities. *Historische und politische Aufsätze*, pp. 307 ff. See also Freytag-Loringhoven, *op. cit.*, 106.

11. For a full account of his career, Kurt von Priesdorff, ed. *Soldatisches Führertum*, VII, 189 ff.; Friedrich Karl, *op. cit.*, II, 20. Voigts-Rhetz was head of the General War Department of the War Ministry in 1859 and was one of the strong advocates of the Krupp gun.

12. *Bismarcks grosses Spiel. Die geheime Tagebücher Ludwig Bambergers*, ed. by Ernst Feder, p. 29; Albrecht von Stosch, *Denkwürdigkeiten*, ed. by Ulrich von Stosch, p. 107; Priesdorff, *op. cit.*, VIII, 59 ff.

13. Blumenthal, *Tagebücher*, p. 9.

14. J. von Verdy du Vernois, *Im Hauptquartier der Zweiten Armee 1866*, pp. 32 f.; Ulrich von Hassell, *Tirpitz. Sein Leben und Wirken mit Berücksichtigung seiner Beziehungen zu Albrecht von Stosch*, pp. 17 f.; Priesdorff, *op. cit.*, VIII, 307 ff.

15. See Hajo Holborn, "Moltke and Schlieffen," in *Makers of Modern Strategy: Military Thought from Machiavelli to Hitler*, ed. by Edward Mead Earle, Gordon A. Craig and Felix Gilbert, pp. 181 ff. On the Prussian staff's use of railways, see E. A. Pratt, *The Rise of Rail Power in War and Conquest, 1833–1914*, pp. 104 f. For Moltke's early interest, see his essay of 1843, "Welche Rücksichten kommen bei der Wahl der Richtung von Eisenbahnen in Betracht?" *Gesammelte Schriften*, II, 235 ff.

16. This worried Bismarck and led to a brush between Moltke and him, but the Chief of Staff insisted that it was necessary to secure equality of numbers with the enemy

in the main theater of war and he had his way.

17. Friedjung, *op. cit.*, II, 11 ff.; Bigge, *op. cit.*, II, 164 f.

18. *Ibid.*, II, 163.

19. On this meeting, see especially Kaiser Friedrich III, *Tagebücher, 1848-66*, ed. by H. O. Meisner (Leipzig, 1929), p. 424; Friedrich Karl, *op. cit.*, II, 13 f.; Blumenthal, *op. cit.*, pp. 12 f.; Stosch, *op. cit.*, p. 75; Kessel, *op. cit.*, pp. 453 f.

20. For accounts of the movement of the Guards, see Hohenlohe-Ingelfingen, *op. cit.*, III, 225 ff., and R. von Arnim, *Erinnerungen aus dem Feldzug von 1866*, pp. 7-10.

21. Bigge, *op. cit.*, II, 171 f.; Kessel, *op. cit.*, pp. 455 f.

22. Stosch wrote on June 12: "The joke is that we now become the big army and Frederick Charles rattles along behind." Stosch, *op. cit.*, p. 80.

23. See Friedrich Karl, *op. cit.*, II, 17; *Aus dem Leben Theodor von Bernhardis*, VII, 17.

24. Through an intermediary, the Bavarian premier had said: "Does Beck think that Bavaria is an Austrian satrapy?" Beck had answered: "The result will be that we'll be beaten in Bohemia and you in Ba- varia, and we'll both be flat on our backs!" Glaise-Horstenau, *op. cit.*, p. 93.

25. *Ibid.*, pp. 100 ff.

26. *Ibid.*, pp. 102 ff.

27. Verdy du Vernois, *op cit.*, p. 62. See also the Austrian General Staff work on the war of 1866, *Oesterreichs Kämpfe im Jahre 1866*, III, 33 f.

28. Preussen: Grosser Generalstab, *Der Feldzug von 1866 in Deutschland*, I, 89 ff.

29. *Der Antheil des Königlich Sächsischen Armeecorps am Feldzuge 1866*, pp. 29-37; Paul Hassel, *Aus dem Leben des Königs Albert von Sachsen. II. König Albert als Kronprinz*, 262.

30. For the campaign in the west, see Bigge, *op. cit.*, II, 221-241, and Lettow-Vorbeck, *op. cit.*, I, chapters 3-5; Heinrich von Sybel, *Die Begründung des Deutschen Reiches durch Wilhelm I*, V, 26 ff.

31. See Jähns, *op. cit.*, p. 4.

32. Friedjung, *op. cit.*, I, 488.

33. *Ibid.*, p. 489.

34. Bigge, *op. cit.*, II, 178 f.

35. *Moltkes Militärische Werke*, I. *Militärische Korrespondenz*, Zweiter Theil, p. 231.

36. *Ibid.*, p. 234; Preussen: Generalstab, *Der Feldzug von 1866*, I, 94.

CHAPTER 3

1. From a well-known and singable song, "Fridericus Rex, Our King and Hero", by Willibald Alexis (Willibald Häring, 1798-1871). Here Frederick the Great is speaking to his wife before leaving for the field in 1756. For music, see Werckmeister, *op. cit.*, p. 386.

2. As given by Carlyle, Leopold of Dessau's prayer was: "*O Herr Gott*, help me yet this once; let me not be disgraced in my old days! Or if Thou wilt not help me, don't help those *Hundsvögte*, but leave us to try it out ourselves!" *History of Friedrich the Second, called Frederick the Great*, IV, 170.

3. Theodor Fontane, *Der deutsche Krieg von 1866*, I, 280.

4. *The Spectator* (London), XXXIX, 742 (7 July 1866).

5. *The Manchester Guardian*, 3

July 1866, cited in Chaloner and Henderson, *op. cit.*, pp. 133 f.

6. "The Prussian army will be under the command-in-chief of the King,—that is to say, of a parade soldier of at best very mediocre capacities and of weak, but often obstinate, character. . . . The Austrian army is under the unconditional command of General Benedek, who is an experienced officer and who, at least, knows his own mind". *Manchester Guardian*, 20 June 1866, in *ibid.*, pp. 122 f. Here, surely, the crystal ball was very clouded.

7. Ernst Buchfink, *Feldmarschall Graf von Haeseler*, p. 35.

8. Friedrich Karl, *op. cit.*, II, 42. On the purely formal role of Gitschin in Moltke's planning, see Schlichting, *op. cit.*, pp. 10 f.

9. Kessel, *op. cit.*, pp. 467 f.

10. Blumenthal, *op. cit.*, p. 27.

11. Fontane, *op. cit.*, I, 123.

12. Quoted in *ibid.*, p. 139.

13. On all this, see Preussen: Grosser Generalstab: Kriegsgeschichtliche Abteilung, *Studien zur Kriegsgeschichte und Taktik*, VI. *Heeresverpflegung*, especially pp. 100–106, 114, 133.

14. Friedrich Karl, *op. cit.*, II, 40.

15. Preussen: Grosser Generalstab: Kriegsgeschichtliche Abteilung I, *Studien zur Kriegsgeschichte und Taktik*, III. *Der Schlachterfolg, mit welchen Mitteln wurde er erstrebt?*, p. 170; Buchfink, *op. cit.*, p. 36.

16. Friedrich Karl, *op. cit.*, II, 41.

17. *Ibid.*, pp. 38 f.

18. Friedjung, *op. cit.*, II, 16; *Benedeks nachgelassene Papiere*, p. 366.

19. Hassel, *op. cit.*, II, 262 ff.

20. A. von Voigts-Rhetz, ed. *Briefe des Generals der Infanterie Voigts-Rhetz aus den Kriegsjahren*

1866 und 1870–71, p. 5; Friedrich Karl, *op. cit.*, II, 44.

21. *Moltkes Militärische Werke*, I. *Militärische Korrespondenz*, Zweiter Theil, p. 237.

22. Friedrich Karl, *op. cit.*, II, 47.

23. Friedjung, *op. cit.*, II, 22 f.; Lettow-Vorbeck, *op. cit.*, II, 181 ff.

24. *Oesterreichs Kämpfe*, III, 59.

25. See Hassel, *op. cit.*, II, 273 ff.

26. Friedjung, *op. cit.*, II, 25.

27. Fontane, *op. cit.*, I, 157.

28. *Oesterreichs Kämpfe*, III, 59–63. Nine officers and 97 men were killed; 17 officers and 230 men wounded; 555 were known prisoners, and 140 missing. Part of the discrepancy in casualties resulted from poor Austrian marksmanship. Prussian Jaeger, as they retired from the first phase of the fight, shouted to their comrades: "Shoot low! They're all firing too high!" Fontane, *op. cit.*, I, 159.

29. Hassel, *op. cit.*, II, 276 f.

30. See Friedrich Karl, *op. cit.*, II, 48 ff.

31. Generalstab, *Heeresverpflegung*, pp. 108, 119 f.; Arnim, *op. cit.*, pp. 13–15, 48 ff.; Hohenlohe-Ingelfingen, *op. cit.*, III, 234 ff. These accounts make it clear that there was no absence of problems, and that some of the units were hungry on the eve of Königgrätz. But because the army was moving on a broad front it did not put too heavy requirements on the supply lines or the countryside, and transport from the rear and requisitioning both worked better than in the case of the First and Elbe Armies.

32. Verdy, *op. cit.*, p. 51.

33. Generalstab, *Schlachterfolg*, pp. 174 f. The authors of this study were nevertheless inclined to believe that Benedek had already waited too long and that the Crown Prince

could have held on until the First Army arrived. Given Frederick Charles's propensity to delay, it is an open question.

34. Friedjung, *op. cit.*, II, 32 f.

35. *Ibid.*, p. 34.

36. Priesdorff, *op. cit.*, VII, 59 ff.; Fontane, *op. cit.*, I, 284 ff.

37. Verdy, *op. cit.*, p. 42.

38. Schlieffen, *op. cit.*, I, 100.

39. For a characterization, see Friedjung, *op. cit.*, II, 43 f.

40. See Alfons Freiherr von Wrede, *Geschichte des K. u. K. Mährischen Dragoner Regimentes Fr. Franz IV Groszherzog von Mecklenburg Schwerin No. 6*, pp. 5, 560 ff. Ramming seems to have thought he had more horse than was actually available. The Austrian cavalry was outnumbered.

41. Verdy, *op. cit.*, p. 92.

42. See the accounts in Friedjung, *op. cit.*, II, 44–52; Fontane, *op. cit.*, I, 290–316; *Oesterreichs Kämpfe*, III, 70 ff.; Preussen: Generalstab, *Der Feldzug von 1866*, I, 130 ff.

43. *Oesterreichs Kämpfe*, III, 93; Generalstab, *Der Feldzug von 1866*, p. 146.

44. Blumenthal, *op. cit.*, pp. 9 f., 14; Buchfink, *op. cit.*, p. 33.

45. See C. Junck, *Aus dem Leben des k. k. Generals der Kavallerie Ludwig Freiherrn von Gablenz*; and Reinhold Lorenz, "Ludwig Freiherr von Gablenz" in *Neue Oesterreichische Biographie, 1815–1918*, Erste Abteilung, VIII, 60 ff.

46. See Friedjung's excellent account of the Austrian victory, *op. cit.*, II, 58–65, and the official Austrian version in *Oesterreichs Kämpfe*, III, 95 ff. The Prussian General Staff work is critical of Bonin and his

divisional commanders. *Der Feldzug von 1866*, I, 118 ff.

47. The Austrians had 1,104 dead, 1,900 wounded, 980 prisoners, 803 missing; the Prussians, 244 dead, 1,008 wounded, 86 missing.

48. Verdy, *op. cit.*, p. 95; Generalstab, *Der Feldzug von 1866*, I, 162.

49. Schlieffen, *op. cit.*, I, 110.

50. Friedjung, *op. cit.*, II, 78 f.

51. *Ibid.*, pp. 80–85. But cf. Schlichting, *op. cit.*, p. 63.

52. Verdy, *op. cit.*, p. 97.

53. Hohenlohe-Ingelfingen, *op. cit.*, III, 246.

54. Verdy, *op. cit.*, p. 100.

55. Hohenlohe-Ingelfingen, *op. cit.*, III, 249 ff.

56. The fight is described in *Oesterreichs Kämpfe*, III, 126 ff.; Preussen: Generalstab, *Der Feldzug von 1866*, I, 172 ff.; Friedjung, *op. cit.*, II, 89 ff.; Lettow-Vorbeck, *op. cit.*, II, 282 ff.; and, with the greatest amount of detail, in Fontane, *op. cit.*, I, 322 ff. Austrian casualties included 882 dead, 881 wounded, 2,829 prisoners, 985 missing; Prussian casualties, 296 dead, 1,056 wounded, 13 missing.

57. In this fight the Second Guard Regiment particularly distinguished itself. See Col. von Pape, *Das Zweite Garde Regiment zu Fuss in dem Feldzuge des Jahres 1866*, pp. 29 ff.

58. Jähns, *op. cit.*, p. 45; Fontane, *op. cit.*, I, 392–414; Friedjung, *op. cit.*, II, 103–110; Lettow-Vorbeck, *op. cit.*, II, 296–312; Schlichting, *op. cit.*, pp. 50–53.

59. *Oesterreichs Kämpfe*, III, 153; Preussen: Generalstab, *Der Feldzug von 1866*, I, 171.

60. Schlieffen, *op. cit.*, I, 116 f.

CHAPTER 4

1. The lines from *Punch*, despite their flippancy, have an undertone of concern that is as serious as that voiced by the more sober-sided English journals after the battle of Königgrätz.

2. Fontane, *op. cit.*, I, 167.

3. *Ibid.*, pp. 169-181; Friedjung, *op. cit.*, II, 153 ff.

4. Jähns, *op. cit.*, p. 46; Fontane, *op. cit.*, I, 182.

5. *Moltkes Militärische Werke*, I. *Militärische Korrespondenz*, Zweiter Theil, p. 239.

6. Friedrich Karl, *op. cit.*, II, 54 ff., 58 ff.

7. See Francis Watson, *Wallenstein, Soldier under Saturn*, pp. 140, 296.

8. *Wilhelm und Caroline von Humboldt in ihren Briefen*, edited by Anna von Sydow, IV, 40; Fontane, *op. cit.*, I, 205 f.

9. Friedjung, *op. cit.*, II, 158.

10. For a brief biography, see Priesdorff, *op. cit.*, VII, 110 ff.

11. Fontane, *op. cit.*, I, 191 ff.; Friedjung, *op. cit.*, II, 163-64.

12. *Oesterreichs Kämpfe*, III, 192, 206; *Der Antheil des Königlich Sächsischen Armeecorps*, p. 125; Schlichting, *op. cit.*, p. 42.

13. Fontane, *op. cit.*, I, 223 f.; Hassel, *op. cit.*, I, 278 ff.

14. Schlieffen, *op. cit.*, I, 122 f. See also Friedjung, *op. cit.*, II, 171.

15. *Der Antheil des Königlich Sächsischen Armeecorps*, pp. 135 ff.

16. *Ibid.*, pp. 141 ff.; Hassel, *op. cit.*, II, 285 ff.; *Oesterreichs Kämpfe*, III, 212; Preussen: Generalstab, *Der Feldzug von 1866*, I, 218.

17. Friedrich Karl, *op. cit.*, II, 63 f.

18. Voigts-Rhetz, *op. cit.*, p. 7.

19. For details, see Friedjung, *op. cit.*, II, 131-135; Fontane, *op. cit.*, I, 420 ff.; Arnim, *op. cit.*, pp. 23 ff.

20. Already on June 28 he had issued a general order that bayonet charges should no longer be ordered until the enemy had been weakened by careful artillery fire. *Benedeks nachgelassene Papiere*, p. 369.

21. *Ibid.*, pp. 371 f.

22. *Ibid.*, p. 375; Beck, *op. cit.*, pp. 112 f. Beck left Königgrätz feeling that this was the only solution. *Ibid.*, p. 116.

23. Friedjung, *op. cit.*, II, 198.

24. Beck, *op. cit.*, pp. 118 f.

25. See *Oesterreichs Kämpfe*, III, 246 f.; Friedjung, *op. cit.*, II, 211 f. Schlichting, *op. cit.*, pp. 85 f., defends Benedek's decision, as does Regele, *op. cit.*, p. 430.

26. Jähns, *op. cit.*, p. 53.

27. See *Ibid.*, and, for a complete listing, Preussen: Generalstab, *Der Feldzug von 1866*, II, Anlage 1. Some details of the movement of this suite to the front are given in Hermann Graf von Wartensleben-Carow, *Ein Lebensbild, 1826-1921*, pp. 32 f.

28. Bismarck, *Gesammelte Werke*, IX, 268.

29. *Moltkes Militärische Werke*, I. *Militärische Korrespondenz*, Zweiter Theil, pp. 239 f.

30. Schlieffen, *op. cit.*, I, 132.

31. On this see Verdy, *op. cit.*, pp. 127 ff.; Friedrich Karl, *op. cit.*, II, 68 f.; Kessel, *op. cit.*, pp. 472 f.; and Friedjung, *op. cit.*, II, 203 f.

32. This is based on Fontane's spirited account, *op. cit.*, I, 457 ff.

33. Friedrich Karl, *op. cit.*, II, 71 ff.

34. See Schlieffen, *op. cit.*, I, 134 f., who believes, more emphatically

than other authors, that Frederick Charles tied Moltke's hands.

35. *Moltkes Militärische Werke,*

I. *Militärische Korrespondenz,* Zweiter Theil, p. 244.

CHAPTER 5

1. A song of the war of 1813 by Max von Schenkendorf (1783–1817), a volunteer in the fight to liberate his country from French domination.

2. Bleibtreu, *op. cit.,* p. 14; Friedjung, *op. cit.,* II, 215.

3. *The Spectator,* XXXIX, 772 (14 July 1866).

4. *Oesterreichs Kämpfe,* III, 261 ff.; Preussen: Generalstab, *Schlachterfolg,* pp. 179 f.; Lettow-Vorbeck, *op. cit.,* II, 415 ff.

5. Preussen: Generalstab, *Schlachterfolg,* p. 179.

6. *Benedeks nachgelassene Papiere,* pp. 376 f.

7. Friedjung, *op. cit.,* II, 217 f.

8. *The Times,* 11 July 1866, p. 9.

9. Bleibtreu, *op. cit.,* p. 16; Hohenlohe-Ingelfingen, *op. cit.,* III, 267.

10. *Der Antheil des sächsischen Armeecorps,* p. 176; Lettow-Vorbeck, *op. cit.,* II, 424 ff.; Verdy, *op. cit.,* p. 182.

11. *Oesterreichs Kämpfe,* III, 266 f.; Anton Freiherr von Mollinary, *Sechsundvierzig Jahre im oesterreich-ungarischen Heere, 1833–1879* II, 155–57; Lettow-Vorbeck, *op. cit.,* II, 426 ff.; Bleibtreu, *op. cit.,* pp. 12 ff.

12. Bleibtreu, *op. cit.,* p. 18.

13. Friedrich Karl, *op. cit.,* II, 76 f.

14. Rupert Furneaux, in *The Breakfast War,* has written of the excellent coverage of the Russo-Turkish war of 1877 by British newspapers. The achievement of *The Times* in 1866 was equally notable. *The Saturday Review* wrote on July 14 (XXII, 31): "For the

first time we have had a great battle described immediately after it had taken place by narrators who have followed the fortunes of either army. *The Times* has supplied English readers with a description of the battle of Sadowa as it appeared to an observer on the Prussian side, and also with a description of it as it appeared to an observer on the Austrian side. We have never had this done before with anything like the same amount of fulness and graphic power." The *Illustrated London News* sent an artist to the scene of war, but he was detained at Gitschin until after Königgrätz, and his drawings of that battle are based on sketches made by Major von Verdy of the Crown Prince's staff. See *Illustrated London News,* XXIX, 150, 153. *Le Siècle* had a correspondent with the Second Army; and the *Illustrierte Zeitung* appears to have had a staff artist at the front.

15. *The Times,* 11 July 1866, p. 9.

16. Voigts-Rhetz, *op. cit.,* p. 43; Friedrich Karl, *op. cit.,* II, 88 f.

17. *Ibid.,* p. 77.

18. *The Times,* 11 July 1866, p. 9.

19. See Richter, *op. cit.,* pp. 149 f.

20. Friedjung, *op. cit.,* II, 224.

21. R. von Keudell, *Fürst und Fürstin Bismarck: Erinnerungen aus den Jahren 1864–1872,* pp. 282 f.

22. Friedrich Karl, *op. cit.,* II, 80; Kessel, *op. cit.,* p. 477.

23. Bismarck, *Gesammelte Werke,* VII, 206.

24. Schlieffen, however, believed that Benedek might have been able to mount an attack over Nechanitz,

pushing Herwarth aside and taking Frederick Charles in the flank (*op. cit.*, I, 137). Later in the day, even an Austrian offensive in the center did not seem impossible to some Prussian commanders.

25. Kessel, *op. cit.*, pp. 477–78.

26. Duke Ernest of Koburg-Gotha wrote later: "Prince Frederick Charles always regarded the famous and extraordinary course of the tactical developments on the 3rd of July as a blow from a malevolent fate against his own fame and self-esteem." He was never jealous of the Crown Prince's well-deserved renown, but he resented the fact that Moltke's orders had made it impossible for his battalions to play the role he had planned for them and that, in consequence, their great services were not sufficiently appreciated by public opinion. See Friedrich Karl, *op. cit.*, II, 95 ff.

27. *Der Antheil des sächsischen Armeecorps*, pp. 183 ff.; Hassel, *op. cit.*, II, 294 f.; Lettow-Vorbeck, *op. cit.*, II, 446 ff.; Jähns, *op. cit.*, pp. 168 ff.

28. On all this, see especially Preussen: Generalstab, *Schlachterfolg*, p. 182; Lettow-Vorbeck, *op. cit.*, II, 452; Friedrich Karl, *op. cit.*, II, 85 f.; Preussen: Generalstab, *Der Feldzug von 1866*, I, 264 ff., 357 ff.

29. *The Times*, 11 July 1866, p. 9.

30. Fontane, *op. cit.*, I, 496.

31. *Ibid.*, p. 504.

32. *Ibid.*, pp. 512 f.

33. Preussen: Generalstab, *Der Feldzug von 1866*, I, 355; Lettow-Vorbeck, *op. cit.*, II, 465.

34. Jähns, *op. cit.*, p. 216.

35. *Ibid.*, p. 217.

36. Lettow-Vorbeck, *op. cit.*, II, 467.

37. Friedrich Karl, *op. cit.*, II, 89.

38. Priesdorff, *op. cit.*, VII, 242 ff. On Fransecky see also his most interesting memoirs, *Denkwürdigkeiten des Preussischen Generals der Infanterie Eduard von Fransecky*, ed. by Walter von Bremen; and on the crucial importance of his role on July 3, see Général H. Bonnal, *Sadowa*, pp. 112, 135, and especially 179 f.

39. Bleibtreu, *op. cit.*, pp. 17 f.; Friedjung, *op. cit.*, II, 231 f.

40. Fontane, *op. cit.*, I, 518 ff.; Lettow-Vorbeck, *op. cit.*, II, 437.

41. Jähns, *op. cit.*, p. 126.

42. Bleibtreu, *op. cit.*, p. 19.

43. Lettow-Vorbeck, *op. cit.*, II, 437 ff.; Friedjung, *op. cit.*, II, 232; *Oesterreichs Kämpfe*, III, 286 ff.

44. Fontane, *op. cit.*, I, 527, 528 f.

45. Friedjung, *op. cit.*, II, 233.

46. *Oesterreichs Kämpfe*, III, 297.

47. Friedjung, *op. cit.*, II, 235.

48. *Oesterreichs Kämpfe*, III, 292 f.

49. Fransecky, *op. cit.*, II, 307; Jähns, *op. cit.*, p. 138.

50. *Feldmarschall* Graf von Loë, *Erinnerungen*, pp. 75 f.

51. Friedjung, *op. cit.*, II, 236 f.

52. Jähns, *op. cit.*, p. 143.

53. Bleibtreu, *op. cit.*, pp. 71 f.

54. Loë, *op. cit.*, pp. 102 ff. and, for other versions, Wartensleben, *op. cit.*, p. 29; Moltke, *Gesammelte Schriften*, III, 423; Moltke, *Briefe an die Braut und Frau*, II, 325n.

55. Kessel, *op. cit.*, p. 479.

56. Richter, *op. cit.*, p. 150.

57. Kessel, *op. cit.*, p. 479; Friedrich Karl, *op. cit.*, II, 91.

58. Friedjung, *op. cit.*, II, 242 f. The news had been sent earlier, but as usual had got lost.

CHAPTER 6

1. A salute to the Guard Corps by Theodor Fontane (1819–1898) who, before he won fame as a novelist of manners, wrote excellent histories of the wars of 1864, 1866, and 1870–71.

2. Arnim, *op. cit.*, pp. 28 f.

3. Lettow-Vorbeck, *op. cit.*, II, 454.

4. Hohenlohe-Ingelfingen, *op. cit.*, III, 267 ff.

5. Verdy, *op. cit.*, p. 143; Preussen: Generalstab, *Schlachterfolg*, I, 305.

6. Hohenlohe-Ingelfingen, *op. cit.*, III, 268.

7. Friedrich Karl, *op. cit.*, II, 76 f.

8. Verdy, *op. cit.*, p. 147.

9. Hohenlohe-Ingelfingen, *op. cit.*, III, 269 ff.

10. Pape, *op. cit.*, pp. 78 f.

11. *Illustrated London News*, XXIX, 153 (18 August 1866).

12. Verdy, *op. cit.*, pp. 152 f.

13. Bleibtreu, *op. cit.*, p. 40.

14. Blumenthal, *op. cit.*, pp. 33 f.

15. Friedjung, *op. cit.*, II, 241 f.

16. *Ibid.*, p. 244n.

17. *Ibid.*, p. 247; Mollinary, *op. cit.*, II, 164.

18. Schlieffen, *op. cit.*, I, 142.

19. Friedjung, *op. cit.*, II, 254.

20. Hohenlohe-Ingelfingen, *op. cit.*, III, 272 f.

21. *Ibid.*, p. 273; Lettow-Vorbeck, *op. cit.*, II, 458.

22. *Oesterreichs Kämpfe*, III, 313; Hohenlohe-Ingelfingen, *op. cit.*, III, 275 f.; Lettow-Vorbeck, *op. cit.*, II, 459.

23. *The Times*, 11 July 1866, p. 9.

24. Richter, *op. cit.*, pp. 150f.

25. Verdy, *op. cit.*, p. 155.

26. Lettow-Vorbeck, *op. cit.*, II, 471.

27. Friedjung, *op. cit.*, II, 258.

This was the famous occasion on which Manstein, when he received Moltke's counter-order, said, "That's all very well, but who is General von Moltke?" and insisted that his orders must come from Frederick Charles. See Wartensleben, *op. cit.*, p. 44. This was probably the last occasion on which Moltke's authority to command was challenged.

28. *Moltkes Militärische Werke*, I. *Militärische Korrespondenz*, Zweiter Theil, 244 f.

29. *Der Antheil des sächsischen Armeecorps*, pp. 201 f.; Hassel, *op. cit.*, II, 296.

30. Preussen: Generalstab, *Der Feldzug von 1866*, I, 362 ff.; Fontane, *op. cit.*, I, 482 ff.; Lettow-Vorbeck, *op. cit.*, II, 482 ff.; *Oesterreichs Kämpfe*, III, 330 ff.; Friedjung, *op. cit.*, II, 280 ff.; *Der Antheil des sächsischen Armeecorps*, pp. 215 ff.; Hassel, *op. cit.*, II, 296 ff.

31. Fontane, *op. cit.*, I, 486n. Schulz's gallantry impressed his own troops and the Prussians, particularly the Thirty-fourth Regiment, which came into Ober Prim just after his death. The Thirty-fourth had served with him before the war in the federal fortress of Rastadt. Schulz was buried with honors at Ober Prim on July 4, but was later exhumed on orders of Emperor Francis Joseph and buried in Königgrätz churchyard. It was discovered at that time that he had been wounded by infantry fire, not twice, but five times.

32. Lettow-Vorbeck, *op. cit.*, II, 484–86.

33. Hassel, *op. cit.*, II, 296.

34. *Ibid.*, pp. 296 f.

35. Preussen: Generalstab, *Schlachterfolg*, p. 183.

36. Fontane, *op. cit.,* I, 492.

37. See Max von Apel, *Geschichte des 3. Niederschlesischen Infanterie-Regiments Nr. 50,* pp. 26 ff.; and Oberst von Boguslawski, *Geschichte des 3. Niederschlesischen Infanterie-Regiments Nr. 50 von seiner Errichtung 1860 bis 1886,* pp. 126 ff.

38. Lettow-Vorbeck, *op. cit.,* II, 461 f.

39. Hohenlohe-Ingelfingen, *op. cit.,* III, 278.

40. *Ibid.,* p. 282.

41. Arnim, *op. cit.,* pp. 32 f.

42. Fontane, *op. cit.,* I, 562, 564 f.

43. Friedjung, *op. cit.,* II, 270.

44. Fontane, *op. cit.,* I, 563.

45. Arnim, *op. cit.,* p. 33. For his spirited leadership in the attack, Arnim was awarded the *pour le mérite.*

46. Preussen: Generalstab, *Der Feldzug von 1866,* I, 328 f.; Lettow-Vorbeck, *op. cit.,* II, 474 f.; Friedjung, *op. cit.,* II, 267 f.; Bleibtreu, *op. cit.,* p. 79; *Oesterreichs Kämpfe,* III, 342 f.

47. Preussen: Generalstab, *Der Feldzug von 1866,* I, 329; Fontane, *op. cit.,* I, 564 f.

48. Hohenlohe-Ingelfingen, *op. cit.,* III, 285 f.; Fontane, *op. cit.,* I, 565 f.; Verdy, *op. cit.,* pp. 160 f.; Friedjung, *op. cit.,* II, 271; *Oesterreichs Kämpfe,* III, 350 f.

49. *Ibid.,* III, Beilagen, p. 30.

50. Friedjung, *op. cit.,* II, 272.

51. Lettow-Vorbeck, *op. cit.,* II, 476.

52. *Ibid.,* p. 477; *Oesterreichs Kämpfe,* III, 348 f.

53. See Fontane, *op. cit.,* I, 573–83.

54. *Ibid.,* pp. 584–88; Friedjung, *op. cit.,* II, 266; Apel, *op. cit.,* pp. 29 ff.; Boguslawski, *op. cit.,* pp. 136–142. The Austrian staff work points out that the ammunition of some of the retiring units was virtually exhausted. *Oesterreichs Kämpfe,* III, 352 f.

55. See Lettow-Vorbeck, *op. cit.,* II, 478.

56. See, for example, Friedrich Karl, *op. cit.,* II, 96 f.

57. Lettow-Vorbeck, *op. cit.,* II, 498.

58. Hohenlohe-Ingelfingen, *op. cit.,* III, 289.

CHAPTER 7

1. As Jähns has pointed out (*Die Schlacht von Königgrätz,* p. 375), this speech of Mephistopheles from Goethe's *Faust* (Part Two, Act IV) comes close to describing the culminating phase of the battle of 3 July 1866, if one allows for certain changes of direction.

2. Friedjung, *op. cit.,* II, 272 f.; *Benedeks nachgelassene Papiere,* pp. 378 f.

3. This supposition was correct, as Benedek reported to the Emperor on the evening of the 3rd.

4. *The Times,* 11 July 1866, p. 10.

Friedjung cites some excerpts from this despatch.

5. Friedjung, *op. cit.,* II, 275 f.

6. Verdy, *op. cit.,* pp. 165 f. In his memoirs, Stosch firmly describes the fire as coming from Austrian batteries. Stosch, *op. cit.,* p. 93.

7. At Auerstedt, on 14 October 1806, the French Marshal Davout defeated the Prussians under the Duke of Brunswick, on the same day that Napoleon triumphed at Jena.

8. For the King's remarks to Boyen as he sent him on this mission,

see M. von Poschinger, *Kaiser Friedrich in neuer quellenmässiger Darstellung*, II, 234.

9. Verdy, *op. cit.*, pp. 167 f.; Stosch, *op. cit.*, p. 93.

10. Hohenlohe-Ingelfingen, *op. cit.*, III, 289–91.

11. A hero of the Liberation period, Major von Schill had risked court-martial for treason during Austria's war against France in 1809, by leading Prussian volunteers against French troops in Westphalia.

12. Pape, *op. cit.*, p. 108.

13. *Ibid.*, pp. 108–109.

14. Fontane, *op. cit.*, I, 594 ff.; Jähns, *op. cit.*, p. 344.

15. *Generalfeldmarschall* von Hindenburg, *Aus meinem Leben*, pp. 28–30. For his capture of the guns, Hindenburg received the Order of the Red Eagle. The pierced helmet he kept on his desk until the end of his life. In 1933, when being treated by Gustav von Bergmann, the famous Professor of Internal Medicine at the University of Berlin, Hindenburg complained of a headache and, under questioning, said he guessed it came from the blow on the head that he had received at Königgrätz.

16. Fontane, *op. cit.*, pp. 601 f.; Arnim, *op. cit.*, pp. 42 ff.

17. Hohenlohe-Ingelfingen, *op. cit.*, III, 292.

18. *Ibid.*, pp. 294–96.

19. Jähns, *op. cit.*, pp. 348–50; Preussen: Generalstab, *Der Feldzug von 1866*, 1, 386.

20. A. O. Meyer, *Bismarck: Der Mensch und der Staatsmann*, p. 310; Fontane, *op. cit.*, I, 609.

21. *Fürst Bismarcks Briefe an seine Braut und Gattin*, ed. by *Fürst* Herbert Bismarck, p. 573. See also *Kaiser Wilhelms des Grossen Briefe, Reden und Schriften*, ed. by Ernst Berner, II, 133 (Letter to Queen Augusta, 4 July 1866).

22. *Oberst* von Zychlinski, *Der Antheil des 2. Magdeburgischen Infanterie-Regiments an der Schlacht von Königgrätz*, pp. 34–36. As the fight in the *Swiepwald* ended and the general advance began, Zychlinski and General von Gordon rode forward on captured Austrian horses, leading what was left of their forces; and it appears from Zychlinski's account that they may have reached Lipa before the King and Frederick Charles. "As I had since the evening of the 1st played the role of the point," he writes, "so was I to continue this to the end. For now I pushed myself, as such, in between the two victorious armies, the First to the right and the Second to the left, as the only troop of the 7th Division which had the good fortune to witness this victorious moment in the middle of the battlefield."

23. Bleibtreu, *op. cit.*, p. 130.

24. *The Times*, 11 July 1866, p. 10.

25. Friedjung, *op. cit.*, II, 288.

26. Hozier (*op. cit.*, p. 252) speaks of a "cuirass brigade led by an Englishman in the Austrian service of the name of Beales." The Austrian staff work does not mention him, but does speak of a Colonel Berres, commanding the Ferdinand Cuirassiers. *Oesterreichs Kämpfe*, III, 367.

27. See Lettow-Vorbeck, *op. cit.*, II, 502–504; Fontane, *op. cit.*, I, 611–615; Jähns, *op. cit.*, pp. 382 ff.; Preussen: Generalstab, *Der Feldzug von 1866*, I, 405 ff.; *Oesterreichs Kämpfe*, III, 366 f.; Wrede, *op. cit.*, pp. 571 ff.

28. Lettow-Vorbeck, *op. cit.*, II, 504-505; Fontane, *op. cit.*, I, 616-20; *Oesterreichs Kämpfe*, III, 364ff.;

Preussen: Generalstab, *Der Feldzug von 1866*, I, 409ff., 413ff.

29. See Lettow-Vorbeck, *op. cit.*, II, 506; Schlieffen, *op. cit.*, I, 147; Preussen: Generalstab, *Schlachterfolg*, p. 185; Wrede, *op. cit.*, I, 576.

30. Jähns, *op. cit.*, pp. 358 ff.; Lettow-Vorbeck, *op. cit.*, II, 488; Friedjung, *op. cit.*, II, 292.

31. *Oesterreichs Kämpfe*, III, 359 ff.; Friedjung, *op. cit.*, II, 291 ff.; Fontane, *op. cit.*, I, 601–604.

32. See Friedjung, *op. cit.*, II, 293 ff.; Lettow-Vorbeck, *op. cit.*, II, 508; *Oesterreichs Kämpfe*, III, 373.

33. Preussen: Generalstab, *Heeresverpflegung*, p. 121.

34. Hohenlohe-Ingelfingen, *op. cit.*, III, 300.

35. Verdy, *op. cit.*, pp. 193–195.

36. Friedrich Karl, *op. cit.*, II, 102.

37. *Moltkes Militärische Werke*, I. *Militärische Korrespondenz*, Zweiter Theil, p. 245.

38. Lettow-Vorbeck, *op. cit.*, II, 520.

39. Kessel, *op. cit.*, p. 481.

40. *The Times*, 11 July 1866, p. 10.

41. Fontane, *op. cit.*, I, 625. During the crossing the Berezina River, 26–29 November 1812, Napoleon's Grand Army, retreating from Moscow, lost over 20,000 men.

42. This is largely based on Friedjung's account, *op. cit.*, II, 300–303.

43. Blumenthal, *op. cit.*, p. 35; Friedrich Karl, *op. cit.*, II, 104.

44. Kaiser Friedrich, *op. cit.*, p. 451; Poschinger, *op. cit.*, II, 195.

45. Blumenthal, *op. cit.*, pp. 35 f.; Verdy, *op. cit.*, pp. 189 f.

46. Hozier, who witnessed the day's events, was impressed by efforts to care for the wounded. He wrote later: "Conspicuous in the hospitals, working diligently in their voluntary labour, were the Knights of St. John of Jerusalem. This Order of Knighthood, renewed lately for the succour of the weak and suffering, had sent here a large hospital establishment, under the direction of Count Theodore Stolberg. From the voluntary contributions of the knights, hospitals were maintained in the nearest towns and in the field, all necessary hospital stores were carried by the Order, and means of transport accompanied the army, hospital nurses were provided, and by their aid many wounded were carefully attended to who could not have been looked after by the ordinary arrangements." Hozier, *op. cit.*, p. 253.

47. Jähns, *op. cit.*, pp. 466 f.

48. Moritz Busch, *Tagebuchblätter*, II, 80; Richter, *op. cit.*, p. 470.

49. Jähns, *op. cit.*, p. 470.

50. *Benedeks nachgelassens Papiere*, pp. 405.

CHAPTER 8

1. From the most melancholy of all *Soldatenlieder* and one of the most widely known, "Morgenrot" ("Red of Morning") by Wilhelm Hauff (1802–1827). Werckmeister, *op. cit.*, p. 409.

2. Buchfink, *op. cit.*, p. 48.

3. *Oesterreichs Kämpfe*, III, Beilage, p. 38. The Austrians lost 187 guns, the Saxons one.

4. Preussen: Generalstab, *Der Feldzug von 1866*, I, 434, II, Anlage 23 and 24.

5. See Friedrich Karl, *op. cit.*, II, 110 ff.

6. *Bismarcks Briefe an seine Braut*

und Gattin, p. 573. The conduct of the Prussian troops in Bohemia was correct, and the situation quite unlike the French war, when looting and plunder became common on both sides. See Howard, *op. cit.*, pp. 378 ff. Bismarck's words here nevertheless constitute an unconscious criticism of the supply services, whose issue shoes seemed to be as bad as the bread they provided.

7. See Arnim, *op. cit.*, p. 45.

8. *The Times*, 11 July 1866, p. 10.

9. Friedjung, *op. cit.*, II, 328 ff.

10. Details of the order of march are given in Jähns, *op. cit.*, pp. 482 f.

11. See Glaise-Horstenau, *op. cit.*, pp. 122 f.

12. On Tobitschau and Roketnitz, see *Oesterreichs Kämpfe*, IV, 89–108; Preussen: Generalstab, *Der Feldzug von 1866*, I, 493–506; Friedjung, *op. cit.*, II, 337–40; *Benedeks nachgelassene Papiere*. pp. 391 f.

13. On these events, and the fight at Blumenau, see *Oesterreichs Kämpfe*, IV, 108 ff., 151 ff.; Preussen: Generalstab, *Der Feldzug von 1866*, I, 534 ff.

14. Keudell, *op. cit.*, p. 297.

15. On the negotiations with Napoleon and the struggle with the soldiers, see Craig, *op. cit.*, pp. 198–204.

16. The texts of the Prussian treaties with Austria and Saxony are in *Oesterreichs Kämpfe*, IV, Beilage, pp. 29–40.

17. Schüssler, *op. cit.*, p. 81.

18. Herbert Michaelis, "Königgrätz: eine geschichtliche Wende," *Die Welt als Geschichte*, XII (1952), 196.

19. Wilhelm von Humboldt, *Gesammelte Schriften*, XII, 77.

20. *The Spectator*, XXXIX, 737 (7 July 1866).

21. *Ibid*. See also *Illustrated London News*, XXIX, 3 (7 July 1866).

22. Jähns, *op. cit.*, p. 493.

23. *Ibid*.

24. Howard, *op. cit.*, p. 5 and note. See also Berdrow, *op. cit.*, pp. 193 f., 197, 208, 219.

25. *The Spectator*, XXXIX, 743 (7 July 1866).

26. *Manchester Guardian*, 6 July 1866, reprinted in Henderson and Chaloner, *op. cit.*, p. 139.

27. Jähns, *op. cit.*, p. 146. This is very similar to what Moltke said himself, in a memorandum of June 1869: "Superiority is no longer to be found in the weapon, but in the hand that carries it." *Moltkes Militärische Werke*, II. *Die Thätigkeit als Chef des Generalstabes der Armee im Frieden*, Zweiter Theil, p. 195.

28. Stoffel, *op. cit.*, pp. 2 f.

29. *Moltkes Militärische Werke*, II. *Die Thätigkeit als Chef des Generalstabes der Armee im Frieden*, Zweiter Theil, p. 74. A French critic agreed, going so far as to describe Königgrätz as "une série de luttes de l'infanterie contre l'artillerie autrichienne." Bonnal, *op. cit.*, p. 183.

30. *Moltkes Militärische Werke*, II, *Die Thätigkeit als Chef des Generalstabes der Armee im Frieden*, Zweiter Theil, pp. 126, 130.

31. *Ibid.*, pp. 132 f.

32. *Ibid.*, pp. 111, 114 ff., 119–26.

33. See Kessel, *op. cit.*, pp. 512 f.; Delbrück, *op. cit.*, p. 309.

34. *Moltkes Militärische Werke*, II. *Die Thätigkeit als Chef des Generalstabes der Armee im Frieden*, Zweiter Theil, p. 279.

35. *Moltkes Militärische Werke*, II. *Die Thätigkeit als Chefs des Generalstabes der Armee im Frieden*, Zweiter Theil, p. 173.

36. *Ibid.*, p. 286.

37. Cited in Kessel, *op. cit.*, p. 515.

38. For Moltke's views on this, see *Moltkes Militärische Werke*, II. *Die Thätigkeit als Chef des Generalstabes der Armee im Frieden*, Zweiter Theil, pp. 74 f. See also Kessel, *op. cit.*, p. 517.

39. Ludwig Reiners, *Bismarck gründet das Reich*, p. 184.

40. Kessel, *op. cit.*, p. 492.

41. Friedjung, *op. cit.*, II, 545.

42. *Benedeks nachgelassene Papiere*, p. 384.

43. *Ibid.*, p. 401.

44. *Ibid.*, pp. 405 ff.

45. The article is reproduced in Friedjung, *op. cit.*, II, 546 ff. See also Regele, *op. cit.*, pp. 491 ff.; Alter, *op. cit.*, pp. 494 ff.

46. *Benedeks nachgelassene Papiere*, p. 407.

BIBLIOGRAPHY

Alter, Wilhelm. *Feldzeugmeister Benedek und der Feldzug der k. k. Nordarmee 1866* (Berlin, 1912).

Apel, Max von. *Geschichte des 3. Niederschlesischen Infanterie-Regiments Nr. 50* (Stuttgart, 1910).

Arnim, R. von. *Erinnerungen aus dem Feldzug von 1866* (Hannover, 1868).

Benedeks nachgelassene Papiere. Herausgegeben und zu einer Biographie verarbeitet von Heinrich Friedjung (Leipzig, 1901).

Berdrow, Wilhelm. *The Krupps* (English translation, Berlin, 1937).

Bernhardi. *Aus dem Leben Theodor von Bernhardis* (8 vols., Leipzig, 1893–1906).

Bigge, W. *Feldmarschall Graf Moltke: ein militärisches Lebensbild* (2 vols., Munich, 1901).

Bismarck, Otto von. *Die gesammelten Werke* (1st ed., 15 vols., Berlin, 1924 ff.).

Bismarck. *Fürst Bismarcks Briefe an seine Braut und Gattin,* edited by Fürst Herbert Bismarck (Stuttgart, 1900).

Bismarck und der Staat, edited by Hans Rothfels (2nd edition, Stuttgart, 1953).

Bismarcks grosses Spiel. Die geheime Tagebücher Ludwig Bambergers, edited by Ernst Feder (Frankfurt am Main, 1932).

Bleibtreu, Carl. *Königgrätz.* (Stuttgart, n.d.).

Blumenthal, Leonhard Graf. *Tagebücher des Generalfeldmarschalls Graf von Blumenthal aus den Jahren 1866 und 1870/71,* edited by Albrecht Graf von Blumenthal (Stuttgart and Berlin, 1902).

Boguslawski, Oberst von. *Geschichte des 3. Niederschlesischen Infanterie-Regiments Nr. 50 von seiner Errichtung 1860 bis 1886* (Berlin, 1887).

Bonnal, Général H. *Sadowa. Etude de stratégie et de tactique générale* (Paris, 1901).

Brix, Rittmeister. *Das Oesterreichische Heer in seiner Organisation und Stärke, Uniformirung, Ausrüstung und Bewaffnung* (Berlin, 1866).

Bronsart von Schellendorf, Paul. *Duties of the General Staff* (3rd revised English edition, London, 1908).

Buchfink, Ernst. *Feldmarschall Graf von Haeseler* (Berlin, 1929).

Busch, Moritz. *Tagebuchblätter* (2 vols., Leipzig, 1899).

Carlyle, Thomas. *History of Friedrich the Second, called Frederick the Great* (4 vols., New York, 1864).

Chaloner, W. H. and Henderson, W. O., editors. *Engels as Military Critic* (Manchester, 1959).

Craig, Gordon A. *The Politics of the Prussian Army, 1640–1945* (Oxford, 1955).

Delbrück, Hans. *Historische und politische Aufsätze* (2nd edition, Berlin, 1907).

Demeter, Karl. *Das deutsche Heer und seine Offiziere* (Berlin, 1930).

Die deutsche Soldatenkunde, edited by Bernhard Schwertfeger and E. O. Volkmann (2 vols., Berlin, 1937).

Eckardt, W. and Morawietz, O. *Die Handwaffen des brandenburgisch-preussisch-deutschen Heeres 1640–1945* (Hamburg, 1957).

Fontane, Theodor. *Der deutsche Krieg von 1866* (2 vols., Berlin, 1871–72).

Fransecky. *Denkwürdigkeiten des Preussischen Generals der Infanterie Eduard von Fransecky*, edited by Walter von Bremen (2nd edition, 2 vols., Berlin, 1913).

Frauenholz, Eugen von, "Feldmarschalleutnant Alfred Freiherr von Henikstein im Jahre 1866," *Münchener Historische Abhandlungen*, 2. Reihe, 3. Heft.

Freytag-Loringhoven, Freiherr von. *Die Grundbedingungen kriegerischen Erfolges: Beiträge zur Psychologie des Krieges im 19. und 20. Jahrhundert* (Berlin, 1914).

Friedjung, Heinrich. *Der Kampf um die Vorherrschaft in Deutschland 1859 bis 1866* (9th edition, Stuttgart and Berlin, 1912).

Friedrich III, Kaiser. *Tagebücher, 1848–1866*, edited by H. O. Meisner (Leipzig, 1929).

Friedrich Karl, Prinz von Preussen. *Denkwürdigkeiten aus seinem Leben*, edited by Wolfgang Förster (2 vols., Stuttgart, 1910).

Furneaux, Rupert. *The Breakfast War* (New York, 1958).

Geschichte des deutschen Unteroffiziers. Herausgegeben vom Reichstreubund ehemaliger Berufssoldaten. Edited by Hauptmann a. D. Freiherr Ferdinand von Ledebur (Berlin, 1939).

Glaise-Horstenau, Edmund von. *Franz Josephs Weggefährte* (Zurich, Leipzig and Vienna, 1930).

Hassell, Paul. *Aus dem Leben des Königs Albert von Sachsen. II. König Albert als Kronprinz* (Berlin and Leipzig, 1900).

Hassell, Ulrich von. *Tirpitz. Sein Leben und Wirken mit Berücksichtigung seiner Beziehungen zu Albrecht von Stosch* (Stuttgart, 1920).

Hindenburg, Feldmarschall von. *Aus meinem Leben* (Leipzig, 1934).

Hohenlohe-Ingelfingen, Prinz Kraft zu. *Aus meinem Leben, 1848–1871* (4 vols., Berlin, 1897–1907).

Holborn, Hajo, "Moltke and Schlieffen," in *Makers of Modern Strategy: Military Thought from Machiavelli to Hitler*, edited by Edward Mead Earle, Gordon A. Craig and Felix Gilbert (Princeton, 1943).

Howard, Michael. *The Franco-Prussian War* (New York, 1961).

Hozier, H. M. *The Seven Weeks' War* (London, 1871).

Hubka, Gustav von. "Ludwig Ritter von Benedek," in *Grosse Oesterreicher: Neue Oesterreichische Biographie ab 1815*, XII (Zurich, 1957), 52 ff.

Humboldt, Wilhelm von. *Gesammelte Schriften*, edited by Königlich Preussischen Akademie der Wissenschaften (15 vols., Berlin, 1904).

——. *Wilhelm und Caroline von Humboldt in ihren Briefen*, edited by Anna von Sydow (5 vols., Berlin, 1906–1916).

Jähns, Max. *Die Schlacht von Königgrätz* (Leipzig, 1876).

Junck, C. *Aus dem Leben des k. k. Generals der Kavallerie Ludwig Freiherrn von Gablenz* (Vienna, 1874).

Kessel, Eberhard. *Moltke* (Stuttgart, 1957).

Keudell, R. von. *Fürst und Fürstin Bismarck: Erinnerungen aus den Jahren 1864–1871* (Berlin, 1901).

Lettow-Vorbeck, Oscar von. *Geschichte des Krieges von 1866* (4 vols., Berlin, 1892–1899).

Loë, Feldmarschall Graf von. *Erinnerungen* (2nd edition, Stuttgart, 1906).

Lorenz, Reinhold. "Ludwig Freiherr von Gablenz," in *Neue Oesterreichische Biographie 1815–1918*, Erste Abteilung, VIII (Vienna, 1935).

Meyer, A. O. *Bismarck: Der Mensch und der Staatsmann* (Stuttgart, 1949).

Michaelis, Herbert. "Königgrätz: eine geschichtliche Wende," in *Die Welt als Geschichte*, XII (1952), 196 ff.

Mollinary, Anton Freiherr von. *Sechsundvierzig Jahre im oesterreich-ungarischen Heere, 1833–1879* (Zurich, 1905).

Moltke, Helmuth von. *Briefe an die Braut und Frau* (Leipzig, 1894).

Moltke, Helmuth von. *Gesammelte Schriften und Aufsätze* (2 vols., Berlin, 1892).

Moltkes Militärische Werke. I. *Militärische Korrespondenz* (Berlin, 1896).

——. II. *Die Thätigkeit als Chef des Generalstabes der Armee im Frieden* (Berlin, 1900).

——. III. *Kriegsgeschichtliche Arbeiten* (Berlin, 1904).

Muhlen, Norbert. *The Incredible Krupps* (New York, 1959).

Oesterreich: Armee: Generalstab. *Oesterreichs Kämpfe im Jahre 1866: Nach Feldacten bearbeitet durch das k. k. Generalstabsbureau für Kriegsgeschichte* (5 vols., Vienna, 1868).

Ollech, Major von. "Reyher," in *Militärwochenblatt*, Beihefte, 1879, Nrs. 5, 6.

Pape, Oberst von. *Das Zweite Garde Regiment zu Fuss in dem Feldzuge des Jahres 1866* (Berlin, 1868).

Poschinger, Margarete von. *Kaiser Friedrich in neuer quellenmässiger Darstellung* (3 vols. in 1, Berlin, 1899–1900).

Pratt, E. A. *The Rise of Rail Power in War and Conquest, 1833–1914* (New York, 1915).

Preussen: Armee: Grosser Generalstab: Kriegsgeschichtliche Abteilung. *Der Feldzug von 1866 in Deutschland* (2 vols., Berlin, 1867).

——. *Studien zur Kriegsgeschichte und Taktik*. III. *Der Schlachterfolg, mit welchen Mitteln wurde er erstrebt?* (Berlin, 1903).

——. *Studien zur Kriegsgeschichte und Taktik*. VI. *Heeresverpflegung* (Berlin, 1913).

Priesdorff, Kurt von, editor. *Soldatisches Führertum* (10 vols., Hamburg, 1936 ff.).

Redlich, Josef. *Emperor Francis Joseph of Austria: A Biography* (New York, 1929).

Regele, Oskar. *Feldzeugmeister Benedek: Der Weg nach Königgrätz* (Wien, 1960).

Reiners, Ludwig. *Bismarck gründet das Reich, 1864–71* (Munich, 1957).

Richter, Werner. *Bismarck* (Frankfurt am Main, 1962).

"Rühle von Lilienstern," in *Militärwochenblatt*, Beihefte, October-December, 1847.

Sachsen: Armee: Generalstab. *Der Antheil des Königlich Sächsischen Armeecorps am Feldzuge 1866* (Dresden, 1869).

Schlichting, von. *Moltke und Benedek: Eine Studie über Truppenführung* (Berlin, 1900).

Schlieffen, Generalfeldmarschall Graf Alfred von. *Gesammelte Schriften* (2 vols., Berlin, 1913).

Schnabel, Franz. *Deutsche Geschichte im neunzehnten Jahrhundert* (4 vols., Freiburg im Breisgau, 1925 ff.).

Schüssler, Wilhelm. *Königgrätz 1866: Bismarcks tragische Trennung von Oesterreich* (Munich, 1958).

Schwertfeger, Bernhard. *Die grossen Erzieher des deutschen Heeres: Aus der Geschichte der Kriegsakademie* (Potsdam, 1936).

Stadelmann, Rudolf. *Moltke und der Staat* (Krefeld, 1950).

Stoffel, Baron. *Militärische Berichte erstattet aus Berlin, 1866–70* (Berlin, 1872).

Stosch, Albrecht von. *Denkwürdigkeiten,* edited by Ulrich von Stosch (Stuttgart, 1904).

Sybel, Heinrich von. *Die Begründung des Deutschen Reiches durch Wilhelm I.* (2nd edition, 7 vols., Munich, 1890).

Srbik, H. Ritter von. *Aus Oesterreichs Vergangenheit* (Salzburg, 1949).

Verdy du Vernois, J. von. *Im Hauptquartier der Zweiten Armee 1866* (Berlin, 1900).

Voigts-Rhetz. *Briefe des Generals der Infanterie Voigts-Rhetz aus den Kriegsjahren 1866 und 1870/71,* edited by A. von Voigts-Rhetz (Berlin, 1906).

Von Scharnhorst zu Schlieffen, edited by F. von Cochenhausen (Berlin, 1933).

Wartensleben-Carow, Hermann Graf von. *Ein Lebensbild, 1826–1921* (Berlin, 1923).

Watson, Francis. *Wallenstein, Soldier under Saturn* (New York, 1938).

Wilhelm I, Kaiser. *Kaiser Wilhelms des Grossen Briefe, Reden und Schriften,* edited by Ernst Berner (2 vols., Berlin, 1906).

Wrede, Alfons Freiherr von. *Geschichte des K. u. K. Mährischen Dragoner Regimentes Friedrich Franz IV. Groszherzog von Mecklenburg Schwerin Nr. 6* (Brünn, 1907).

Ziekursch, Johannes. *Politische Geschichte des neuen deutschen Kaiserreiches* (3 vols., Frankfurt-am-Main, 1925 ff.).

Zychlinski, Oberst von. *Der Antheil des 2. Magdeburgischen Infanterie-Regiments an der Schlacht von Königgrätz* (Halle, 1866).

INDEX

205